Wake Up!

Hip Hop Christianity and the Black Church

Cheryl Kirk-Duggan
and
Marlon Hall

Abingdon Press
Nashville

WAKE UP!
HIP HOP CHRISTIANITY AND THE BLACK CHURCH

This book is printed on acid-free paper.

Library of Congress Cataloging-in-Publication Data

Kirk-Duggan, Cheryl A.
  Wake up! : hip-hop Christianity and the Black church / by Cheryl Kirk-Duggan and Marlon Hall.
    p. cm.
  Includes bibliographical references.
  ISBN 978-1-4267-0301-0 (pbk. : alk. paper)
  1. African American youth—Religious life.   2. Hip-hop—Religious aspects—Christianity.   I. Hall, Marlon. II. Title.
  BR563.N4K585 2011
  248.4089'96073—dc22

                                                                    2010054429

All scripture quotations are taken from New Revised Standard Version of the Bible, copyright 1989, Division of Christian Education of the National Council of the Churches of Christ in the United States of America. Used by permission. All rights reserved.

11 12 13 14 15 16 17 18 19 20—10 9 8 7 6 5 4 3 2 1

MANUFACTURED IN THE UNITED STATES OF AMERICA

To the bards, young and not so young,

whose contributions in the form of Hip Hop
made this volume possible

To our immediate, intimate sojourners,

who've listened, encouraged,
and loved us well

Contents

Preface

It's Bigger Than Hip Hop

Divine synchronicity, human curiosity, and a commitment to creativity framed by faith launched the inception, process, and creation of *Wake Up! Hip Hop Christianity and the Black Church*. This collaborative project brought together the lived experiences of Marlon Hall and Cheryl Kirk-Duggan. Hall, a missionary, columnist, anthropologist, filmmaker, and pastor, helped found The Awakenings Movement, a grassroots Christian church and movement that holds worship in coffee shops, art galleries, and bars in Nairobi, Houston, and Detroit. The Awakenings Movement is designed to challenge and equip ordinary people to live extraordinary lives through the love and power of Christ. Hall grew up in Hip Hop culture as a participant and an observer, living and loving its music. Interdisciplinary scholar/minister/musician Cheryl A. Kirk-Duggan—a prolific author, preacher, professor, poet, performer, prophet, and priest—came to Hip Hop as a professor/learner. Synchronicity emerged during the spring of 2008, when one of Kirk-Duggan's students, then-Minister Leon Parker, came to her asking if she would teach a class on Hip Hop. She responded that if he could get eight people to sign up for the course, she would teach it as a readings course in fall 2008. In the summer of 2008, Abingdon Press editor Kathy Armistead phoned Kirk-Duggan and asked her if she would be interested in writing a book on Hip Hop. Kirk-Duggan initially stated that she had already made a commitment to say no to any new projects. However, since she had just agreed to teach a course on Hip Hop, she was willing to invest in the project.

Armistead went on to introduce Kirk-Duggan to Hall by emailing a couple of articles written from Hall's column in *Outreach Magazine, Awakening Faith,* which talked about his passion for people and his work at Awakenings as a "cultural provocateur": one who provokes culture from a life of mediocrity to dream, believe, and then live out his dreams. One article stated how the Awakenings Movement community is a group of "Social Visionaries who are called by God to make an indelible mark on humanity that no one can erase. Our community is a dynamic Christ-Centered movement that discovers God in unorthodox public settings. At Awakenings, we learn to excavate God's extraordinary presence from the remnants of ordinary life and spaces. This movement allows us to share the never changing story of Christ's life, love, death, and resurrection to an ever-changing world." Curiosity was ever present once Kirk-Duggan's interest as a musician and scholar was piqued earlier when she wrote an article, "The Theopoetic Theological Ethics of Lauryn Hill and Tupac Shakur," for the volume *Creating Ourselves: African Americans and Latino/as, Popular Culture, and Religious Expression,* edited by Anthony Pinn and Ben Valentine (Durham, N.C.: Duke University Press, 2009). Students' curiosity moved the course with engaged and creative dialogue, which brought in speakers and a local radio producer. Mid-semester, Hall spoke to the Hip Hop class via teleconference. Kirk-Duggan revised her course content in conversation with Hall, and they crafted the table of contents and began the writing process. The two have yet to meet face to face.

For the dialogue partners, the process has been one of growth and discovery. Hall's mission and anthropological study in Kenya and work in the Awakenings community have supported his commitment to this project. Kirk-Duggan's work with her students and the interest that arises when she talks about the project have fueled her joy in this venture. Both authors acknowledge that music has always been central to the African and African diasporan lived experience, central to community, worship, and praise. Historically, traditional African people did not have a sense of performing music for others; music was participatory. Both writers were primed to engage in this work as a next step in their understanding of who God wants them to be and how they are to engage in ministry in the worlds of the church and the academy.

Hall's most memorable experience of hearing "It's Bigger Than Hip-Hop," by underground rap group Dead Prez, was in a crowded movie theater while watching Dave Chappelle's concert documentary, *Block Party*. "It's Bigger Than Hip-Hop" is a song that honors a movement in music that has become a culture. Hall and his friends were all stuffed in a movie theater, and not one seat was open. Dead Prez slowly and deliberately walked onto the stage, and as soon as the first few chords of the song were heard, everyone in the movie audience stood as if the film screen had come to life and they were experiencing a concert in real time. Some jumped, others bounced, but everyone stood to honor this musical anthem that lyrically celebrates the potential of Hip Hop music as a cultural phenomenon and not just a fad marked by gold teeth and baggy pants.

M1, a member of Dead Prez, once described Hip Hop as one word with two meanings. The music is "Hip" because it is sensitive and vulnerable to relevant issues and "Hop" because it is a dynamic movement not bound by conventional processes and practices. This music has its finger on the pulse of human possibility and pain. Hip Hop is a viral phenomenon that has reached an internationally diverse populace in a matter of years.

In many ways, this is like the movement of Christ. In a matter of years, a message of love, redemption, and self-sacrifice became a cultural phenomenon. The good news of God in the flesh moved across continents in a matter of years. From Africa to Asia to Europe, what began as a message became a movement.

For Hall, no phenomenon has the potential to mirror the gospel of Christ like Hip Hop. The church of Christ and the Hip Hop movement share a passion for human interest and sensitivity to human pain. They have an influence that stretches like a rubber band beyond cultural contexts, continents, and time. When it comes to human development, they have a connection that is indivisible and a future that is undeniable.

Some, like Brad Jordan, also known as Scarface, argue that Hip Hop is not a culture but only a fad. It is a gag. It is a get-rich-quick scheme. The powers that be got involved and turned it into a gag gift. Hip Hop was intended to be a gift to the world but now it is a gag. Our stories were so blunt and to the point that they had to be dumbed down. Those in power had to dumb down our method of communicating to the masses. It should be a way of life. Hip Hop will continue to be a gift to listeners who want to hear our story.

Kirk-Duggan got involved with exploring the complexities of Hip Hop while researching the life and times and music of Tupac Shakur and in work on Lauryn Hill. Shakur's complicated life—moving more than twenty times before his teen years, his intellectual prowess, and his Machiavellian, self-destructive nature toward the end of his life—invoked such a sense of tragedy that the disjointedness of such a reality was an intriguing lens through which to read his life story and explore the theological implications of his music. When Lauryn Hill received a Grammy for her CD *The Miseducation of Lauryn Hill,* her use of this term first made popular by historian Carter G. Woodson in his 1933 classic, *The Miseducation of the Negro,* also struck a chord. As an interdisciplinary scholar, Kirk-Duggan often uses cultural artifacts and cultural productions to do research in theology, ethics, Bible, music, and women's studies. When the opportunity to teach a class on Hip Hop presented itself, it was an opportunity to do further research on the music, the culture, and the influence this music and culture have on youth in general and in particular on the youth at the church where she serves on staff as an associate minister. Young Missionary Temple Christian Methodist Church, Raleigh, North Carolina, has helped produce a quartet of young men known as Leviticus, who sing Christian Hip Hop music. Leviticus is on the move and has made their national debut at Apollo Theatre in Harlem, New York, in August 2010. Time spent watching them grow up and do keyboard work with their mentor, Reginald Caldwell, has coalesced many ideas around Christian Hip Hop for Kirk-Duggan.

The process of coauthoring this volume has mirrored some of the experiences of Generation X and the Millennial Generation. Kirk-Duggan and Hall have communicated via texting and e-mail, with an occasional phone conversation. Kirk-Duggan retrieved articles through Epsco, part of the ATLA religious database. No time was spent going through library shelves or microfiche, which was the practice in times past. Books were accessed through online orders or through interlibrary loan. VH1 and BET were sources for viewing Hip Hop videos. This process has been a dialogical spiritual journey. Both writers have dealt with professional issues and personal and family health issues while working on this project. And so, we offer *Wake Up!* as a testimony and witness to the phenomenal creative grace of God and of God's children who take their gifts and their talents and produce marvelous songs of praise and worship of social commentary and of angst, pain, and celebration.

When we fail to listen to someone who is different, whether that person is dressed in the garb of a different age, gender, race, sexuality, class, or creed, we diminish a cosmological sense of the holy. Since the earth is the Lord's and the fullness thereof, the entire world is God's sanctuary: everything that has breath is to praise God; thus we ought not dismiss those capable of praise. According to sociocultural critic Derek Greenfield, over the last thirty years, Hip Hop has provided a venue of voice for many of the voiceless. This cultural praxis has also engaged movement, spoken word, and graffiti to acknowledge and affirm the presence of persons forgotten and overlooked, initially in the bowels of Bronx ghettos. Greenfield distinguishes between Hip Pop and Hip Hop. Hip Pop is the capitalistic, consumerized, idiomatic, and formulaic diatribe fraught with misogyny, violence, and objectification of female bodies. Hip Hop is a revolutionary force for acknowledging human capacity and frailty. To say "I feel you" is an engagement of heart and head, which permeates Hip Hop.

Hip Hop is a complex culture, in which boomers have left a legacy and Generation Xers are engaged in making a statement amid an ethos that claims democracy and freedom are available to all even though they are not. Many, particularly the young and the poor of all colors, cannot access transformative education, decent pay, and a promise for the future. Since persons of African descent were stolen from the continent, they have been able to survive and often flourish through community solidarity, using music as a bolster and therapeutic process toward healing and change. The music of Hip Hop culture, just as blues, rock and roll, boogie-woogie, and rhythm and blues before, has engaged the social and sacred life of the people. What became gospel music emerged from the Spirituals and other so-called secular black music, and the same with Hip Hop. Today, many youth music ministries have created, developed, and included Hip Hop music as part of the worship liturgy. Like gospel music before it, Hip Hop music has not entered worship without contention. Some adults say that Hip Hop music is too secular and is ill suited for saving souls. Some youth contend that adults just do not understand their worldview, their music, and the way they connect with God.

Wake Up! Hip Hop Christianity and the Black Church is a book that invites a conversation, which uses the culture, particularly the music, to create opportunities for new, intergenerational conversations toward building community inside and outside of churches around the experience of salvation in Christ Jesus. The text employs the language of today's youth and that of baby boomers who helped found Hip Hop to wrestle with faith and life in their totality. Engaging this topic involves exploring questions regarding theology, ethics, anthropology, music, and spirituality. Interdisciplinary methods and perspectives frame our discussion of theory and praxis toward effecting social change.

Chapter 1 describes the methodology used, and provides an analysis of terms, contexts, and the role of violence, generational tensions, and Hip Hop as a response; and it explores the experience and placement of physical bodies and embodiment, the emotional engagement and objectification of the body, physicality and rhythm, the body in Christian thought, sexuality, and the devastation of sexism and misogyny.

Chapter 2 explores musical characteristics from African roots, the use of language, and the technical aspects of music to major Hip Hop artists, their signatures, and music as a vehicle of the sacred.

Chapter 3 wrestles with the connections among God, Hip Hop, and spirituality: matters of ontology, existential realities, salvation, freedom, sin, salvation, and prophetic Hip Hop voices within communal life.

Chapter 4 reviews lived theology in the disciplines of black and womanist theologies and explores the role of music and the history of denominations, matters of justice, liberation, and generational tensions around faith and liturgy.

Chapter 5 reflects on the effect of Hip Hop on the black church.

Chapter 6 explores the needs of youth and the intergenerational church for transformation. Specifically, the chapter investigates youth, their worldviews, and their pain and angst; intergenerational and youth challenges in the world; developing youth ministries and practicing faith with those deemed "other"; and the intergenerational future of mission, movement, and evangelism.

The volume closes with an epilogue. We give thanks for the opportunity to signify for a generation that wants to testify and incarnate "Jesuz"!

For those who remain skittish about Hip Hop, it seems that this culture and music, notably in its Christian genre, is here to stay. Hip Hop is not just for thug life. Numerous poets and scholars participate in spoken word. Philosopher Cornel West has produced several Hip Hop projects, and many projects honor his work: for example, "Sketches of My Culture" and "The Cornel West Theory." Courses that include Hip Hop culture abound in universities and seminaries. Churches are opening their doors and hearts to Hip Hop worship just as they used coffeehouses in the 1960s for outreach. We invite you to read *Wake Up!* and to listen to Hip Hop music with your kids and grandkids, if you need translation. Note that there are censored and milder versions of some tunes. Listening with your children, youth, and young adults might open up some doors that you have long desired would not remain closed.

Acknowledgments

Coauthors' Tribute

Our sincerest thanks to Kathy Armistead, our project editor/sojourner at Abingdon Press for her support. Her vision and energies made this book possible. For her great ideas, helpful critique, and genuine passion and compassion for a healthy exchange of ideas, we give thanks.

Marlon Speaking

While developing this book, Cheryl taught me to use metaphors as a way to energize my writing. When it came to these acknowledgments, I was exhausted by the task of thanking the right people the right way so I decided to use metaphors to inspire the words for the people who inspire me.

So here goes. To my writing partner and mentor, Cheryl: you are the *Peacock; beautiful, humble, yet bold*. To the Awakenings Movement (Houston, Detroit, and Nairobi): you are *Still Waters;* reflecting heaven, restoring our cities, and teeming with life beneath the surface. To my first teacher and Mommy: you are the *Minor Chord Triad; intervals of passionate patience, educated wisdom, and infinite support*. To my first coach and Dad: you are a *Warrior's Cry; courageous, vulnerable, and piercing to the soul*. To my sister and inspiration Chelsey: you are the *Needle and Thread; you get straight to the point and always keep us in stitches*. To my sister and crying partner Nikole: you are the *Flamingo; pretty, elegant, and always found in Miami*. To my sister and heart Tiff: you are the *Psalm; prayerful, a powerful statement, and a song*. To my nephew and comrade Cody: you are the smallest *Anchor ever; deep, strong, and agelessly insightful*. To my beloved friend, editor, and ministry partner, Danielle: you are the *Drawing Compass; sharp like the point, creative like the pencil, and well rounded*. To my sweet wife and ride-or-die chick, Regina: you are the *Sun; radiant, life giving, and super hot!* To our daughter, Phoenix: you are *God's promise fulfilled and a little girl who resurrected our burned expectations from the ashes*. I love you all.

Cheryl Speaking

My deepest thanks to students in THE 591: Readings in Theology and Ethics, who engaged in significant dialogue about Hip Hop culture, life, and music; who grew with me, taught me, and encouraged me to press forward with this manuscript: Macy Jones, Gregory Messick, Craig Neill, Leon Parker, Christopher Paul (interviewed for the volume), James Utley, and Michael Whiting. Colleagues from Shaw University, and particularly from Shaw University Divinity School, have been incredibly supportive. Special thanks and kudos go to Lizette Tapp, research and interlibrary loan librarian at the James Cheek Library at Shaw University. Kudos and gratitude to the group Leviticus (Timothy Caldwell, Jared Caldwell, Joseph Ragland, and Ashton Howard) and to their mentor, Reginald Caldwell, who embody the best of Christian Hip Hop, and to our church family, Young Missionary Temple CME Church, who serves as an incubator for their creativity. Many thanks go to persons willing to share their experience around Hip Hop through interviews, contacts, and conversations of support, including: Derek Greenfield, James Stackhouse, Kevin White, Pamela P. Martin, Carl Kenney, Chanequa Walker-Barnes, Tina Pippin, Dedurie Kirk, Deborah Boatner, Latanya Sanders, Edward Thomas, Lilipiana Darensburg, Allison Franzetti, and Rona Drummer. Special thanks to my beloved, my sweet potato pie, the Honorable Mike Kirk-Duggan, who, even during his recent illnesses, has always supported my work and loved me when I had to be away—my first editor and biggest champion.

CHAPTER ONE

I'm Bound to Wreck Your Body and Say Turn the Party Out[1]

Physical Bodies and Embodiment

Hip Hop as Cultural Phenomenon

Historian Carter G. Woodson, in his classic volume *Miseducation of the Negro,* warned us of the generational problems and traumatic loss that occur when society and the church miseducate their own. Miseducation affords distraction, loss of focus, lack of critical thinking, and irresponsible actions or passiveness. Miseducation creates an enslaved mentality. When slave runners stole God's children from Africa and brokered in human cargo, they did not believe that the slaves had souls or could even think. So slave runners were content to limit their restraints to the physical. However, allowing enslaved persons to read or write was illegal once they were on shore in the United States. Limited and segregated life and education made miseducation a systemic reality. Similarly, Jesus' disciples were miseducated, for they did not listen well, interpret, or process information given to them, either.

In Matthew 16, after a confrontation with the Pharisees and Sadducees, Jesus had to deal with his disciples who, yet again, did not "get Jesus" or his message; particularly, they did not understand Jesus' use of bread as a metaphor after feeding the five thousand with five loaves and two fish. Later, when Jesus took his disciples to Caesarea Philippi, he asked them about the identity of the Son of Man. They tried to dodge the question by stating what "some say." But Jesus wanted to know who they said he is. Simon Peter responded that Jesus is the Messiah, the Son of the Living God. Jesus blessed him and recognized that divine wisdom allowed Simon Peter this knowledge. Jesus then said, "You are Peter [*petros*], and on this rock [*petra*] I will build my church, and the gates of Hades will not prevail against it" (Matt. 16:18).

1

We begin this chapter by situating how we came to Hip Hop as we reflect on Hip Hop as a cultural phenomenon. We explore the sociohistorical context in which the music began and the dynamics of East Coast/West Coast/Southern musical and sociocultural sensibilities; the emotional engagement and objectification of the body in Hip Hop; the function of physicality and rhythm; the role of violence, sexuality, and sexism in this genre; and the effect of the Internet in the development and popularity of Hip Hop. Marlon Hall speaks as one who grew up on Hip Hop. We first hear his voice as he recounts how his own sense of agency and coming-of-age parallel the birth and development of Hip Hop.

The Humanity of Hip Hop

Birthed in the 1970s on street corners and at block parties by DJs and MCs, Hip Hop went from being considered "underground" to "Top 40" when Sugarhill Gang made "Rapper's Delight." There are three key trajectories of Hip Hop. The first began in the 1970s and went into the early 1980s and was generated by Afrika Bambaataa, Cold Crush Brothers, DJ Kool Herc, Grandmaster Flash, Kool Moe Dee, Kurtis Blow, Sugarhill Gang, Treacherous Three, and Ultramagnetic MCs. The gangsta rap part of this trajectory emerged from Compton, California, in 1989 and involved an outlaw script and a derrière-shaking beat. From the 1990s came the work of N.W.A., Schoolly D, Ice-T, and Too Short; then came Ice Cube, Dr. Dre, Eminem, Snoop Dogg, Coolio, Warren G, the Notorious B.I.G., Master P, Juvenile, Cash Money, Jay-Z, Ja Rule, Ruff Ryders, Eve, and DMX.

The second trajectory, Hip Pop, also known as Pop Hop, had risqué lyrics that at one time no black radio station would play. These Hip Pop artists included the Beastie Boys, Heavy D, Biz Markie, Will Smith, Run-DMC, LL Cool J, Slick Rick, Salt-N-Pepa, TLC, Missy Elliott, Foxy Brown, Tone-Loc, MC Hammer, Young MC, Da Brat, Jermaine Dupri, Vanilla Ice, Kris Kross, Busta Rhymes, Naughty by Nature, Puff Daddy, D'Angelo, R. Kelly, Mary J. Blige, the Notorious B.I.G. (gangsta and Hip Pop), Lil' Kim, and Sisqo.

The Radicals, the third trajectory, are more revolutionary, politically engaged, and historically aware in their music, where they view themselves doing edu-taining as opposed to entertainment. These artists include include Big Daddy Kane, Queen Latifah, EPMD, Public Enemy, Boogie Down Productions, Eric B. and Rakim, Tupac Shakur, Nas, Redman, Wu-Tang Clan, Raekwon, Method Man, De La Soul, Gang Starr, Jungle Brothers, A Tribe Called Quest, Leaders of the New School, Pete Rock & CL Smooth, Arrested Development, Outkast, The Roots, Erykah Badu, Black Eyed Peas, Common, Mos Def, Fugees, Lauryn Hill, and Wyclef Jean. The once-dominant New York political themes of activism in the 1980s began to diminish in the 1990s.[2]

I (Marlon) grew up *with* Hip Hop, not just around it. I literally grew up *with* the music. The music and I were born around the same time in the 1970s, after the civil rights movement of the 1960s. Together we grew and learned to navigate our way around an ever-changing world. We were raised like second cousins, this music and me. This kindred music visited me from all over the nation, by way of my Sony Walkman and headphones, sharing stories and life experiences that would reflect and shape my own.

My first fight was coached by the East Coast group Brand Nubian,[3] who taught me that "punks step up to get beat down."[4] My second public dance routine was choreographed by West Coast cousins Digital Underground,[5] who taught me the "humpty dance." In the humpty dance, you move the midsection of your body while your arms move in a wing-like motion. Even the fire that fueled my last crush on a teacher, Mrs. "Got It" Gibbs, was energized by the muscle-bound rapper and actor LL Cool J (Ladies Love Cool James), who told me I needed a girl (or teacher) "who's as sweet as a dove for the first time in my life, I see I need love."[6] This music has been a well-traveled and experienced relative and friend to me, and to many others of my generation. This music is a companion and not just a culture, which has a compelling quality that connects with masses of people in personal ways.

Hip Hop seems human or biological in the way it has spawned an original art form, dance expressions, and styles of dress. Its set of shared attitudes, values, and practices are infectious. This inspiration positively and virally travels like it is airborne. Here are some of its characteristics: (1) sudden involuntary motor and repetitive vocal expressions when clever metaphors are spoken at varying volumes; (2) grimaces that resemble a person eating sour lemons

3

when particular chord progressions are heard; and (3) sporadic head nods with facial frowns when acute drum patterns are played. Hip Hop is an international human phenomenon that draws us in, one song and metaphor at a time.

Hip Hop lives and breathes with us like a person; and unlike most cultural movements in human history, Hip Hop is human. It effortlessly connects with what makes us human because it is human. Because it was unconsciously shaped by the meek and not manufactured by the affluent, Hip Hop has a freedom and truth that is distinctly human. By exploring the vulnerability, passion, and truth of Hip Hop, we discover what it means to be more fully human.

Hip Hop Is Human

I realized that Hip Hop was a living and breathing phenomenon at the age of sixteen. I traveled to Eastern Europe a few weeks after the Iron Curtain fell in 1989. I was there to distribute an unlikely combination of gifts on the streets that would have had me and my delegation jailed just two weeks before. As a delegate of the United States Youth Council, I had a mission to pass out condoms and Bibles. The novelty of our mission was only overshadowed by the unique culture shock I experienced as the only African American delegate. We traveled to places in Moscow and Leningrad where black people had never been seen in person. The only experience many of the Eastern Europeans had had with young black men was through media images and entertainment portrayals of life in the United States.

Many older folks grimaced at me, while others called me "monkey" or "darkie" as I walked the streets. Some even spit on the ground to show their disgust as I walked past. This was not a shock because to some degree I had experienced this treatment at home. The real shock, however, was the way young people in Moscow and Leningrad treated me. They treated me like the young prince of the 1989 cult classic film *Coming to America*, starring James Earl Jones and Eddie Murphy.[7] Often running up to touch my skin and smiling as I moved about the city, they made me feel like family. Some even stopped to do random break-dance moves and awkwardly attempt to give me handshakes that were authentic to the urban streets of Houston. These Russian youth

4

made me feel human and valuable because, through Hip Hop, we could communicate, as together we experienced the heart and vibe of a global culture. Even across continents, Hip Hop connected us as members of a distinguished clan and gave a voice to the voiceless.

Recently freed from the oppression of Communist reign, they saw me as a baggy-jeans-wearing freedom fighter sent to guide them into the new world of freedom. The humanity of Hip Hop went before me in every province and town we visited. To the young people, I was a human brother and not a monkey—a kindred member of a redeemed people.

This charismatic phenomenon that we call Hip Hop draws people of different ethnic backgrounds and experiences together all over the world because it has an honest, rich, and authentic life that makes room for everyone. Many wonder how this music has been able to bridge gaps between so many in such a short time. How can this ghetto music have such a compelling glamour that it seduces the bodies, minds, creative sensibilities, and clothes closets of dancers, artists, and designers everywhere? A response to this question may come from the personality of the music. The music allows us to be creative expressions of a living culture rather than products of dying neighborhoods.

Not Mere Products

In a world in which people are often seen as only products of their environment, Hip Hop believes that we are more than manufactured; we are creative. Hip Hop boldly tells the world that we are not "products of our environment," but "creations of God."[8] Music made from the discarded B-side[9] of classic albums, dance studios made from cardboard, and fantastic moves made by our bodies make us a force to be reckoned with.

Black migrants, from Southern plantations, moved north in search of a better life in such cities as New York, Detroit, and Philadelphia. They found jobs in manufacturing plants and on assembly lines, which made them instruments of industry. When the industry jobs dried up during the Great Depression,[10] their communities became desperate and even dangerous. Crime escalated because of a lack of jobs, and alcoholism increased as people

5

sought to self-medicate the pain of hardship. These transplanted communities from plantations became islands of poverty and then ghettos.

Soon the children of these disenfranchised former sharecropping farmers received more education and began a movement to gain civil rights and black power. The civil rights and the Black Power movements gave these ghetto communities, in both the North and South, an antagonist to combat and a reason to come together. They began to gain momentum as a creative force that was more than a product. Bus boycotts, sit-ins, marches, and voter registration efforts made these descendants of former slaves more than mere products of a workforce; they were organized masses of social and political creativity.

However, the presidency of Ronald Reagan in the early 1980s thwarted many of the gains of the civil rights movement and Black Power initiatives. "Reaganomics" led to more job loss, economic challenges, and social desperation. The desperation coupled with a cheap and deadly combination of cocaine and baking soda (crack) turned the need to self-medicate into a minefield of unrealizable dreams. Landmarks of African American development, like New York's Harlem and Houston's entrepreneurial Dowling Street, that once lifted blacks up became landmines where drug cartels and gangs planted the explosive drug crack in the pockets of metaphorical suicide bombers who killed themselves and the people around them. Neighborhoods that were once safe villages were transformed into graveyards where dead-men-and-women-walking abused drugs. The descendants of once-freed slaves became enslaved once again.

In the throes of the violence and tension of urban community, DJs such as Afrika Bambaataa[11] and DJ Kool Herc[12] brought music that "stood in the cracks of our brokenness."[13] Hip Hop came along in this time as a voice of freedom and truth. It worked to dispel the crippling message that we are products or slaves of any environment. Pioneers like Sugarhill Gang[14] and Kurtis Blow[15] came to give a voice of hope to a community shattered by drugs, violence, and despair. And the horror of death and poverty became the matrix that forged the power of Hip Hop music.

From Broken to Beautiful

> The thing that drew me into Hip Hop was that it was a rebellious
> music. It was a ghetto folk music that was not supposed to have
> a voice. Here is this symbolic art form called Hip Hop where the
> music aspect was us only taking what was there. We had the
> record and that was what we used. That is what Flash used, that
> is what Herc used, that is what Bambaataa used.[16]

Hip Hop takes broken shards of promise, dance, and music and
makes a mosaic. It does not hide brokenness; rather it discovers art
and beauty within. I experience this art and beauty as a kindred
spirit. Its sound, my second cousin, is skilled at taking discarded
stuff and making of it dynamic objects of art: found-object art.

I have many memorable experiences with this kindred sound,
but one of my first was seeing rapper Biz Markie[17] for the first time
on *Yo! MTV Raps*.[18] Biz Markie was my hero. His layers of "dookie
rope chains" dangled freely from his rather large neck. The gold
jewelry was the stuff of the Hip Hop rich and famous.

Believe it or not, this was the coolest image of manhood that I
had ever seen on TV. As one of the premiere beatboxers of his time,
Biz Markie used his mouth to move a nation. A beatboxer is a performer who uses his or her voice, mouth, lips, and tongue to imitate the sound of musical instruments, especially percussion
instruments, to create musical beats, rhythms, and melodies. His
"I'm Bound to Wreck Your Body and Say Turn the Party Out"[19]
made its way, everywhere, into souls and minds of rap artists and
listeners alike.

From "Vapors,"[20] a song that was a tale of a reject's revenge, to
"Make the Music with Your Mouth, Biz"[21] in which Biz used his
mouth as an instrument; he became a spokesperson for all self-
declared and societally affirmed underdogs like me. Biz Markie
taught a generation that we could use what we had to be great,
even with our oversized lips and bellies. He taught us that what
others saw as flawed could be beautiful.

Biz's music was introduced on discarded cardboard dance
floors, used microphones, and borrowed turntables. These inaus-
picious beginnings led many critics to believe that the music was
a temporary fad that would fade like the jeans worn by its sup-
porters. These critics thought Hip Hop would simply drift off into

pop-culture obscurity when the cardboard wore out and the secondhand instruments broke, but it did not. Even after some thirty-nine years from its origins, Hip Hop remains one of the most prolific and powerful cultural standards in the world. As I continue to travel today from New York to Prague and beyond, I am welcomed by young people and respected by the old as a young black man who is a part of their cultural family. This is because Hip Hop continues to pave new pathways for the powerless, rejected, and disenfranchised.

However, this cultural phenomenon grew not only in spite of its cardboard-thin foundations, but also because of them. Hip Hop music is for displaced people—young and old. This music and its accompanying cultural experience are accessible, relevant, tangible, and honest. Here, lonely latchkey kids find love; recluses find companionship.

Issues of Method: Interviews

Rather than speak simply as researchers and analysts, we, the authors, decided to let the music speak for itself. Hip Hop wordsmiths, artists, and musicians themselves best document this broken-to-beauty story. For them, the music is the means to tell gripping human stories. This approach will allow the story about the music, culture, and the people of Hip Hop to tell itself. The interviews are the heart of the book, and our observations and research are woven in and about. Relevant and emergent artists respond to key questions so that by the end of this book, you will have a new window on your own life.

The first interview is with Brad Jordan, also known as Scarface.[22] Brad is Hip Hop's metaphorical photographer. He seeks to find the right setting, adjust the lens, and project the lighting necessary to capture images of hope, pain, and promise in ghetto life.

Is Hip Hop a Cultural Phenomenon?

Brad Jordan's manager called me and said that Brad had thirty minutes to talk in between holes as he played his daily round of golf.[23] Because I was driving at the time, I frantically pulled into an empty parking lot, placed the interview questions on my laptop computer, plugged my recording device to the phone, and dialed the number. As the phone began to ring, I thought about his role in the architecture of The Geto Boys,[24] and I began to tap my fingers on the steering wheel. I also thought about his solo career and ambassadorship as a Southern rapper working with artists such as Nas[25] and Freeway[26] and the record label Def Jam South[27] that signed unknowns such as Ludacris.[28] When he finally picked up, I realized that my palms were sweaty and that I was speaking in an octave deeper than normal. I was nervous.

Brad Jordan, born in Houston in 1971, is a Hip Hop icon for his entrepreneurship, poetic prose, and insightful storytelling. He was a founding member of The Geto Boys, one of the most prolific rap groups in the world, with such hits as "Mind Playing Tricks on Me"[29] and "Gangster of Love."[30] These songs continue a tradition of storytelling that honors the legacy of Langston Hughes[31] (1902-67), poet, novelist, playwright, short-story writer, and columnist, who wrote about the Harlem Renaissance.

After introductions and pleasantries, I realized that this golf-playing rapper was a really nice guy. I started by asking him if Hip Hop was a cultural phenomenon, and after a long pause, a deep breath, and a Southern-styled "Mannnn," he responded:

> Hip Hop was once a culture, but today it is not a culture; it is a fad. It should be a way of life and a gift, but right now it is a gag gift sold at a discounted price. It is a get-rich quick scheme and not a culture. The powers that be got involved and turn it into a gag gift.

When he finished his statement, it started to rain hard. I thought that it would be hard for me to hear him, but his voice got louder and grew more passionate. You could tell he was beginning to speak out of a painful, disappointing place when he said:

> It was intended to be a gift to the world, but now it is a gag. It will continue to be a gift to listeners who want to hear our story, but our stories were so blunt and to the point that it had to be dumbed down. They had to dumb our method of communicating down to the masses.[32]

This interview transpired a few months after he had publicly denounced Hip Hop. Blogs and online magazines reported that the artist formally known as Scarface was asking audiences to no longer refer to him by his rap name. He wanted to be known as Brad. This former rapper and record-label president of the most influential label in Hip Hop gave up rap and decided to shift to a career in golf.

This man cared about the music that he loved and lived for, but he had decided no longer to be associated with it. This may seem extreme, but Brad's decision communicates a larger cultural truth about the tarnished quality of the music. The "gift" of Hip Hop to the world is truth and authenticity. Without those, the music has nothing to say.

East Coast/West Coast/South/Global: Sociohistorical Context

As one who came later to Hip Hop, Cheryl has listened to this music, researched the culture and select musicians, and taught classes on Hip Hop, particularly around its sociocultural reality as it relates to intergenerational relationships and education within Christianity and their related communities. Below is her analysis.

Hip Hop is a cultural movement that originated in the 1970s from urban African diasporan peoples in New York City and Jamaica, amid the changes of urban renewal, white flight, resegregation, busing, and interstate highways that demolished many black and brown communities. Now it is a global phenomenon, which includes political activism, fashion, slang, double-Dutch moves (complicated jump roping), and beatboxing. Vocal scratching (imitating turntable skills) involves singing and simulating various musical instruments and replicating sound effects. Though some think of Hip Hop as being the same as rap music, many understand Hip Hop as the cosmology or cultural context and rap as a musical by-product of Hip Hop.

In many ways, for sociologist Derek Greenfield, the line from the song that heads this chapter, "I'm bound to wreck your body and say turn the party out," embodies the best of what Hip Hop endeavors to do. Here the Pacific Northwest takes the spotlight. Certain geographic regions, other than the East Coast and West

Coast, have voices that need to be heard. Benedict Anderson's imagined community[33] concerns the creation and global spread of the "imagined communities" of nationality—the personal and cultural feeling of belonging to the nation. According to Greenfield, Anderson's concept of imagined community (the East and West Coasts) could be brought to explicate hip hop's definition of authentic spaces; in turn, the culture could be challenged to broaden beyond the East/West paradigm so people could give voice to their particular experiences all over the world. Thus, there is both a commonality and a kind of ontological space that is just for a particular region, with its own needs, styles, and interests. This shift begins to challenge and deconstruct the limitations of an East/West paradigm and reveals the complexity and diversity of Hip Hop and of its global paradigm, which go beyond East Coast/West Coast.

Geologic, a Filipino Hip Hop artist, sees an opportunity in Hip Hop, in general, and in "Nobody Beats the Biz," in particular: the opportunity to challenge and struggle against political oppression and to be able to find one's place in terms of scripture, a sensibility that goes so much beyond only a local perspective. Such music raises issues of people around the world being critical consumers of information regarding politics, church, and education, making it a global phenomenon. While our physical world is vast, modern technology reduces time and space in a way that we now live in a small world, because we are so connected. The irony of living in a small world is that Greenfield knows Blue Scholars such as Geologic, who goes by Geo, personally.

The global experience of Hip Hop is a culture that has been the sound track and blueprint for a great deal of progressive social action worldwide: for example, it is a force that propelled and affirmed young people in South Africa in their struggle against apartheid. And we continue to hear from other youth whose contextual conditions in their own lands move them to use Hip Hop music.[34]

The sociopolitical influence of Hip Hop through popular culture, often seen as antiestablishment, continues to influence the music, style, fashion, and sense of purpose of youth. But Hip Hop is not monolithic having become quite diverse over the last four decades. This genre engages multiple age groups and geographic regions, beyond East Coast/West Coast polarities, and involves diverse racial-ethnic groups. Hip Hop is global; it emerged as a multilingual, multiracial, multicultural phenomenon, and it continues to live with multiple tensions, particularly the focus on profit versus the focus on politics.

The makeup of the people involved reflects different sociocultural and historical realities. Amid this flurry of activity, Hip Hop provides an opportunity for the galvanizing of poetry, imagination, and rhythm, which can spark interest in creativity and learning. Author S. Craig Watkins posits that the internal debate rages about how the Hip Hop movement can reestablish commitments and responsibilities to the robust, growing, diverse, youth-based community. Hip Hop is part of youth reality, in which it serves as a venue for them to speak truth to power, to imagine their world in optimistic, insightful ways, cognizant of how systems and situations can thwart their capacities to affect the world in which they live.[35]

Hip Hop engages the most pertinent, contemporary sociopolitical issues and provides a forum for youth dealing with and having dialogue about "real world issues that frustrate the Hip Hop nation."[36] Early on, critical figures such as Afrika Bambaataa (born Kevin Donovan) thought that Hip Hop could bolster and encourage young people to transform their lives. Groups such as Public Enemy that began as a protesting, ghetto subculture movement forced the discussion of disenfranchisement, racism, history, politics, incarceration, violence, generational differences, miseducation, and media misrepresentation that produced socially conscious, relevant, revolutionary commentary and also opened the door for lyrics that are raw, graphic, aggressive, and antiestablishment. With this shift came reality music that privileged the market over the message, sensationalism over education; the focus shifted to street hustling, crack, and crime. By the mid-1990s, song themes ceased to be politically provocative and by the twenty-first century focused a lot more on gangsta swagger, hypercapitalism, pop posturing, misogyny, guns, ghetto reality, and street credibility, which often expressed the death of the souls and bodies of black folk, as it became the language of media moguls in corporate United States.[37]

East Coast "conscious rap" stands in contrast with West Coast gangsta rap. Hip Hop continued in a festive rap frame through the late 1980s, as gangsta rap emerged. By this time, two well-defined cohorts—the East Coast's Public Enemy from Long Island, New York, and the West Coast's N.W.A (Niggaz with Attitude), a Compton, California-based Hip Hop group—articulated unorthodox styles of revolution, framed by metropolitan, postindustrial realities shaping young African diasporan male identity. Public Enemy invested in the black radical tradition and intentionally referred to icons or idols of black militancy.[38]

Christian Hip Hop

Christian youth engaging in Hip Hop have no geographic or ethnic boundaries. When the youth sing about the harshness of life without Christ, they avoid rhyming about misogyny, money, or mayhem. Ministries such as Tampa's Without Walls and New York City's Metro Ministries' Club Life provide space for youth to sing, fellowship, and dance to Christian words and Hip Hop music.

The popular beats and positive lyrics of the Hip Hop nation emerging within the rule of God draw the youth to ministries dedicated to preaching Christ's good news. Pastors such as Gerald Durley of Atlanta remind youth that although they think they listen to the beat and not to the words, they need to be aware of the subliminal power of the violent, sexually explicit lyrics that can harm their spiritual growth. Pastor Edwin Rucker of Virginia notes that youth interface with church culture to appease their parents and with Hip Hop culture to be with their friends.

When teens feel disconnected, disenfranchised, and abandoned without responsible adult support, the Hip Hop culture offers a way to connect with community. Harry Young, who ministers to youth in Chesapeake, Virginia, posits that Hip Hop music supports merciless honesty, even if wrapped in vulgarity, as it describes the ravages, frustrations, and confusion of urban places, and shows how social institutions fail to help youth. Like the 1970s Jesus movement, today's Hip Hop movement can offer venues in which youth can come to know the gospel message in their own context.[39]

Another type of aggressive emotional violence occurs when artists are distracted, are panicky, have self-doubt, and are filled with anxiety or are intimidated. Some MCs or DJs intentionally threaten others, criticize others' lack of skill or Hip Hop expertise, or use language of sexual violence to oppose and denigrate others' appearances. Some MCs strive to maintain internal silence in order to concentrate and to keep self-consciousness and self-doubt in check. Brett Edaki, cultural critic, notes that, ironically, the male MCs' internal quiet supports their homophobia, misogyny, and machismo, though they deny any homoeroticism or homosexuality. When the music is pitched in deafening decibels, in either Hip Hop or "new wave" Evangelical services, it brings the crowd to a frenzied state. To insiders, this wall of sound ensures isolation. And silence, the space between the pattern of sounds, is needed for the message to be heard and absorbed.[40]

Emotional Engagement and the Body

Historically, the body in Christian thought has been a tradition of paradox, misunderstanding, contradictions, and with significant distortions. While Jesus becomes incarnated in bodily form and St. Paul talks about the church as Christ's body, there exists a great deal of distorted thought about the body, which often plays out in popular culture. Mary Timothy Prokes, theologian and Franciscan Sister of the Eucharist, identifies eight reasons for these distortions, in which people experience, represent, or reflect on the body as an object of shame, fear, and unworthiness.

- First, people often fear the unknown and create taboos around things wrongly considered dangerous or misunderstood, particularly the female life cycle of menstruation, pregnancy, birth, and nursing: issues about sexuality and fertility. Powerful folk customs and belief systems, inhibitions, and shame about the human body have a tremendous effect on the human psyche and human behavior.
- Second, ignorance concerning women's bodies and the mysteries surrounding human procreation remain the source of fascination and fear, of cynicism and control. In the twenty-first century, many people are embar-

rassed to talk about the female body and continue to objectify it as if women were property.

- Third, early Western philosophical and theological systems supported mind/body, body/spirit, spiritual/material dualisms. Constructing these dualisms in which mind or spirit were superior to body and the material, some thinkers would press these polarities to make men superior to women, with the understanding that males were superior to females, that females were imperfect, and that females could only become perfect and, for some Christians, ultimately saved by becoming male. Some early theologians have a lot of ambivalence about the body. This mentality caused some to become martyrs; and during the times of persecution, others became ascetic, as they sought to escape desire and the carnal. Even so, some theologians came to see the interconnectedness of body and spirit.
- Fourth, influences and results of invasions by warring tribal groups and crusaders, pitting Christianity against Islam, quieted asceticism and brought about the split among the body, mind, and spirit as people just tried to survive. Monastic life provided greater balance, and the twelfth and thirteenth centuries found new insights and a new appreciation for the body.
- Fifth, with Aquinas's revival of Aristotle's thought and the move from monasteries to universities, dualism again emerged, leaving confusion and misunderstanding regarding the body, the roles of men and women, sexuality, and procreation.
- Sixth, there was confusion and ecclesial abuse around the sacraments, including the collection of relics from saints, and the selling of indulgences flourished within a climate rife with such diseases as the bubonic plague and political instability because of war.
- Seventh, Enlightenment dualism signaled by Rene Descartes' famous dictum, *cogito ergo sum* ("I think therefore I am") split the cosmos in two, separating the mind from the body in lasting and profound ways.

• Last, twentieth-century technological advances promoted distortions around the human body and a material universe, as we can now dissect matter into tiny
particles not visible to the naked eye.[41]

In the twenty-first century, while we speak more intentionally
about holistic beings, we nevertheless tend to live and express ourselves in compartmentalized ways, often wedded to the notion that
the spirit is strong, but the flesh (or body) is weak (Matt. 26:41).

Human Sexuality and the Body

Studying the body in Christian thought means dealing with
human sexuality, about which there is much ambiguity and
ambivalence. Christine Gudorf notes that we are in a crisis, for the
scriptures do not have all of the answers, and many church and
societal traditions are skewed. Often neither churches nor other
systems within society address sexual sin and sexual violence;
hence we choose sexual ignorance. She posits that we need a new
framework—a theological framework—for sexuality; we need to
deal with Christian moral blindness, sexism, homophobia, and the
glorification and cheapening of sexuality. Society and the church
fail to celebrate sexual activity and the pleasure of sex. We need to
integrate sexuality into our larger human experience and deal with
the problems many of us have regarding sexual language and intimacy more generally. Because we do not teach that sexuality is part
of the beautiful reality of being human, shame, guilt, and fantasy
around sexuality create sensationalism, violence, and heightened
objectification of the body.[42]

Physicality and Rhythm

Physicality relates to the way we see, feel, experience, and move
our bodily, material, or corporeal selves in any given space. A discussion about physicality and Hip Hop is also a dialogue about
how Hip Hop music helps define a person's literal place in the
world. For many in Western culture, space, understood as property, is commodified. The more you own, the more power you
have over other people and is directly proportional to your value

as a person. This is the concept of *real* estate. In our postcolonial culture, how much earth you own and can claim determines your worth or real value. Some use Hip Hop as a way to claim space often denied because of systemic oppression.

Nasir "Nas" Jones's musical testament, "Whose World Is This,"[43] was a way for him to process his lack of space when he lived in the projects as a child. His "the world is yours"[44] was a declarative statement that he shared with a fictitious character from *Scarface*, the docudrama that featured an exiled Cuban immigrant.[45] Tony Montana[46] found himself with no space in his native land or in the land in which he found refuge, so he worked hard to acquire a place in the world by amassing a huge piece of property with a mansion that had a neon sign pasted on a rotating globe reading, "The World Is Yours."

The regional nature of Hip Hop helps the artists and their artistry authenticate the value of where they are in the world. Tupac's *California Love*, Nas's *New York State of Mind*, and Outkast's *Southerplayalisticadillacmuzik* are manifestos that tell the world that we are here and are beautifully connected to where we are in the world.[47] The regional sensibility of Hip Hop also gives listeners in other regions a glimpse into the life of young people in other places, erasing the space that separates them. While some may never be able to travel across the country, through listening to a song, they can travel in a moment's notice. Outkast in Atlanta, Jay-Z in New York, Common in Chicago, and N.W.A. in Los Angeles reflect ghetto documentarians who tell stories about life in other neighborhoods across the country. The music has a way of erasing the boundaries of space and time. Hip Hop is a magical experience that can bring the East to the West and the South to the North in a matter of minutes through the music.

Another way Hip Hop displays physicality is through the use of body movement, and in this, B-boying is the ultimate. Who would have ever in a million years thought about dancing as spinning on your head or doing windmills (having your legs kick off and wheel)? Who would have thought that a person could spin on one hand?[48]

Hip Hop dancing is an expression with multiple purposes. Dancing in time to the rhythm with no regard to your location is a way to escape and be where your imagination takes you. It is literally a way to release stress and emote in a manner consistent with the vibe, beat, tone, and lyrical content of the music. Hip Hop dance battles gave people a chance to go to war and prevail in an area and arena that belongs to them and to win at night when they have lost and have felt lost all day.[49]

Physicality also involves the movement and gestures of the DJ and the infamous, often sexually suggestive "booty calls" made popular through clips and videos from BET (Black Entertainment Television) and MTV (Music Television) where they are so prevalent. The physical dance movements are often sexualized and suggestive; the garments are often provocative, too tight, and often reveal too much. The movements sometimes simulate sexual activity and objectify women dancers, in particular. Earlier dance movements connected with Hip Hop were largely B-boying and break-dancing. With the commercialization of Hip Hop serving as a catalyst to create Hip Pop, sexualized gyrations have become normative. Some would posit the impetus for physicality, regardless of the style or type of movement and dance, is the heightened importance of rhythm in Hip Hop.

Rhythm, in Hip Hop, can frame a person's perception of his or her mortality. Rhythm, the symmetry or flow of the beat, the pulse of the music that involves alternating stressed and unstressed elements as it incorporates sound and silence, helps young people process and understand that they may or may not have to live. Biggie Small's[50] "Machine Gun Funk"[51] was his way of partnering with the rhythm to help him process what he thought was his limited time on earth. The sound of bullet rounds inspired the pattern for his rhythm. Smalls actually wrote to the rhythm of the same kind of bullet that would tragically take his life in March 1997.

The violence of a community in poverty and the victims left behind are an alarm clock for many black youth. Music is a way of keeping time until the clock runs out. The rhythm of a machine gun or the vibrant sound of a drum rim is a way for a generation to dance with death personified; a way to "live for this funk and die for the funk."[52] Such music affords an escape that rhythmically forces you to lose track of time in the rhythm. The rhythm is a carpet ride that gives us an escape out of our problems and into the music.

In some respects then, Hip Hop music does what music always does: it provides an aesthetic matrix, a venue in which one can imagine and recreate a reality of beauty and nobility; a world that can make sense amidst the daily tragedy of crime and hard time, transforming the mundane into the sublime even as one comes of age. Music that appeals at such a visceral level provides leverage against annihilation from societal and familial oppression. Hip Hop music tells its devotees "You matter" when Momma and Daddy cannot or do not care. Music, at its best, soothes, inspires, and anchors one when, in the words of the great Chinua Achebe, "things fall apart."[53]

Role of Violence

An essential building block of Hip Hop culture is "keeping it real," or to have an authenticity and credibility. Since the 1990s, the authenticity that once challenged white supremacist oppression— the language of black consciousness-raising, often nationalism— has shifted toward dysfunction and pathology, with pathology becoming normative. Notions of authenticity vary, as the issue of underground versus commercial Hip Hop still must contend with issues of poverty, class, race, ethnicity, money, and capitalism.[54] Principalities of systemic oppression and violence often targeted the poor, serving as catalysts for violence on the street.

The institutional powers that are ambivalent if not utterly dismissive of urban communities, the locus of Hip Hop's origins, include police, banks, and the welfare bureaucracy. These institutions respectively (1) protect economic boundaries, protecting property not people; (2) participate in global economics and care nothing for urban poor; and (3) humiliate and dehumanize the poor, while working against wholeness and support in order to manipulate and control. "Humans who wield violence and imagine they control it are actually in bondage to it. They have become its minions and servants and victims."[55] Thus, the powers and principalities of incarnated and embodied systemic violence wreak havoc on communities and cause corporations to become monsters absorbed in greed, enriching themselves by any means necessary.[56]

Gangsta rap, a subcategory of Hip Hop, promotes sexual violence and misogyny while achieving economic success by being outrageous and viciously exploiting black women. Such misogynistic sensationalism, as depicted in N.W.A.'s "Efil4zaggiN," made platinum because white T.B.W.A.s ("teenage boys with attitude") purchased the albums and marketed them through word of mouth. Gangsta rap went from being to and about street homeboys and about their lived realities and secrets to being commercially successful Hip Hop to targeting a white audience[57] with an increasing use of violent language.

There is the old question, "Does art imitate life, or does life imitate art?" Likewise, is Hip Hop a mirror of a violent reality, or is reality a mirror of violent Hip Hop? To these questions, we have to say both. To the question: Does violence lead to Hip Hop or does Hip Hop generate violence? Again, we answer both. In some ways the violence reflects U.S. culture, and in some ways Hip Hop's use of violence reflects how particular racial-ethnic communities have been oppressed.

Those most affected by violence are often people who lack the resources and hope they need to live a successful life. You do not blame a thermometer because you have a fever. Hip Hop in many ways is a thermometer that is just gauging the political climate and social conditions of our time. However, on the other side, some artists have used the platform of Hip Hop as an economic opportunity to exploit and extol violence and a violent way of life, which then becomes appealing to young people, who often feel disembodied in society and are looking for some ways in which they can have purpose. So violence begets anger and aggression. Fighting becomes a way for people to have a sense of ownership, not to excuse but to explain and understand that streak of violence, particularly in a culture that promotes male violence. Ironically, Greenfield notes that violence can be appealing to young people who otherwise do not feel they have public control of their bodies, and they may use violence as a tool and expression of self-ownership to resist dominant representations that marginalize them.[58]

Although Hip Hop contains misogynistic lyrics, it should not be scapegoated for the societal problems of the United States. Writer/filmmaker/critic Cheo Coker posits that rather than question the misogyny in Hip Hop, one should ask why leadership fails to question other places in society that support and promote misogyny. Thus, if one critiques the sexism in Hip Hop, one also needs to critique the corporate structure that creates, manufactures, and distributes the CDs and DVDs.[59]

Sexuality and Sexism

Three terms are significant for us as we wrestle with the depths of violence, particularly against women, and the power and pain it generates within Hip Hop culture: patriarchy, sexism, and misogyny. Narrowly construed, *patriarchy* refers to hierarchical social systems, relationships, and ways of thinking, historically derived from Greek and Roman law. The word *patriarch* comes from the Greek words *patria*, meaning "father," and *arché*, meaning "rule"; that is, "the rule of the father," in which the male head of the household has absolute legal and economic power or governance over his dependents, the female and male family members of his household. Broadly construed, patriarchy means the manifestation and institutionalization of male dominance over women and children in all social systems in particular (family, religion, economics, politics, wealth, authority, status, interpersonal relationships, and self-image) and the extension of male dominance over women to society in general. In patriarchal societies, men hold power (dominance, supremacy) in all-important societal institutions, and women are deprived of access to such power. In these societies, gender relations, structured on a principle of male responsibility and authority, correspond to female protection and submission. This does not mean that women are either totally powerless or totally deprived of rights, influence, and resources. Yet property, for example, is usually inherited from father to son. In the Bible, Paul contradicts this system when he asserts that within marriage, women and men are equal sex partners (1 Cor. 7:1-7). If patriarchy is part of the larger social context, sexism is the specific oppressive use of power against another because of gender.

Sexism is a belief and philosophy, along with the resulting related behaviors, that people of one sex, or gender, are inherently superior to people of the other sex. Such prejudice, which leads to hatred or discrimination based on gender, can be institutional, communal, and personal. The prejudice focuses on the interpretation, beliefs, and feelings about a person's physical, mental, or

21

spiritual characteristics that define male and female and cultural and psychological definitions of femininity and masculinity. Sexism involves unfair treatment or bigotry, inequity, or bias based on a difference of gender, which cause disadvantage or unequal opportunity because of the cultural dominance of one gender over the other.

Misogyny is hostility, hatred, strong prejudice against, or pathological aversion to women; it is an antonym of philogyny, which is an overfondness of women and an aggravated form of male sexism. Those holding misogynistic beliefs can be of either sex. Although misogyny is sometimes confused with misanthropy, the terms are not interchangeable, for misanthropy refers more generally to a hatred of humanity.

A myth of male superiority and great sexual and mental prowess justifies male pleasure at any cost and embodies sexism and gender oppression in forms of misogyny and male supremacy. Some men, engaging in sexism, simultaneously pursue intense political, economic, and erotic pleasure. Other men dehumanize others through dysfunctional behavior. Some male supremacist behaviors include experiencing powerlessness when relating to people who are different and then transferring responsibility for that feeling of powerlessness onto what becomes the victim.

Art often imitates what people practice in real time. During the 1960s and 1970s, movies shifted from covert misogyny or sympathetic indifference to brutality and violent abuse. Contemporary film, pornography, and music objectify women, place them in lewd and lascivious poses, and depict enactments of rape and physical, mental, and emotional abuse.[60]

Women who embrace an epistemology—or a way of knowing and learning related to connectedness—often relate to the discomfort and pain of the other one, her male partner. The oppressed or battered woman often puts concern about others over concern for self or at the expense of herself and usually cannot focus on her own needs, especially if she believes her needs conflict with those of her partner. Some women do not protect themselves as they try to change their abuser. Women are often fearful when displaying power because they view this behavior as arrogant, prideful, or selfish. Ultimately, women end up having to choose between saving their economic well-being or saving their physical safety and emotional well-being.[61]

Sexual and gender oppression manipulates, violates, and diminishes the energy of the victim, and the perpetrator believes and behaves as though the victim is merely his or her personal property. The emotional intensity and skewed identity of gender predators and their victims emerge in life and in popular cultural representations such as film, music, and literature—including the Bible.

In his research of Hip Hop and popular culture, Greenfield notes that in many ways, Hip Hop reflects global misogynist culture as a whole. The song "Tip Drill," by artist Nelly, is a poignant example of the complexity of sexism in American society. In this song's video, Nelly, surrounded by dozens of scantily clad women at a pool party, swipes a credit card between the buttocks of a bent-over woman (whose face is never seen in the video) as if to purchase her. On the one hand, it is a deeply disturbing and demeaning image. On the other hand, some who watch the video will proclaim that she is complicit in her own oppression. This may be true, but inflicting humiliation on oneself is still humiliation. Yet the larger sociopolitical implication—because we live in a culture that encourages us to consume objects and merchandise—is that if she does not do it, someone else will.[62]

The reverse scenario of a man being portrayed in this way will never happen, because that is not an image that is marketable in the United States. Such a reality speaks to Hip Hop culture or individuals acting in the social drama; more important, it also stands as commentary on our appetite for sexism and female objectification in mainstream U.S. culture.

One could also tie the imagery in the video to heterosexism and male dominance. That is, the man in the video needs to validate his heterosexuality. So, the more women a man can have, consume, or buy, the more manly he is perceived to be.[63]

For women who grew up in the Hip Hop culture, with its appeal of contagious rhymes and experiences of beats pulsating in one's head and body, the conundrum is dealing with the blistering, misogynistic words, particularly when women are more involved than men, yelling out the words, tapping their toes, and dancing harder to the beats of this music. The raw creative genius that has built a billion-dollar Hip Hop empire has nurtured the ability of youth to create an organism, a sociocultural musical industry. As this industry increases in size, it ultimately can crush the very ones who created Hip Hop. The young people who birthed the music and its culture lose creative control as popularity and institutionalization of this music as genre in the music industry grows. That is, the beauty of its beginnings, gone mainstream and literally taken hostage by suits in the music industry, has such a weight that it can destroy those who first created and loved the music. Black male Hip Hop participants largely fail to see how destructive their language can be. For twenty-year-olds, Hip Hop culture mirrors their generation's experience of life's harsh and syrupy realities.[64]

In 2000, many persons, including some rappers, stated that Hip Hop had become an expression of depravity, violence, hypersexuality, and misogyny. Tupac Shakur and Biggie Smalls's hard-core rap has been seen as a precursor to "booty call" videos that signify pimping and obsession with "bling bling," flashy, elaborate jewelry. Many Hip Hop artists, scholars, aficionados, and some who do not listen to this music complain that the sexualized, violent, misogynistic language and acts on videos are excessive. Some old-school and new-school rappers express concern about the messages and the sensationalism that have emerged. Others dismiss these concerns and say that they sing about the reality of their cosmos, of their experience, which includes drugs, murder, sex, money, and pimping. Some old-school rappers such as Ice-T, while allowing for scatological language, still view much recent music as mediocre. According to Mos Def, today's Hip Hop promotes vacuous, tired music proffered by the music industry. Some rappers, such as Chuck D, critique the sinking level of intelligence within rap because it glorifies thugs and embraces stereotypical minstrelsy.

For many young men, Hip Hop seems to be a venue for getting rich quickly, to get where they believe black folk should be, whether from middle-class, educated families or from the projects. Community members, teachers, and parents realize that Hip Hop has appeal because it is so accessible, and many school districts and parents do not have the funds to make other options available. They wonder about the effect of Hip Hop videos on their sons and daughters, videos that feature disturbing portrayals of black women and men. The overwhelming layers of consumerism, greed, violence, hypersexuality, and excess in the United States, beg the question of whether Hip Hop reflects its context or shapes it.[65]

Impact of Internet and Downloading

Internet and downloading have had a major influence on Hip Hop, both a good and a bad influence. The effect of the Internet and downloading is like a double-sided LP album. The A-side label reads "progressive," and the B-Side "regressive." The Internet is a global data communications system, an infrastructure that connects us like a spider web to people all over the world. You can grab files of information from this network and receive data to your computer and cell phone from remote hubs. The transfer of this data is called downloading.

This dynamic technology has been a momentous tool and a powerful entanglement. Such double-sidedness has made the music more accessible to international communities, but it may have cheapened it as well. The Internet gives everyone a voice to speak for Hip Hop. Both exceptional and unacceptable are given a virtual mic (microphone) to say something or nothing for a music made from free speech. This means that although there is more diversity, this diversity has diminished the quality of the music. Seemingly, all you need to be considered a Hip Hop artist is a MySpace page and some version of your music in MP3 format. This creative tension has increased the opportunities for more artists to enter the industry, but it has also almost eliminated the divide between the novice and the expert, those talented and those merely tolerated. Hip Hop has become accessible but cheap, reachable but a novelty only.

The Value of Trouble

Hip Hop has been an expensive cultural commodity since early in its history. If you were not hunting down an album in a music store, you were going through the trouble to engineer your own mixtape. One Maxell ninety-minute cassette tape, a dual tape deck, and an hour later you had the quintessential rap tape. While complex and possibly illegal because of copyright law and the rights of the artist, the trouble a person might get into to get the music gave the music more value.

As everyone knows, the interplay between supply and demand is a fundamental principle of economics. The cost and value of diamonds are high because we are told there are so few diamonds in the world that it makes them precious stones. Cubic zirconium producers mass-produce low-quality imitations of diamonds because they cannot compete with the limited supply of the precious stones. Even though the Internet has given more people access to listen to the music through downloading and sites like YouTube, it has also oversaturated the market with cubic zirconium rappers who overshadow the true rap artists. Artist development, like mining and polishing a diamond in the rough, takes a backseat to the mass production of music with lower quality.

Individuality and authenticity are the cornerstones of Hip Hop. Urban youth used Hip Hop as a tool to help them mine what was special about them out of their own personal pain and challenging experience, from cut-off jean jackets worn by break-dancers, to signature tag art that graffiti artists left on subway trains. But now the market is so saturated with "artists" who imitate one another that they decrease the value of the culture and the economy of Hip Hop.

The Valueless Production

As we have already stated above, as Hip Hop became more accessible, its value decreased. This resulted in record companies challenging artists to spend less time producing good music and to spend more time kicking out more music just to compete.

The producers and manufacturers were driven by an economic model that did not mirror the resonant origins of Hip Hop music. Hip Hop was a music that spoke, signified, and honored the heart of a hurting generation. But now the soul of Hip Hop is being sucked out of the music that was once meant to express the soul of people. Hip Hop developed a pop culture presence in the world of music, but each song now only has a kernel of its original depth. The pressure of mass production turns this "meaty" music into a candy-coated treat.

In addition, rap audiences do not buy an entire album for an extended musical experience; instead, they connect only with singles heard on the radio, songs sold one at a time in little sound bites. Record companies coerce artists to do an entire project full of isolated, single marketable bites rather than to create a conceptual journey from the first song to the last.

As a youth, I (Marlon) saw LL Cool J's "Radio" video on *Yo! MTV Raps* and made it my mission to get the music in my hand. I saved my allowance, negotiated a ride to the record store, combed threw the rap section, and proudly walked out with the first purchase that I made without my parents' help. The music motivated many firsts like mine all over the world. Saving, planning, and engineering were all a part of the lived reality of Hip Hop.

Expertise

The technological advancement in the music industry and the Internet have just about made the novice into the expert. The line between a professional and an amateur engineer has been blurred with such laptop-ready software as Garageband and Fruit Loops. These programs technically have the same mechanics as full-scale studios. Some artists have even created entire albums on laptops and recorded them in bedroom closets.

Using the diamond analogy again, Hip Hop artists are now cheap and ill-shaped by a lack of professional development and clarity. For instance, the journey of a single from an album now is different from what it once was and even could be again, with some creative checks and balances. A song no longer has to go through the traditional filters to affirm the balance of authenticity. Today, the same effort and initiative on the part of the listener are not needed to get a Hip Hop song and album produced and on the market. You can buy it on iTunes, download a song on a pirated web page, listen to the song on the MySpace page of the artist, or just listen to it on YouTube without going through the effort to buy it. This makes the music accessible, but it has diminished the character and quality of the music in the process. A flooded market of "almost but not quite" rappers who are here today and gone tomorrow weakens Hip Hop. Young people who were born to be innovative gems of science, business, religion, education, and literature, for example, are choosing "almost but not quite" careers of Hip Hop instead.

CHAPTER TWO

Hip Hop Is Dead

Musical Characteristics

"Hip Hop Is Dead," a song composed by Nas, one of the veterans of Hip Hop, reflects irony and evokes humor. Hip Hop aficionado Christopher Paul,[1] notes that Nas took a break from Hip Hop before he came out with the album of the same name. Nas has been a Hip Hop artist since the 1980s, so his saying that Hip Hop is dead is like providing a correction for the music and culture.

There are differences between Hip Hop music and Hip Hop culture, but there is also a direct connection between the two—Hip Hop culture transcends the music. Christopher Paul says that in the last couple of years, Hip Hop music has evolved, has expanded to be eclectic, and is open to other forms of music. But Hip Hop is not simply defined by its music, for it is ever-changing: it hops here; it hops there. Hip Hop last year is not the same as Hip Hop this year; next year it will not be the same either. Every month new artists come out with something new, and then everybody jumps on that. Things do not remain static. Hip Hop also is open to other forms of music. This is reflected in all of the heavy sampling of other genres of music: blues, jazz, big band, and rock music. Lil Wayne's music is an example of Hip Hop's collaboration with rock music.

Nas has come back to Hip Hop to say that he wants to bring back the fun and the joy of Hip Hop. In the album *Hip Hop Is Dead*, Nas deals with Hip Hop's debauchery and the negative press, offering the critique that Hip Hop has gotten away from what it was and that it needs to get back to its roots. His claiming that "Hip Hop is dead" is to say the current artists have killed it and that he, Nas, is its resurrecter. To make his point he portrays Jesus in his videos. (To see one of Nas's videos, go to www.youtube.com and search for the song "Hate Me Now," featuring Puff Daddy.) In the video for "Hate Me Now," Nas portrays Jesus, and Puff Daddy performs the chorus of the song: "I won't stop now. I can't stop now." Nas's use of irony reminds us of the wisdom literature in the Bible (Psalms, Proverbs, Job, and Ecclesiastes). In Ecclesiastes 8:1, the sage draws a parallel between a wise person and one who can interpret things, for the gift of wisdom illumines and takes away hardness of heart. Listening to "Hip Hop Is Dead" with the Ecclesiastes text in mind helps us grasp the power of this kind of experience and question what it means, and it urges us to live life and do music with integrity and an openness for change.

This chapter explores the musical traditions and recourses that exist in Hip Hop. Following deliberation on African roots, origins, and retentions in Hip Hop, the chapter continues with reflections on language, instrumentation, essentials of musical style, and chief players and their musical signatures.

African Roots, Origins, and Retention in Hip Hop

Roots of African diasporan performance practices in general and those of African Americans in particular did not emerge within a vacuum. Africans who were kidnapped by those who supported colonialist, imperialistic oppression came to our shores with worldviews, religions, and musical traditions. From early Spirituals and work songs to R&B, soul, and Hip Hop—the souls of black folk revel in, communicate through, and engage in political protest and storytelling through recitation and song. Experience—the sacred and profane—materializes in song.[2] Black folk empower others in community and seek justice and mutuality in relationships through creative expression, especially through song. Slave bards and ghetto (rap) artists, like traditional African griots, speak or sing to share their wisdom as they call attention to society's accountability. Grounded in collective communal history and significant memories, these poets tell stories. They remind us of the past, analyze and offer proclamation about the present, and sometimes predict the future.[3]

A black eschatological (or goal-oriented) vision in Spirituals and much Hip Hop music helps those subjugated and exploited experience a reality not limited to present historical moments. It enables these people to reckon and ultimately work toward a reality shift in which they experience salvific wholeness, that is, freedom from systemic oppression, and can be in a place and space that honors their creation in God's image.

Spirituals and much Hip Hop music embrace African philosophy in which sacred and secular are not distinctive frameworks; rather, they exist synergistically. For example, in Bantu thought, language classification pertains to words, not to grammar. In this language system, four categories or forces of reality and existence occur: *kuntu* (modality), *hantu* (time and space), *kintu* (thing), and *muntu* (human being). Things converge at the point of *Ntu*, where opposites are not contradictory realities. *Ntu*, Being itself, pertains to the meeting point of the Divine (Being) and the created (being). Traditional African worldview includes the living, dead, and unborn, known as the *Muntu*. This intelligent force controls *nommo*, the living and the ancestor's word force. God, the great *Muntu*, begets or creates the ancestors; *Muntu*, divine and human life force, along with word power, or *nommo*, together create life. The relationship between the Divine and humanity is that of paradox, incomprehensible, beyond the articulation of human words or understanding.[4] Such talk about God or theology provides the framework for how one talks about human behavior and the values that frame that behavior, or ethics.

In his discussion of African and African American social ethics, Peter J. Paris explores seven selected related moral virtues: beneficence, forbearance, practical wisdom, improvisation, forgiveness, justice, and public and private ethics. Practicing these virtues bolsters one's own moral sensibility and that of the community. One of the virtues of particular importance to African and African diasporan music in general and to Hip Hop in particular is the experience of improvisation. African American instrumentalists and vocalists, in all music forms, including Hip Hop, engage improvisation as authentic musicality as a part of communal praxis. As the soloists, signifying African griots or primary keepers of communal history, Hip Hop artists improvise over/with other musicians, mirroring the relationality of person in community. Improvisation provides opportunity for individual creative freedom that bolsters the esteem of all participants, for black music-making is always communal. In the past, improvisation allowed enslaved bards to retain African traditions and to intermingle them with cultural forms and norms in this new world. Couched in oratorical, ceremonial, and musical performance, the enslaved bards signified and eloquently made something new out of virtually nothing.

Improvisation, a process of inventive, capricious variation on a theme, makes the old novel, as one invokes spontaneity, creativity, and communal well-being. As African and African diasporan art (music, dance, and poetry) has an aesthetic intent to help persons experience and know beauty, it also helps them surrender to tragedy. Observing and exercising the moral virtue of improvisation has motivated civil rights movements and social protest, chronicling these events in accessible cultural ways.[5]

Sometimes the poets use irony and paradox, reflecting life's chaos, challenges, and constructive, pathological oppressions. These lyricists incorporate multiple texts, sacred and secular, framed by personal experiences to hone and share their redacted narratives. Like slave bards, traditional Hip Hop artists offer celebration and challenge and agonize over disruptive, death-dealing sociocultural practices that signal the need for change. Artists, then and now, signify against colonialism and its accompanying oppression.[6] Like the Spirituals, Hip Hop music from its inception addressed daily life, while it also protested and agonized over injustice, calling for alternatives to the oppressive practices that ignored the humanity and dignity of black folk. These songs of life-giving vitality have evolved over time, expressing a vast range of emotions about all stages and cycles of human life. Such expressions tell stories that announce key motifs and themes to help a community see itself, as they honor rituals and confront myths to provide meaning and help individuals in society understand who they are while also communicating their differences. Such practices emerge out of a traditional African philosophical ethos, in which people are inherently religious and religious tenets frame their entire worldview and way of being,[7] often with a poetic bent. Hip Hop artists are the most recent poets who represent this long tradition of poetic expression.

In the 1930s, more than a one-sixth of Harlem residents were from the West Indies, and the block parties of the 1980s were similar to *sound systems* in Jamaica.[8] Sound systems were large parties, originally outdoors, thrown by owners of loud and expensive stereo equipment, which they could share with the community or use to compete among themselves, who began speaking lyrics or toasting. Later, during the mid-twentieth century, changes in American music also influenced the musical culture of the

Caribbean. As early as 1956,[9] DJs were toasting (an African tradition of "rapped out" tales of heroism) over dubbed Jamaican beats. It was called *rap*, which expands the word's earlier meaning in the African American community as an informal discussion or debate.

During the late 1960s civil rights movement in the United States, a group of poets and musicians—beginning with Felipe Luciano, Gylan Kain, and David Nelson, and eventually including Abiodun Oyewole, Umar Bin Hassan, Alafia Pudim, and percussionist Nilaja Obabi—formed the Last Poets. Their name derives from a poem by Keorapetse Kgositsile, a South African revolutionary poet who claimed that he was part of the last era of poets prior to a takeover by guns. Formed in 1968 on Malcolm X's birthday, May 16, the group made it to the U.S. Top 10 album charts, and many dub them the godfathers of rap. Their performances fused rhymed street-smart and often politically charged poetry with musical backgrounds, invoking black consciousness and Black Nationalism. Oyewole notes that the Last Poets pulled inspiration and influences from the Spirituals, rhythm and blues, jazz, and salsa and that Hip Hop mirrors wherever the poet is. Experiencing a bit of decline in the 1970s, the Last Poets have had a resurgence and have garnered renewed interest with the rise of rap music. Thus, it comes as no surprise that some of the Last Poets have collaborated with rap music artists.[10]

Having grown up on Hip Hop, Christopher Paul notes that a sense of community in Hip Hop emerges out of traditional African philosophy. He also sees that today, the primary division occurs not along race lines, but along age and demographic lines—as there are subcultures even within black culture. Hip Hop is a youth thing that many elders do not get; and young people love that because they have something of their own. Adults often cannot understand youth talking over beats with rhymes in Hip Hop. Hip Hop is marketable, fun, and a positive means of expression, not a negative one. If artists say what they want to say over a beat, it is a problem for some people. For those in Hip Hop, music-making is a right of freedom of speech.

Along with the connection with traditional African philosophy amid a sense of community, a spiritual component exists. Such an element can be seen in the Hip Hop community, its culture, and its relationships. The way Hip Hop draws people together also involves spirituality. Hip Hop music "is ours, it redefines itself, it changes, and it is being embraced by the Hip Hop community. Whether good or bad, we embrace our own."[11]

Music videos, now a mainstay for Hip Hop and other popular music, emerged with the birth of MTV, formerly Music Television, a cable television station launched August 1, 1981. There is a difference between only hearing/listening to music and seeing a music video, which is an art form in itself. Some Hip Hop aficionados suggest that people should not get mad at Hip Hop when they can watch girls in skimpy clothing in videos because Hip Hop holds a mirror up to the culture so it can see itself. If Hip Hop is about prostitution or drugs, is Hip Hop being responsible, or is it a fair object of criticism? Perhaps the mirror is not the problem, but the people are.[12] Mirrors reflect what stands before them, and a critical reflective feature of Hip Hop is its language and use of this powerful tool.

Language

Language, which is key to communication, constitutes or creates our reality and affects our experience of where and how we live, think, act, know, and value. The language of Hip Hop provides an arena for persons to develop their identities and their sense of pride and power. Hip Hop allows its aficionados to connect globally with other youth and young adults, many of whom grew up on Hip Hop. Sometimes they use Hip Hop language for protest, targeting hegemonic, oppressive thought and attitudes. This language helps people deal with and speak to political, sociocultural, and economic realities.

While parents, mentors, teachers, and other adults often overlook or disavow the interests of youth, everyone—both young and old—needs to be heard. When heard, people feel respected, empowered, and valued. As youth develop and mature, with adult support, they invent their own realities, identities, worldviews, and worlds. They are able to share their own stories, signifying matters of friendship, adventure, love, respect, and purpose.[13]

One significant tool of language critical in music-making as storytelling is metaphor. Metaphor, a figure of speech in which an expression refers to something that it does not literally mean to suggest or imply a similarity, is a tool of the trade for Hip Hop artists as they critique, analyze, and offer commentary on marginalized voices. Artists use metaphor to talk about things that often defy literal description. Metaphors can give succinct, compact expression and offer ways to create new concepts and visions about reality. This type of figure of speech can let one illumine new problems and help communities gain new understandings of and insights into communal experiences.

African American Hip Hop music is highly metaphoric. Key themes of this metaphoric language include: space and place of neighborhood, unemployment, underground economies, sex acts as objectification, materialism, and black-on-black crime. Critics of Hip Hop music need to remember that not all Hip Hop is gangsta rap. Hip Hop artists use metaphor to respond to the socioeconomic, political, and cultural problems collectively experienced by many black communities. Listening to and having informed conversations about metaphorical language in Hip Hop can help us learn to see and understand the concerns and challenges youth face daily.[14]

In Hip Hop, artists use words that may say one thing and mean another, reflecting another connection with the Spirituals. Like the Spirituals, Hip Hop consciously and unconsciously employs biblical metaphors. Christopher Paul notes that Hip Hop has experienced a lot of bad press, and folk want to throw out the baby with the bath water. Yet in talking about their background, many artists address God in some manner. Some other artists, however, acknowledge that they are not godly at all. For example, Young Jeezy notes that "when I get to Hell, Lord knows I'm going to fry," in reference to his ungodly lifestyle. Jay-Z's lyrics tend to denigrate the church. He calls himself J-hova. Jay-Z does not bash Christ but says things that are anti-Christian, such that those knowledgeable about Hip Hop music in the church are beginning to critique him.

There are artists of many different faiths. In the 1990s, many youth engaged in Hip Hop joined the Five Percenters. The Five Percenters is a derivative of the Nation of Islam, founded in 1964 by Clarence 13X. Clarence 13X was a minister in Mosque no. 7, under the mentoring of Malcolm X.[15] Some members of Wu-Tang Can as well as Erykah Badu, who participates in the neo-soul genre, engage in a type of syncretistic spirituality.[16]

For many students, Hip Hop music represents a space where they can be themselves and study things that are important and significant to them. Studying Hip Hop provides a venue where students can awaken to a type of social consciousness in which they examine and analyze the ethos and values of their own society, particularly those practices that are hegemonic and ideological. Studying Hip Hop requires an awareness of the music, and involves personal and cultural comprehension for the complex development and reality of Hip Hop culture. Students' identity development has an impact on how they learn and experience teaching and learning. When teaching Hip Hop or any subject, teachers, likewise, get to see how their identities and sociohistorical and cultural contexts also affect the educational experience. When students, teachers, and clergy engage in social inquiry, such a process of learning can be emotionally, ethically, aesthetically, and intellectually appealing. Part of a healthy study of Hip Hop includes dealing with the kind of internal colonialism found in culture, as capitalism has successfully marketed pathological images of Black women and men. Thus, it becomes important to heighten awareness about the deadly anti-intellectualism and complicit behavior when viewing Hip Hop videos that consistently celebrate violence and thug life, and objectify females by having them gyrate in scanty clothing. When studying Hip Hop, in the schools and church, one must include a focus on matters of personal values and social relevance, generational matters and ways of knowing. Studying Hip Hop also reflects how popular culture can subvert dominant models of life and sociopolitical systems by treating students as burgeoning experts, who can inform the learning process of themselves and their secular and sacred teachers.[17] One of the most contentious battles around word usage in Hip Hop is the "N word."

We must be mindful of the concerns and challenges that arise for parents, educators, and clergy when dealing with Hip Hop music, and the reasons for their resistance. Bronwen Low pushes the envelope by wrestling with using the N-Word as a limit-case for exploring using Hip Hop music as a pedagogical tool. Limit-case pertains to that place where we incur the breakdown of intelligibility, communication, and sociability, which paradoxically means that at these various points of seemingly concrete, impassable boundaries, real possibilities actually begin, following the work of Paulo Freire. Low based the findings on actual classroom work studying writing and poetry traditions, including performance workshops, framed by student interest in Hip Hop music and its culture. When working with students, teachers did not want to play the role of censor or reject any music because of the language, either in the classroom or during public performances. Most disagreed with Cornel West's argument that the N-word be discarded completely and that other words of affection be substituted, like sister, brother, or comrade. The study shows that people vary greatly and are sometimes ambivalent about using the N-word, notably about whom, when, and how this word can be used. That is, questions of authority, timing, and context are prevalent. Some African American youth posit a difference between using the words *Nigger* and *nigga*; that the latter is not pejorative or mean-spirited, whereas the former is hateful and demonizing. For some students, it appears these are two different words, which clearly signals intergenerational tensions. While language is critical for self-identity and expression for all age groups, the time of adolescence and the challenges and disconnects of high school make this time particularly challenging and stressful. This self-defining and reshaping of self-moments are often intentionally shaped to pit themselves over against adult opinion and judgment. Hip Hop culture often rejects standard English language practices and often embraces political, social, and racial resistance. Hip Hop musicians are intrigued with language and develop their own particular glossaries and lexicons, and make distinct choices and give words new meanings. African American Hip Hop generation members use language in ways reflecting their post-civil rights, post-segregation lived experience, that has known the ravages of decline of public schools, growth of a prison industrial complex that criminalizes and disproportionately imprisons black youth, high unemployment, and an onslaught of low-paying service jobs. Use of the N-word is a matter of judgment, communication, and the politics of interpretation. Some feel overwhelmed by the awful, painful, oppressive, racist history that birthed the term. Others view its usage as an act of rebellion, self-actualization, and community empowerment. The space of the N-word is one of discomfort; a discomfort necessary for intergenerational communication, fraught with joy, struggle, challenges, and negotiation.[18] This scenario repeatedly occurs around our use of language and understanding its meaning.

Artistically, words have great power and are an art form. Language has a powerful effect; it is not what you say, but how you say it. Thus, Soulja Boy has been a phenomenon. Although he is not known for his lyrical prowess and does not rap well, what he says is catchy, fun, and influences his dance (called the Soulja Boy dance). He even did his own successful marketing on YouTube.

Christopher Paul notes that many Hip Hop musicians get a contract after making a name and gaining a following; they do not have to worry about sales initially, because they can place their music online to get visibility. They get exposure, and then an agent picks them up; once they get exposure they can put out a mixed CD that people can buy. But if they want to go big, they still have to sign with a recording company. People knew Soulja Boy and his dance before he had a contract. No one else is doing what he was doing.

Hip Hop anticipates change. But this dependence on novelty is a challenge, because artists have to keep reinventing themselves. In Hip Hop, you cannot keep doing the same thing. This makes it different from Gospel and R& B, in which no one expects, for example, Shirley Ceasar to sound like Kirk Franklin or Tye Tribbett. However, with Hip Hop, the music genre changes so much that artists have to stay current if they want to last. Older Hip Hop artists work with younger people to help themselves stay current. The Hip Hop music that is coming out now is different from the Hip Hop Paul listened to a few short years ago. For example, Mos Def, as popular as he is, will never sell platinum. He has a loyal fan base. However, he will not become mainstream, because his music is not what enough of today's buyers want. A contrasting example is Sade, who came out with a new album in 2010, her first in over a decade. Her fan base is so solid that they want to hear what they have always heard. However, with Hip Hop, you have to continue to reinvent yourself. Reinventing oneself involves sharing awareness and knowledge, and can lead to teaching, or pedagogical, moments.

Pedagogical, or teaching, techniques in courses focusing on literacy are valuable for teaching scripture, about God, and Christian traditions and values. A Christian educator or pastor can draw parallels between Hip Hop rhymes and scripture or traditional phrases that communicate doctrine, often found in hymns, gospels, and Spirituals: assurance of Jesus; God's amazing grace; God's unconditional love; God's promises never to forsake us. Some fear using Hip Hop, under the guise that all of it is negative, abusive, sexist, and disrespectful of women. By sharing such concerns with you, and by taking time to listen to the variety of Hip Hop music, educators and pastors can be selective in the music they use. Their youth and young adults can advise them of the music they prefer, and participate in dialogue together, about the content and meaning of Hip Hop music, particularly the rhymes. This can be an educational experience for everyone. Young people get to tell their stories and then "hear" how their stories played out in earlier generations. This intergenerational dialogue can come to see how poets, from the ancients to those of the Harlem Renaissance to twenty-first century hipsters, all use imagery, rhythm, grammar, syntax, and typography to create their texts. Writing scripture and other music as Hip Hop music and then taking Hip Hop music and rewriting it as scripture or hymns help students learn to think and practice their faith in creative ways, and help them to understand how socio-historical contexts and individual and communal values have changed or stayed the same. Such exercises allow youth opportunities to build their communication skills, to explore who they are, to learn how to challenge systemic injustice, and to learn how to view, think about, and address matters close to their hearts, which affects their lived realities with respect to issues of family, peers, and self.[19]

When James Stackhouse, who grew up with Hip Hop and now writes Christian Hip Hop music, thinks of language in Hip Hop, he believes that whatever one wants to talk about, it has to be infused with energy. Life is the subject of Hip Hop. While Hip Hop does have its own language and unique ways of wording and phrasing, Stackhouse says one needs to try to find a way to take a topic and use Hip Hop language. Therefore, people listening to the music can relate and still understand what is being talked about. For example, if he wanted to use biblical language to speak about a particular topic, Stackhouse would take it and then relate a scriptural experience to a contemporary scenario. For example, one could make the story about the rich young ruler in Luke 18:18-23 into a modern story, in which someone could see it happening in his or her own world. The principles are the same and can be expressed in a modern story.

Artists often convey popular biblical stories in rap songs. Stackhouse usually abstracts the principles and concepts from a story and adds them to his songs, without referencing the particular biblical reference, as with the prodigal son.[20]

Hip Hop music is an ongoing U.S. literary tradition. The continuing effect of enslavement and racism, joined with the ways in which persons from various racial ethnic traditions communicate publically, helps reorient Hip Hop toward twenty-first-century political and economic realities in the United States. Hip Hop artists such as Mr. Lif bemoan issues of acquisitiveness and divine retribution, corruption, and malaise in ways similar to seventeenth-century American Puritanism. Puritanism and Hip Hop both decry the fantasy and delusion of materialism.[21] Yet Hip Hop is also part of a global literary tradition because it is a hybrid of different global influences in sync with black musical and other oral traditions.

What effect, then, do words have in Hip Hop? Which is more important: the words or the music? Can listeners actually tune out words and only focus on the beat? As a child growing up in New Orleans, Louisiana, a city that has had many firsts in music, Christopher Paul, like many other kids, knew Hip Hop songs before he learned nursery rhymes. His older brother played Hip Hop all the time. When other kids were watching *Sesame Street* and learning their ABCs, Paul was listening to "New Orleans bounce music," a Hip Hop genre unique to New Orleans.

This kind of Hip Hop took elements from New Orleans chant and brass bands, including repetitive catchy phrases. Bounce music is chanting over a simple beat; an artist may be singing while he is rapping. It can even be a song full of chants; for example in TT Tucker and DJ Erv's "Where Dey At?" someone says "where dey at" repetitively; the song then chimes out. This style began in the early 1990s, before other places had heard this music.

Music as Magic:
Impossible Feats, Natural Means, and Instrumentation

Magic is a performing art that entertains an audience by creating illusions of the seemingly impossible.[22] Postmodern illusionist and magician David Blaine gave a speech at TED (Technology Entertainment Design) about his greatest illusion during which he held his breath underwater for twelve minutes. He said, "Magic, whether I am holding my breath or shuffling a deck of cards, is pretty simple. Magic is practice, training, and experimenting while pushing through the pain to be the best that I can be."[23] Hip Hop is a magical story of a people who pushed through the pain to be the best they could be with what they had been given. There are four primary forces and musical characteristics in Hip Hop that mysteriously came out of nowhere to redefine music everywhere: sampling, beatboxing, scratching, and lyrical cadence. Like the African American Spiritual, each of these characteristics is a vessel for the sacred longings and imagination of a generation.

Sampling: Ancient-Future

Sampling is the act of physically copying sounds from one recording to another through use of digital technology.[24] An example of sampling is James Brown's "It's a Man's, Man's, Man's World," used in Alicia Keys's "Fallin'," Big Daddy Kane's "Mortal Combat," and Ice Cube's "It's a Man's World." While musicians have always used and reused melodies and rhythmic patterns from other music, Hip Hop has taken this borrowing to another level.

The mirroring of styles and ideas is a kind of evolution that is taken from one musician by another who replicates and advances the sound. Hip Hop artists were pioneers, charting new musical territory with little or no formal musical training. Rather than play a chord or measures of the original music, Hip Hop composers rerecorded, dissected, and reassembled pieces of the exact music to make a totally different song. Sound bites of funk hooks and measures of jazz riffs excavated from old record collections are the playground for producers and DJs. Jamaican-born DJ Kool Herc was one of the first to do this. Kool Herc developed break-beat DJing, in which the breaks of funk song—the most danceable part, often featuring percussion—were isolated and repeated for the purpose of all-night dance parties.

Grabbing pieces of preexisting songs, sounds, or other patterns to create new music is a way to honor the past while shaping the future. Sampling is a way to redefine what exists to create the impossible; it makes magic. The old becomes the new, creating value out of the melodies, the beat breaks, and cadences from older albums that are discarded, disregarded, or forgotten. Explaining the heavy sampling found on *The Blueprint: Volume 1*, Jay-Z says, "The first blueprint was soul samples that I grew up on; it was my blueprint."[25]

A former resident of Brooklyn's Marcy Houses project, Shawn "Jay-Z" Carter did not have access to instrumental music lessons, music theory classes, or even after-school music programs. But he did have the records purchased by the generation who raised him, which became the foundation for the career of the one whom many call the best Hip Hop artist alive.[26] For insight on the history of sampling, visit the following website: http://jklabs.net/projects/samplinghistory.

As DJ Flash (Jason Woods) and I (Marlon) walked down the hallway of Flash's home in Houston's South Park neighborhood, it felt like I was walking through a time warp. The walls were hung with album covers from every time period. This walkway of cover art became a time machine that spun and made me dizzy. The closer that we got to our destination, the more I smelled an odd smell. It was almost but not quite stale. Experiencing this smell—a combination of decades-old dust and vinyl—took me back to the 1970s and I remembered a kind of noble funk that personified the funk music of that time. I even imagined that the odor is what a Maceo Parker saxophone solo would smell like if it could be a "scratch and sniff." Experiencing funk, both as music and physically as a pungent odor, spellbound me and made me even more excited about interviewing Flash.

Flash and I finally got to a warmly lit room where thousands of albums of every genre of music were peeking from tall bookshelves that reached the ceiling. The rest of his record collection, carefully placed in milk crates, sat on the floor and formed a maze in and around the room. DJs, producers, and Hip Hop composers commonly use milk crates to store the albums they use to create and spin music. DJ Flash, a local renaissance man, easily found and pulled out two albums from among the thousands. He gently held the ornate album covers, removed the vinyl albums from their sleeves, and placed them on the turntables like a museum curator handling pieces of ancient art.

As he put the albums on the turntable to show me where Kanye West sampled *Drive Slow* and where Common sampled *The Light*, I realized that the instrumentation of Hip Hop is both magical and archeological. The fact that for this book I decided to interview DJs to better understand instrumentation in Hip Hop was no coincidence, because they are the primary composers of the sound, even though many of them play no instruments. They are magicians and archeologists who "dig" for old albums to create new sounds.

My time with Flash affirmed that this music made from golden LPs housed in milk crates is the metaphorical rabbit excavated from the hat of poor neighborhoods all over the nation. No formal musical training, schools without music programs, and homes without the incomes to afford the luxury of music lessons or instruments were contexts for the pain and possibility of the music.

Hip Hop transcends the usual boundaries of music by using rerecorded samples of vocals, beat breaks, and jazz riffs to defy the traditional laws of music. Hip Hop is a new voice that speaks the ancient message of freedom and hope. In many ways, it mirrors the African American Spiritual. How sweet this sound, a sound gracefully squeezed from the tight situations of youth today.

Beatboxing: The Sound behind the Sound

Having no trumpets, saxophones, and drum kits available to them, the musicians created a miracle of sound through beatboxing. In beatboxing, mouths give the illusion of musical instruments, creating, for example, bass drum and rim shot sounds without a drum set. While beatboxing requires no expensive instruments, it nevertheless changed everything in the music industry. Today, there are even beatboxing championships in Japan and Queens, New York.[27]

Beatboxing can be thought of as a modern form of scatting. Although the history of scatting may date back to West Africa, trumpeter Louis Armstrong also made it popular in the United States. When he accompanied blues singer Bessie Smith, for example, Armstrong used his coronet to sound out vocalizations. Beatboxing comes from scatting, made popular by jazz artists such as Ella Fitzgerald. Fitzgerald's mastery of "scat," in which the singer improvises nonsense syllables to imitate a musical instrument, is heard in many of her recordings. Fitzgerald could make her voice sound like a saxophone. Through recordings, concerts, and television appearances, both figures brought scat to a broad public audience.[28]

Beatboxers are admired and imitated throughout the world. Their musical signatures in Hip Hop are beautiful because they signify these young artists as they are. In a world in which Hip Hop musicians are often known and dubbed criminals and the dregs of society, their voices and breath can become powerful instruments. They are connected to the music in a special way because the music makes them too.

As a former beatboxer, I (Marlon) am a retired member of a community of mouth musicians who made good beatbox rhythm with oversized lips—often disrespected by society—and with my hands. Every lively rhythm made with balled-up fists on the cafeteria tables before school made my friends and me living instruments, not deadly weapons. Beatboxing made us value our own bodies and made our experiences into something beautiful.

A Scratch for an Itch

The absence of instruments and musical training was an irritation turned opportunity by turntablists and DJs, as they used purposeful scratching with a slight movement of the vinyl on the turntable to create a new sound—one that could act as a transition between songs in live presentations and a new instrument with a sound that could rhythmically play a role in Hip Hop songs. Scratching is a technique used to produce distinctive sounds by moving a vinyl record back and forth on a turntable while manipulating the crossfader on a DJ mixer.

A fader is any device or object used to increase or decrease audio levels. A crossfader is a component on a DJ mixer that works like two faders connected side-by-side, but in opposite directions. A DJ uses the crossfader simultaneously to fade in one source and fade out the other.

Scratching was developed by early Hip Hop DJs from New York such as Grand Wizard Theodore and DJ Grandmaster Flash, who describes scratching as "nothing but the back-cueing that you hear in your ear before you push it [the recorded sound] out to the crowd."[29] Although previous artists such as William S. Burroughs had experimented with the idea of manipulating a record manually for the sounds produced (such as with his 1950s recording, *Sound Piece*,[30] scratching as an element of Hip Hop became an integral part of music instead of just uncontrolled noise.

Grandmaster Flash was the first person to release a song, "The Adventures of Grandmaster Flash on the Wheels of Steel," with scratching on it in 1981. Grandmaster Flash and the Furious Five were inducted into the Rock and Roll Hall of Fame in 2007, becoming the first Hip Hop/rap artists to be so honored.[31] Some scholars and aficionados note, "His pioneering mixing skills transformed the turntable into a true 'instrument' and his ability to get a crowd moving has made his DJ sets legendary."[32]

There are also particular, distinctive styles of scratching, and Hip Hop artists make up new ones on a daily basis. Two particular modes of scratching include: crab scratching and chirping. Crab scratching consists of moving the record while quickly tapping the crossfader open with each finger of the crossfader hand; it is like taking one syllable and manipulating it in different times and ways. The thumb is on one side of the crossfader and the other fingers lightly tap the other area of the fader.[33] The hand on the record and on the crossfader look like a crab walking.

Chirping occurs when a person puts his hand on the record and all you hear is the forward motion that creates the sound of a bird chirping. A DJ can use the crossfader as a "hatchet," chopping off a portion of the song. In this way, DJs are able to perform "transforms," the transitions of the transformers back and forth, much faster than they could by manipulating the crossfader with the whole hand. Chirping produces a fading/increasing transforming sound.[34]

From scratching to chirping, such is the instrumentation of Hip Hop music, such is the joy of the magic that lets street artists signify with beat, words, and passion.

Style, Tempo, Rhythm, and Other Essentials

Having a working knowledge of basic musical terms supports intergenerational conversation around Hip Hop music. Style pertains to how we express ourselves, how we participate in music-making, and what values we accentuate in the performed work; that is, the distinctive qualities of a particular genre or type of music. Rhythm is measured flow or movement of strong and weak beats or pulses in the flow of sound and silence that involves meter (repeated particular pattern of the beats), accent, and tempo (the speed at which a composition is to be played). In the hands of artists these elements become modes of artistic expression and help a musician express his or her own distinctive worldview. Needless to say, Hip Hop artists use these elements in many different ways.

The culture "du jour" affects the stylistic artistry of Hip Hop, which includes eclectic and multidimensional textures. Hip Hop is versatile, whether it is rap singing or melodic rap over music. What really classifies the music as Hip Hop is the artist performing over the music, which makes the style of rap unique. From outside looking in, people would say that Hip Hop is fast paced with many fast-paced rhythms and beats within the songs and that the actual words are spoken at a fast space. But within the genre of Hip Hop, there is not one particular style, tempo, or rhythm—all have been popular at one time or another. The beat behind the song has always been important. Many would say that the beat is more important than what the artist is actually saying. The beat behind the words needs to be catchy and infectious. But when creating Hip Hop music, the composer has to get a feel for the effect that the beat will have on the public in order to be commercially successful.

The genre of Hip Hop has greatly opened up since the late 1980s through mid-1990s. There is a lot of infusion from other forms of music, including R&B, rock, Latin, country, and jazz. Because of its hybrid nature, on any given day on any given radio or computer, one can hear Hip Hop because of its hybrid nature; this gives Hip Hop a familiarity that it might not have otherwise. Being a hybrid of other forms of music, however, is both good and bad. Good, because it has opened Hip Hop up to so many ways and options of putting music together. But being a hybrid is also a negative because it is harder to know in advance whether people will like it.[35]

At one point, demographic lines defined Hip Hop style: East Coast, West Coast, South, and Midwest. One can tell Southern rappers, for example, because they have a certain beat, certain accent or phrases, and certain slang that reflects their context. A Northerner might say "son" when speaking to a friend, while a Southerner might say "cuz" (for cousin) when doing the same. The music itself now also transcends geographical boundaries; before in the late 1980s and early 1990s, the styles were more distinct. There are now Canadian artists such as Drake, who are top rated in the Hip Hop community. Drake is versatile and has no loyalties to any particular substyle or genre of Hip Hop. Drake does all types of Hip Hop; and everyone loves him, in part because audiences feel included when he performs.

More mainstream artists, however, are more restricted by record companies. The kid who creates his own sound, who is not under contract, can do his own thing. He can do what sounds good to him; if others like it, OK; if not, no problem, they are comfortable in their own skins. Young Hip Hop artists see what Lil Wayne is doing and what Kanye is doing and want to do their own thing.

Fads come and go in the Hip Hop movement but don't necessarily define it. Hip Hop generates its own diverse culture. When young men wearing sagging skinny jeans emerged in the Hip Hop movement, it did not limit Hip Hop. Pants, for example, can (and have gone) from baggy low-riders to the tight skateboarder look.[36] Just like there is a rhythm and beat in the music, the culture also has a diverse pace or tempo.

Tempos, like everything else in Hip Hop, vary; some are very, very slow; some are very, very fast. The purpose of the song shapes the speed of the music. Most Hip Hop albums will have a club anthem, something you can dance to and get many spins. For dancing people want something more upbeat. To accommodate this "felt need" of the buyer, some artists may have a very fast track to show off their lyrical skills: how fast they can rap and yet still be understandable—clear, but fast. Twista, aka Tongue Twista is famous for his speed; he only raps fast. Twista, featured on R&B songs as well, has become more famous because R&B Hip Hop artists like Jamie Foxx and Dream include him in their work, where he will rap fast to their slow songs. Sometimes there is the contrast between the speed of the lyrics and the tempo of the music. In fact, people call the music or track "the beat"; whether it has a melody or not.[37]

Many times with rhythm, more goes into play in the beat itself; with some artists, there is a greater focus on the lyrics and their rhythm of delivery. Currently people globally are gravitating toward a new popular rhythm from the Southern region of the country. Gucci Mane (Southern rapper), for example, is known for his flow or rhythm. His lyric content is not extra special, but the rhythm that he uses gives him a slurred cadence that mirrors the spoken Southern drawl.[38]

Chief Players and Their Musical Signatures

I've known rivers:
I've known rivers ancient as the world and older than the flow.[39]

Langston Hughes was a Harlem Renaissance poet who was an innovator of the new literary art form known as jazz poetry. This poetry flowed in a musical pattern that mirrored the music of its time in cadence and color, and it continued to evolve and find its way into the Bronx years later. Jazz was an outgrowth of the blues that came from African American Spirituals. Thus, it is no coincidence that the lyrical cadence, "spoken or chanted rhyming lyrics with a strong rhythmic accompaniment"[40] or flow, seeped deeply into all African American music, even Hip Hop.

I (Marlon) was sitting in White Oak Grove Baptist Church in Homer, Louisiana, when I heard a preacher conclude his sermon in a way that was reminiscent of Hip Hop. The vibrato and texture of the old man's voice was strangely like the rough sandpaper sound of Leaders of the New School's Busta Rhymes. The congregation's response was immediate, like a shiny-shoe-and-dusty-suit-wearing version of a baggy-pant-and-Timberland-booted crowd being emotionally moved by the words of an MC. Before I knew it, the familiarity became relevant; and quietly, I began to take in the words that meant nothing to my religious sensibility but everything to me as a member of the "Second Church of Hip Hop." The preacher's hoop, tune, and call-and-response were the "Hip Hop to my Hooray."[41]

Rap has deep roots in the ancient oral tradition that began with musical African griots, or storytellers. Rappers can sound like preachers, and preachers can sound like African songsters. The cadence of a preacher is on a continuum of the ancient sounds of

African chants that drove the call-and-response of a song.[42] This experience of music-making is part of the lineage of an oral tradition transmitted from one generation to another. Centuries before Hip Hop music existed, the griots of West Africa delivered stories rhythmically, over drums and sparse instrumentation. Many modern-day griots are spoken-word artists.[43]

Rap is an art made for storytellers and people of God who have something to say but no other way to articulate it. The book *How to Rap*[44] provides different components separated into word content, flow (oral rhythm and rhyme), and delivery (verbal pace of the spoken words). "Flow" is also sometimes used to refer to elements of the delivery (pitch, timbre, and volume). Whether content, flow, and rhyme, or pitch, timbre, and volume, they are all representative of linguistic genes woven into the strain of an African diasporan oral tradition's DNA. They are almost identical in color and tone to the hooping, tuning, and shouting that many preachers still do in traditional churches. Hooping is the heavy delivery at a certain point in a sermon that has a deep breath after each statement. Tuning involves high-pitched tones that are like notes, which follow key words. Shouting is a spiritually charged response to an idea or series of words that consumes a person's state of being. This metaphorical river runs not only through the oratorical styles in preaching, but also in the oral presentation of the blues, jazz music, and Spirituals.

Blues music, rooted in the work songs and Spirituals of slavery and influenced greatly by West African musical traditions, was first played by black people (and some white people) in the Mississippi Delta region of the United States. Grammy-winning blues musician/historian Elijah Wald and others have argued that musicians were rapping the blues as early as the 1920s. Wald went so far as to call Hip Hop "the living blues."[45] Jazz, which developed from the blues and other African American and European musical traditions and originated around the beginning of the twentieth century, has also influenced Hip Hop; and it has been cited as a precursor of Hip Hop, not just jazz music and lyrics, but also jazz poetry. Gil Scott-Heron, a jazz poet/musician/spoken-word performer, wrote and released seminal songs such as "The Revolution Will Not Be Televised."[46]

Old-school flows were relatively basic and used only few syllables per bar, simple rhythmic patterns, and basic rhyming techniques and rhyme schemes.[47] Melle Mel, an old school MC,
epitomizes the old-school flow, according to Kool Moe Dee, who
says:

> From 1970 to 1978 we rhymed one way [then] Melle Mel, in 1978,
> gave us the new cadence we would use from 1978 to
> 1986.[48]...He's the first emcee to explode in a new rhyme cadence,
> and change the way every emcee rhymed forever. Rakim, Biggie,
> and Eminem have flipped the flow, but Melle Mel's downbeat on
> the two, four, kick to snare cadence is still the rhyme foundation
> all emcees are building on.[49]

Artists and critics often credit Rakim with creating the overall
shift from simplistic old-school flows to more complex flows near
the beginning of Hip Hop's new school. Kool Moe Dee says, "Any
emcee that came after 1986 had to study Rakim just to know what
to be able to do....Rakim, in 1986, gave us flow and that was the
rhyme style from 1986 to 1994...from that point on, anybody
emceeing was forced to focus on their flow."[50] Kool Moe Dee
explains that before Rakim, the term *flow* wasn't widely used. From
the griot to the preacher to the blues and jazz orator, this cadence
is a flow in a river of sound that mirrors Hip Hop. One of the catalysts for the birth of Hip Hop music involves oppressive sociocultural realities.

Humble Means to an Eternal End

Dysfunctional school systems, dilapidated neighborhoods, and
harsh housing conditions were sociocultural chains of bondage for
Hip Hop that mirrored the chains of African slaves. The music
became the coded freedom song for a generation that felt trapped
by conditions left by crack cocaine and community centers forced
to close their doors. This beatboxing, scratching, and sampling
sound of the streets is the poetic slave narrative of our time.
Speaking of Hip Hop music at the end of Kanye West's "Crack
Music," poet Malek Yusef said:

Now the former slaves trade hooks for grammies
This dark diction has become America's addiction those who
ain't even black use it. We call it crack music.[51]

The Artists and Their Musical Signatures

Scarface: Photographer of Passion

Scarface passionately captures moments of pain and promise like a photojournalist in hostile territory. He develops urban stories in the dark rooms of his mind so well that the vivid imagery he raps about can be refreshing and often uncomfortable. His lyrics are so transparent and expressive that they reach listeners in an emotional place that is "more tangible than thought."[52] You process Scarface's music not only with your mind but also with your heart.

In many ways his imagery is reminiscent of the work of photo-journalist Jonathan Eubanks (b. 1927) of Oakland, California. A visual chronicler of the Black Panther's activities, Eubanks employed a documentary style that is emotional and descriptive. His photographs explore the personal world of the party leaders and members. In one of his most famous photographs, Eubanks depicted a party member campaigning for the release of Huey Newton, who was arrested in 1967 for killing an Oakland police officer.[53]

Scarface and Eubanks both speak out against social ills through their crafts and artistic activism. Scarface's lyrics communicate imagery that parallels the emotions of Eubanks's portfolio of the Black Panthers' encounters with the police.[54] Listening to Scarface express his own emotions on *Made*, his tenth album, released in 2007, one can clearly hear thoughts that mirror the conspiracy Eubanks's photographs suggest. When I (Marlon) met with Scarface, he denounced Hip Hop because of how it "hurt him." He was available enough to the music to be hurt by it. He poignantly communicated a betrayal of the honesty and beauty of rap. These revealing images and stories are the differential advantage Scarface has in a music culture growing more and more insincere by the song. Without the work of Brad Jordan also known as

Scarface, Hip Hop would not be the self-aware and sensitive music that it is at its best.

Biz Markie: Contemporary Griot Like Sumano

A native of New York, Biz (born Marcel Hall) first came to prominence in the early 1980s. In 1988, he released his debut, *Goin' Off*, which became a word-of-mouth hit based on the underground hit singles "Vapors," "Pickin' Boogers," and "Make the Music with Your Mouth, Biz." A year later, he broke into the mainstream when "Just a Friend," a single featuring rapped verses and out-of-tune sung choruses, reached the pop top-ten list and its accompanying album, *The Biz Never Sleeps*, went gold.[55]

Biz's generation embraced his music, which showcased his ability to tell stories in a distinctive language. Through well-crafted tales laced with humor, clever rhymes, and interesting metaphors, he communicated cautionary tales and introduced truisms about life, love, and what success brings. Unbelievably inventive beat-boxing, choruses sung off-key, witty couplets, and resonating accounts of what has happened to Biz Markie and his friends fuse together to become some of the most memorable, singable, and livable Hip Hop anthems. While Biz Markie's career was stalled by a sampling dispute, Hip Hop artists and fans alike still pay homage to him as an MC whose sweat and gifting helped secure the foundation of Hip Hop.

In many ways, Biz Markie is a modern-day griot—a West African poet, praise singer, and wandering musician, considered a repository of oral tradition. His career is similar to that of a griot from Mali named Bakari Sumano.[56] According to Sumano, "The griot has a knowledge of the sociology and anthropology of this country, the whole of oral tradition. He cultivates it by his performances every day, on all occasions. He tries to maintain living values, he has the function of an educator."[57]

Sumano felt he was responsible for communicating the lessons found in the history of his people. Increasingly famous, Sumano has acted as a consultant for UNESCO and participated in many seminars and colloquia on Malian traditions in African, European, and American universities. In 1994, he became head of the Association of Griots of Mali and dedicated himself to restoring the griots (whom he preferred to call "jeli") to a prominent role in Malian life. He toured the continent, connected with foreign leaders, and organized the griot association, putting in place official ceremonies for the naming of head griots in different cities, such as San and Naréna.[58]

Mos Def: Filmographer of Truth

Mos Def is to Hip Hop what Gordon Parks is to the culture in his time. Gordon Roger Alexander Buchanan Parks was the first African American to work at *Life* magazine and was renowned for his photo essays. His gift was seeing extraordinary potential in ordinary people, places, and spaces. He was a sociologist in his head and a humanitarian at heart. Like a sociologist with a cause, he captured the beautiful side of the ugly streets of New York in *Shaft*, his 1971 detective film starring Richard Roundtree, which explored ghetto life through the suave leather-clad black private detective hired to find the kidnapped daughter of a Harlem racketeer. Parks found heroism in a Harlem known for drugs and prostitution. He communicated what was in the dangerous setting of ghetto life but inspired what could be in the noble mission of a black knight who fearlessly took "no mess."

Mos Def continues that legacy. Mos Def, like Parks, sees the beauty in urban life through a kaleidoscopic lens of art. Mos Def once said, "Life is real! Shootings, stabbings, free tray, arrest crush, kill, destroy, cheques. Death. Rebirth. Reach the world but touch the street first." Mos Def and Gordon Parks are both Renaissance men who are not easily boxed into any one label. Their kaleidoscopic vision keeps them multifaceted because they use many different forms of film, photography, literature, and music to share stories of hope. The vision they have is the end, and their art is simply a means to that end.

Dante Terrell Smith-Bey, also known as Mos Def, is bigger than any of the many wonderful things he does. At heart, he is a sociologist of popular culture who happens to be an artist and African American literary enthusiast by trade. At fourteen Mos Def appeared in the TV movie *God Bless the Child*, starring Mare Winningham. He was embraced by young people everywhere for his role as Bill Cosby's assistant in *The Cosby Mysteries*.

Mos Def reinvented his acting career as the gifted but paralyzed rapper who is afraid to commit to a major label in *Brown Sugar*. Star of HBO's spoken-word show, *Def Poetry*, Mos Def won Best Indie Actor at the 2005 Black Reel Awards for his portrayal of Sgt. Lucas in *The Woodsman*.[59] For his portrayal of Vivien Thomas in HBO's film *Something the Lord Made*, he was nominated for an Emmy Award and a Golden Globe and won the Image Award. Parks and Mos Def have a way of translating our greatest longings.

André 3000: Framer of Fearlessness

The work of André 3000 (André Lauren Benjamin) resembles that of painter Archibald John Motley Jr. Motley was an African American painter who studied painting at the School of the Art Institute of Chicago during the 1910s. He is most famous for his colorful chronicling of the African American experience during the 1920s and 1930s and is one of the major contributors to the Harlem Renaissance. Despite their differences, both Motley and André explore and expose the importance of individuality. Motley was highly interested in skin-tone hues and did numerous portraits of women with varying complexions. These portraits celebrate skin tone as something diverse, inclusive, and pluralistic.[60]

Motley's fascination with painting different types of African Americans stemmed from a desire to show each African American's own character and personality. This is consistent with Motley's aims of portraying an absolutely accurate and transparent representation of African Americans; his commitment to differentiating between skin types shows his meticulous efforts to specify even the slightest differences among individuals. In an interview with the Smithsonian Institution, Motley explained his motives and the difficulty behind painting the different skin tones of African Americans: African Americans are not all the same color; they are not all black, so-called high yellow, or brown. Motley tries to give each person character as individuals, which is difficult when you have so many figures to create and still have them have their individual characteristics.[61] Motley's work parallels modern-day Hip Hop artist André 3000 because they both desire to illuminate that which is unique and distinct.

André 3000 is one of the most respected and intellectual Hip Hop artists, and he has now expanded his work to include producing, fashion designing, acting, and writing. While the disciplines he experiments with vary, one common thread runs throughout each of his projects: his desire to demonstrate the importance of being a unique individual. His music, lyrics, and in-person appearances communicate his refusal to succumb to stereotypes, be they racial, generation specific, or Hip Hop related. He carefully chooses his roles so that he conveys a positive effect. His projects tend toward messages of hope, living out dreams, and defying the norm. When asked how he wanted to be remembered during an interview, he said, "I hope that people remember that he had dreams that he wanted to do and just did 'em. He was a dreamer. That's all."[62]

Jay-Z: Author of Aspiration Turned Entrepreneur

Shawn Corey Carter, also known as Jay-Z, is a synergy of art and entrepreneurship. He is business personified because as he puts it, "I am not a businessman. I am a business, man!" As one of the most industrious Hip Hop artists in the world, he had a net worth of over $150 million in 2009.[63] He has sold approximately fifty million albums worldwide,[64] while receiving thirteen Grammy awards and numerous nominations[65] for his musical work.

Jay-Z co-owns The 40/40 Club and the NBA's New Jersey Nets and is the creator of a clothing line. He is the former CEO of Def Jam Recordings,[66] a cofounder of Roc-A-Fella Records and recently, the founder of Roc Nation. He holds the record for the most number-one albums by a solo artist on the Billboard 200.[67] Jason "DJ Flash Gordon Parks" Woods says, "Jay-Z is a chess player. He has strategically been a part of every major movement within Hip Hop from 1996 until now. Even his exit is strategic; he moves on to the next movement while the last is still being celebrated."[68]

Jay-Z has been able to turn his art into a business enterprise; in this he parallels Malcolm Gladwell. Gladwell is a journalist, author, and pop sociologist who studies culture and writes in response to his observations. Both Jay-Z and Gladwell have a keen ability to perceive what is happening around them, see beyond the circumstance, and take their culture to another level of innovation and creativity. Their respective responses are, at the same time, perplexingly strategic and insightful, delightfully entertaining, and provocative. They are the type of person who always seems to be out front, anticipating the next winning move.

CHAPTER THREE

I Used to Love Her

God, Hip Hop, and Spirituality

"I Used to Love Her"[1] signifies Common's feelings about Hip Hop. One grasps a historical, contextual rendering of events, places, and his own persona in this song. Such a call/invitation/confrontation can remind one of the biblical leader Joshua and his pronouncement at the end of the book bearing his name, in chapter 24. In "I Used to Love Her," Common critiques some of Hip Hop's accomplishments and crassness. By implication, Common calls for creative accountability. Joshua recounts Israel's history to his own time based upon what God had revealed to him. The biblical story relays the dynamics of obedience and idolatry. As a prophetic voice, Joshua calls all of the gathered people to choose whom they will serve and declares, "but as for me and my household, we will serve the LORD" (Josh. 24:15b). Both Common's witness and Joshua's sermonic invitation can inspire us to live with integrity and to set right priorities.

Music with a Cleansing Truth

The relationship among God, Hip Hop, and spirituality is evident but paradoxical. Their intersection often fuels the amazing creativity in the production of Hip Hop music and the phenomenal resilience within Hip Hop culture. The content of the music and its context come from a rich legacy of improvisation and imposed contradiction. This genre emerges out of the tremendous African diasporan legacy in which music has always connected with and mirrored a God consciousness along with protest, communal solidarity, and healing empowerment. The lyrics of a single album can poignantly pierce the heart and blush the face with embarrassment.

As an eighth-grade rap enthusiast, I (Marlon) would find a way to sneak an illicit rap cassette tape into my collection only to discover why the music needed a parental advisory[2] label. Those tapes had a strange way of confirming and corrupting what I was being taught by the very parents who should have been advised of its contents. After taking my headphones off and smacking my lips, I would often communicate my disappointment with an "ahh, man," when I realized that my dirty rap tapes were not that dirty. This so-called dirty music had a way of communicating a cleansing truth. This experience kind of confused me and made me feel that I did not get my money's worth.

Some lyrics could have been copied onto a greeting card to a mom while others had to be concealed from her. The harsh lyrical content of some rap artists has even played a part in the creation of the Parental Advisory Label (PAL). The increase in rap music sales made the harsh content more accessible to wider audiences including underage fans of the music. The first Hip Hop album to receive the PAL was Ice-T's debut album, *Rhyme Pays*,[3] released in 1987, whose lyrics were associated with violence and sexually explicit lyrics. On the album's "I Love the Ladies," Ice-T says, "I think it's time that I tell the truth, I been dissin' females since my early youth." This would lead one to believe that Ice-T does not value womanhood, but just a few stanzas later he says, "Because to me women are God's true gift."[4] The rapper "disses" (urban English vernacular for "disrespects") womanhood in one line and worships God for it in another.

The paradox of Hip Hop has led many to discard it as immoral material with no redeeming religious value, but this practice and attitude should not be so. As confusing as this may sound, the moral paradox of Hip Hop is not the absence of spirituality; it is evidence of it. Hip Hop, like all other human endeavors, shows evidence of the friction between right and wrong and the tension between good and evil. From Sam Cooke's "A Change Is Gonna Come" to Bob Marley's "Redemption Song," this music has translated culture's desire to reconcile good and evil.

The friction between what is and what could be drives the Hip Hop movement and its search for God. The Roots' "Dear God 2.0," from their 2010 album, *How I Got Over*, is titled after a famous gospel song.

Black Thought, the lead lyricist, says:

> Why is the world ugly when you made it in your image?
> And why is living life such a fight to the finish?

Being rubbed the wrong way by what is wrong but that could be right inspires important questions that begin a quest for God.

This chapter explores the intersection and relationship among God, Hip Hop, and spirituality. This chapter also reflects on spirituality and empowerment as gift; ontology (being), Hip Hop, and spirituality; existential reality and Hip Hop; the gift of salvation amid freedom, sin, and the sacred; and the experiences of life of the community, prophetic voices, and Hip Hop.

Inspiration that stimulates questions is like a spark that fires a flame. Sparks are like questions in that how we respond to them can stir up our quest for illumination. This section of chapter 3 explores the questionable spark we call Hip Hop and how what appears to be a friction between God and spirituality has inspired an interest that could purify the desire of a generation and irreparably change its state of being. Putting Hip Hop, spirituality, and God together reveals the potential for the inspiring.

Spirituality and Empowerment as Gift:
The Biggie Blessing

On the wings of Hip Hop, some of the gifted can rise from the cavernous depths of emotional and economic depression to soar through a life of financial and social freedom. This ascension does not come without giftedness of the Hip Hop artists. Lyrical and musical gifts of Hip Hop really engage an incarnation of the spirit realm. Hip Hop bards speak for that part of us not seen by the eye but known by the heart. God's Spirit glows out of the skill of gifted people when we give those people an opportunity to express their talent. Biggie Smalls is a case study of a clever artist whose lyrical gift is a spiritual inspiration that exudes social empowerment.

Christopher George Latore Wallace was born in 1972 in Brooklyn, New York. By ten years old, Wallace—or, as other kids called him, "Big," because of his size—was the only child of his single mother. He was a latchkey kid who came home to an empty apartment while his mother worked two jobs to support him. Even though he was an award-winning English student at the Queen of All Saints Middle School, Wallace's many English awards failed to provide the instant gratification that came with having the money he needed to do what he wanted. At twelve years old, he took advantage of the crack cocaine culture that characterized Brooklyn in the 1980s and joined the league of "entrepreneurs" who were making a living selling drugs. Discouraged by teachers who seemed to ignore his intellect, he dropped out of school altogether. Instead, he channeled his energy into selling crack cocaine and into mastering the English language and his new hobby: rapping.

The birth of a daughter, T'Yanna, gave Wallace justification to grow his drug business even larger. He served nine months in prison after being convicted of several offenses, including possession of weapons and crack cocaine. Following his prison stint, Wallace continued to hone his musical skills. He had an unmistakable gift, and Wallace's freestyle recordings became quite authentic and sought after.

An enthusiastic producer gave Wallace an ultimatum in 1993. Wallace took a chance and signed with Uptown Records and later transitioned to be the principal artist on Bad Boy Records as the Notorious B.I.G. His storytelling was surprisingly smart and his personal stories so vulnerable that they resonated with thousands of people. The marriage of his brilliantly clever writing and fearless, confident flow with tracks that were simultaneously old and new gave birth to hit after hit.[5]

Through Hip Hop, Wallace was able to magnify what was beautiful and divine about him. Hip Hop became the mirror through which he saw himself and gave the public a clear lens into his creativity, his spirit. Affirmed and loved, he began "Juicy," his debut single that ascended on the billboard charts, as he "dedicated [the album] to all the teachers that told me I'd never amount to nothing."[6]

On "Juicy," lyric by lyric, we climb with him out of his "one-room shack." We sympathize and empathize with him because "birthdays was the worst days," and we celebrate because "now we sip champagne 'cause we thirsty." Wallace's gift was a refreshing, even spiritual blessing to the Hip Hop world when he released *Ready to Die* in 1994. The album, released at a time when West Coast Hip Hop was prominent in the United States, according to *Rolling Stone*, "almost single-handedly...shifted the focus back to East Coast rap."[7] Not only did his divine gift lift him from his depressed and hopeless life but also it changed the game of Hip Hop, saving the art from dying on the coast of its origin.

Wallace is now celebrated as one of the greatest rap artists and is described by AllMusic as "the savior of East Coast Hip Hop."[8] Using his God-given gift, he exchanged his circumstances and poor decisions for a role as a prophet, immortalized by his ability to make us dance, laugh, think, love, and dream of rising despite the stakes that seem to tether us down. We rise with him when he says, "Damn right I like the life I live, 'cause I went from negative to positive, and it's all good." One could envision Wallace's notion of the shift to positive and the good as an experience of salvation.

Ontology (Being), Hip Hop, and Spirituality

Hip Hop revolutionized culture and continues to change and inspire the lives of many young people as it provides opportunities for self-expression and empowerment. Many find their authentic voice through this medium. Who could have imagined young people returning to poetry or that the protest, begun in the Bronx and Jamaica, would travel the world? While some gangsta rap jars the sensibilities of those not accustomed to "street" language, the message and the sentiments are genuine, powerful, and real, producing a powerful, complex aesthetic.

Black Aesthetic

When speaking of a black aesthetic,[9] one explores the richness of life out of African diasporan realities, in concepts of the folk and the formal: rival forces of the double consciousness of African American life. The folk and the formal define and name ideal motivational aspects of a politically based black life aimed toward improving black spirituality and aesthetics.[10] Hip Hop performance honors the legacy of African sociocultural heritage preserved within living, beautiful poetry—some paradoxical, some filled with irony, some in your face, but always fighting against ancient oppression although formulated in new ways within an expanded double consciousness, a "Du Boisian veiled,"[11] hidden reality.

A veiled aesthetic or frame of beauty involves the folk tradition, which expresses communal values of most African Americans. Beauty reflects the difference between music as art (an in-depth encounter) and music as entertainment (an immediate experience).

In Hip Hop, like the Spirituals before them, powerful music imitates life, in which music makers and listeners can know themselves and know art as life.[12] Studying Hip Hop as interdisciplinary black aesthetics can move us toward discovery, suggesting that those who are not familiar with Hip Hop should not close their eyes, ears, and minds to the possibilities of the generational effect of this music and its lived experience.

Following French philosopher, sociologist, and historian Michel Foucault's understanding of the "archaeology of knowledge," which focuses on questions of what already exists, we can have dialogue about where we trace and analyze knowledge. Using this lens, we can find how language works in Hip Hop music by studying gestures, sentences, and exclamations as statements.[13] These statements can be understood as matrices, dynamic groupings of words and gestures of protest, affirmation, and celebration. Just as civil rights activists sang songs of hope and affirmation, locally and globally, across space and time,[14] Hip Hop musicians have also written about needs and wants, about freedom and respect, about life and death.

Interpretation of Hip Hop involves governing statements that come from their contextual archeology of knowledge or general descriptive themes. In Hip Hop music, a black aesthetic wants to avoid a distanced, compartmentalized perspective in which one understands life and musical expression as divided into theory, beauty, and ethics or behavioral values. Hip Hop defies such stratification. Hip Hop artists—in particular, those who participate in knowledge rap—view the experience of artist and poet as integral to their roles as truth seekers and teachers, as they seek to reflect on realities of our sociocultural, material, historical world. Such reflection, however, in and of itself, includes a distinct philosophical, metaphysical view related to American pragmatism. These street philosophers connect art, thought, and the practical, all of which have value and meaning. Some of the themes that derive from such an aesthetic of blackness include street-smart parables or fables; adages of street African diasporan political consciousness; revolutionary sensibilities; the nature of art; questions of legitimation and social struggles; transformative, progressive practices; and pedagogical strategies around reading, writing, and learning about black history.

Hip Hop artists engage in the immediacy of personal, participatory, and embodied involvement. A full appreciation of the complex aesthetics of Hip Hop music involves a participatory awareness of sound, rhythm, movement, hearing, and dancing. Full appreciation often involves an awareness of ambiguity and irony; gleaning the author's intent while noting how context can shape and reshape the unfolding of the rap; being open to the myriad ways people express and hear language, which can have multiple meanings reflecting diverse social power relations. Most rappers have learned to use indirect communication skills. They can digest numerous texts easily and use themes and words from these texts in their own creative process when the texts are of importance to the artists' lived experiences.[15]

One word that emerges out of and celebrates the black aesthetic, or the sense of beauty in blackness, is *signifying*. Signifying is a process during which one renames or revises various spoken, sung, and written traditions, affecting "double-voicing." Double-voicing involves the text of the words and the text of the music. Signifying involves the cosmos or world within the text itself as a text reiterates, revises, reverberates, reflects, or responds; it is a process of intertextuality. Thus, signifying affords an artist an opportunity to take one text and change it in multiple ways. Here, double-voicing provides a new orientation to a word or words that retain their own meaning. Signifying is African diasporan double voicedness that involves complex, interrelated relations and formal revision.[16] Signifying—part of the sociocultural, musical infrastructure of black language systems—performs like veiled double consciousness. One signifies in singing the Spirituals, implying multiple hidden, coded meanings within the Spirituals themselves, with basic English words. One signifies in doing Hip Hop music as the metaphors may shift their meaning depending upon one's context, the MC, the venue, and the engagement of participants. Signifying involves participatory, improvisatory music-making.

People often convey such language systems in their social rituals, which surround family and communal gathering places as black people talk about talking. This black manner of speaking remains the black person's sign of difference and encodes personal but communal cultural rituals.[17] Such a practice, when used in music and lyrics, involves a rhetorical-musical perspective. A rhetorical-musical view explores words and music, themes, interaction among people, and people's experiences of God and one another toward the meaning that emerges. This engagement involves the creative spirit and treats many levels of meaning and expressions of rich black language traditions as widespread dialogue or meta-discourse, which pertains to the language tradition.[18] Signifying, itself meta-discourse, involves the creative process during which mind, body, and spirit connect internally and externally in community as music-making unfolds with authenticity, beauty, and relationality. Central to one's relationality with one's own person is the notion of what it means to be, that is, ontology.

Ontology or Being Black

Ontological blackness, a philosophy of racial consciousness, emerged in response to the demonization of black people through white racial ideology. This philosophical stance presents an antithetical conversation, a rhetoric that involves sociocultural and religious thought, toward discounting and disproving white racist ideas about black identity.

Philosopher Victor Anderson presses the notion of "beyond ontological blackness" that takes seriously historically contingent factors and our subjective (individual/personal) intentions in dealing with black lived experience. Anderson has five foci in developing his philosophy.

- One, beyond ontological blackness recognizes a way of being that understands that race is a critical category when constructing personal or communal identity and recognizes that these identities are always changing as black people experience different social spaces and communities in which they engage and practice dialogue about morality. Thus, beyond ontological blackness rejects race as the only category and reminds us to examine gender, class, and sexuality as well.
- Two, this philosophy problematizes historical representations of black people and other non-Europeans, deeming them a false species.

- Three, it views black racial identity as corresponding to a blackness created by whiteness; beyond ontological blackness, it focuses instead on black heroic genius of individuals and of the race.
- Four, racial dialogue from ontological blackness conflicts with contemporary black life. Yet, this counter-discourse does not attack but appropriates the logic that supports and frames European racial ideology. Thus, categorical racism serves as a catalyst to a black racial apologetics intended to annul the negative, white racial dialogue definition of black racial identity and to replace it with a positive definition. Discourse of black genius mirrors the collective of European genius, in which black identity is creative, valiant, morally masculine, groundbreaking, and self-determined.
- Five, to press beyond ontological blackness with a grotesque aesthetic framing notions of difference require that critics reveal and challenge cultural practices and institutions that undermine cultural fulfillment of African Americans within a democracy. Going beyond ontological blackness, black theology, then, focuses on alienated persons who exist amidst socio-cultural determinants of catastrophe, struggle, and survival, instead of blossoming, flourishing, or actualizing.[19] Central to black ontology is an inclusive, creative, freedom-based spirituality.

African diasporan spirituality is the catalyst, foundation, and framing of African culture and religion globally, and particularly for African American culture and religion, towards an experience of salvific freedom. Spirituality develops from one's spiritual identity, in which one encounters the Divine, as ultimate intimacy. This experience goes deep down to one's bones and pierces one's heart, where it guides and comforts. Flora Wilson Bridges notes that spirituality is holistic and ontological: it is a way of being, in which body, mind, and soul act together as one relates to the Divine.

Traditional African faith and thought posit the possibility of meeting God in everything, everywhere, at every moment. For

Africans, who became enslaved in these United States, this came from their spiritual identities and temperaments derived from their African heritage/retentions, their communal and personal experiences, and the hybrid of a faith woven from African and European Christian traditions. For Flora Wilson Bridges, such a spirituality locates itself in its African past and in Christian and other scriptures (e.g., marginally the Qur'an) as authoritative, and the protest traditions of black religions and the black church amidst freedom struggles occur because of this hybrid spirituality's own liberative sensibilities, rather than in response to white oppression. This spirituality embraces a unified cosmology or worldview: embodied spirituality as warrant for protest, self-definition by black folk toward human identity, and a pursuit of community, all framed by liberation,[20] which must be relevant, dynamic, and empowering.

When spirituality is irrelevant, static, or oppressive, it cannot meet the needs of people, particularly those who experience unrelenting oppression. Hip Hop artists embrace a spirituality that is relevant, and they critique the church for not speaking to their needs. From the time of the civil rights protests and the call for social change in the 1960s, the church began to fail to meet the needs of many youth and young adults. Toward this end, Karen and Kasimu Baker-Fletcher call for Spirit-church, in which society can reconnect with a freedom vision and in which justice-making is a virtue. Such a vision calls the church to organized, proactive stances of freedom and empowerment. Such a stance also invites the church to critique itself as well.

Many Hip Hop artists offer such a critique and implore Christians to get involved. The Baker-Fletchers call for critique minus condemnation. They remind us that Hip Hop musicians call the church to be the church of liberation, to work for socio-economic change, and to find a new religion if the church's religious experience only produces more misery. This liberation quest involves a spirituality in which we can find God, not only in church, but also in all nature.[21] When we do not place God in a box but engage in intimacy with God, we come to know unspeakable joy.

Unspeakable Joy of Self-expression

Many are oppressed because of gender, class, race, age, and sexual orientation. Oppressed people often use communal rituals to respond to such injustice. That is, they engage a variety of habits, ceremonies, and traditions to communicate and connect with God and with each other to bolster their morale and sustain hope. While many African diasporan spiritual contexts tend to express with shouts and loud praise, there are many black faith communities who do engage in contemplative or meditative practices with distinctive rituals and liturgies as shared experiences. Barbara Holmes reminds us that we experience individual and interpersonal, communal, mysterious life spaces. Communal, spiritual practices of shared worshipful thoughtfulness or discernment is public theology, in which our inward journeys become communal testimony. The beauty, focus, centering, concentration, and energy of communal contemplation are sometimes lost or displaced when we strive toward upward mobility or when dominant cultural norms overwhelm us. Holmes coined the phrase "joy unspeakable" as a metaphor for communal contemplation. By this she means: that which is surprise, drum talk, respite, a space/time/joy continuum that practices freedom and that challenges us to pray and play in the in-between moments. Joy unspeakable quiets one's troubled heart and points a person or community toward transcendence. Holmes explores joy unspeakable through entry, engagement, and effect. In an instant through movement, music, or words, we can enter into a mystical space of worship. As we release control but nevertheless listen and commune with the Spirit, joy unspeakable unfolds.

Engagement involves a readiness to encounter the Holy through one's body and soul. Meeting can be in silence or ecstasy, or one might be reticent or avoid such an experience because of the pain he or she suffers. Through contemplative practices such as prayer and meditation, one can encounter the Divine and be moved to restoration, actionable love, and transformation of the inner and external self.[22]

Communal contemplation can involve prayer, musical expression, and thoughtful dance movements. In these meaningful spaces and experiences, the community experiences joy unspeakable.

African diasporan community life experiences holiness through the everyday living of these cultural values. Through holy encounters, people change, can know a new sense of peace, and experience communal solidarity. One can know joy unspeakable in shouts, dance, hums, moans, or foot cadences. Young, old, and folks in between can know this joy. Moreover, in African diasporan traditions, there is no separation between so-called sacred and secular, for everything derives from incredible spiritual energy. As people and communities grow, their expressions and spiritual needs diversify.[23]

In African diasporan music, just as blues and jazz emerged from the older Spirituals, and rags, house, and rhythm and blues (R&B) came out of blues and jazz, so Hip Hop and rap emerged from the children and grandchildren of the civil rights movement. Rappers signified and made their own way just as African poets and musicians before them, for each generation has a story to tell and is seen as rebellious by the previous generation. Like their predecessors, Hip Hop artists created revolutionary, reformational art forms. They experienced displacement, isolation, trauma, brokenness, deteriorating health, poor education, and sometimes disenchantment and oppression from sociopolitical systems that became fodder for their chanting and rhyming.

Hip Hop artists create music reflecting their sociocultural, political, and religious understandings. Holmes notes that these artists state their identity, as their poetry mocks, reports, and threatens, rejecting the normative, current state of affairs with exaggerated expression and clothing: performance exercised after contemplation. The music and culture of Hip Hop critique subjugated knowledge, that is, knowledge of race, class, gender, and sexuality learned through media, resulting in an impoverishment and a new underclass. These artists feel isolated, and their goals are not the goals of the civil rights generation, who espoused college education, upward mobility, and homes in suburbia. Often they do not have close church connections, but Hip Hop music allows them to redefine their reality, to speak about love and family.

In African diasporan tradition, Hip Hop, like blues and jazz before it, has moved into the churches of black people and white people. Now there are many Christian rappers who blend sacred and secular. For the church to minister to this generation, it must meditate, think about, and discern how to sing new songs. A cultural task of youth is always to revise their language, lives, and musical structures as they make sense of life, and wrestle with differences regarding themselves and their faith. Yet they are also seeking God. Just like preceding generations, they must find their own way to awe and wonder.[24] The unspeakable joy that one wants to experience must also include the existential component of "Why am I here?"

Existential Reality and Hip Hop

Existential Reality of Blackness

Existentialism generally entails studying the uniqueness of each human being's emotions, actions, responsibilities, and thoughts. As a philosophy, it is concerned with an individual making self-defining choices, thus emphasizing freedom of choice and personal responsibility. Some existentialists regard human existence in a hostile universe as unexplainable.

Cornel West connects philosophy with concrete existence and the basic dynamics of a consummate life. He wants to understand how one can make choices while living within systemic oppression. For West, philosophy is a historically conditioned discipline and an existential, sociohistorical response. West's view of the individual remains one of hope and possibility, despite one's disposition or views. A person's capacity to self-express relates to West's notion of existential aptness, based upon three concepts: revolutionary Christian perspective, progressive Marxist thought, and Ralph Ellison's Afro-American humanist tradition.[25] West's prophetic pragmatism involves a democratic faith with existential depth and political awareness.[26]

When seeking to understand one's existential realty, one must always deal with one's own fears, hopes, and dreams. In black cultural expressions, existentialism does not mean self-indulgence or navel gazing. Existentialism involves action, human choice, and taking responsibility, grounded in one's spirituality and one's religious consciousness.[27] Many Hip Hop artists inherently embrace a notion of existentialism, as espoused by Cornel West, who addresses "the fundamental facts of human existence—death, dread, despair, disease, and disappointment."[28]

The popularity of Hip Hop music speaks to its global appeal; it resonates with different peoples, expressing their feelings, pain, questions, concerns, sense of oppression, sexuality, creativity, and energy. It addresses these existential concerns as it engages and marries melody, harmony, and stories amidst marginalization. The existential reality of those who live, breathe, and self-express through Hip Hop can juxtapose their desires and needs. They can live out their freedom to choose and their constraints on being able to choose.

Complexities of Hip Hop's composition and production forge a musical matrix that involves power, survival, and pleasure. Like other types of black music, Hip Hop emerges and evolves from within a particular sociohistorical time frame, and stands in tension to yet has continuity with the other music forms. Tricia Rose notes how Hip Hop has visionary, liberatory, and politically progressive tenets, while coming out of an existential reality fraught with angst. She says that these are postindustrial conditions, which include technological advances, massive loss of industrial factories, reduction of service jobs, restructuring of socioeconomic markets, creation of an impoverished underclass, acceleration of elite greed, deregulation, dwindling federal funding, and declining affordable housing. The horrors of dislocation and disruption, particularly in urban centers, served as catalysts for Hip Hop's development and growth as youth created alternative identities. Because many former support organizations and institutions were torn down, many strong personas moved to other areas, as young people experienced tremendous sociocultural and political changes that forged deep disappointment and alienation.

Hip Hop musicians engage popular culture while also engaging in prophetic rage and proffering social criticism. They signify, naming the abyss between their black lived existence and often-dominant social thinking about so-called equal opportunity and racial inequality. Conversely, rap shares contradictions around gender, race, and class like other types of music and social protest. Hip hop music both kowtows to the music industry's demands and critique, and offers social protest against those systems that often invoke oppression against black communities (e.g., media, government, and police). Within these latter contexts, power brokers often view young black youth as both symbolic and actual threats, and thus these powerbrokers vilify, stigmatize, and approach these young people with hostility. Dominant culture's fear of black youth, which assumes a lawlessness, anger, violence, and amorality, then requires negation and the need to control, particularly ghetto black impoverished youth.[29]

Post Traumatic Slave Syndrome

Oppression is not new to the souls of black folk; it has been generational and much of it has its beginnings in slavery. Sometimes when people have known oppression, once they gain access to a modicum of power, they embrace the crab syndrome: when one gets ahead, the others try to claw him back or take her down. The realities of such angst, miseducation, and cyclical pain emerge in the writings of Joy DeGruy Leary's book, *Post Traumatic Slave Syndrome: America's Legacy of Enduring Injury and Healing.*[30]

Leary notes that there is a historical reason why black people undermine one another individually and in organizations. Some people need to undercut others, just as many African American organizations fall prey to embracing similar undermining behaviors, particularly when it comes to struggles around leadership and finances, producing infighting, cliques, and unhealthy competition. In these situations, the organization loses its original purpose, and the community loses resources.

To our innocent children, a glance can trigger anger, so that proud parents are afraid to praise their children. And out of fear, parents also feel they have to inhibit their children's exploratory instincts. Friends are afraid to celebrate their peers' accomplishments. Black people have become premier consumers and are living beyond their means. Classism, racism, sexism, homophobia, and other pathologies collide internally as hair texture and skin color are topics of discussion pertaining to beauty and physical preferences. Many black people seem to be out of control when it comes to frustration and anger. How prevalent are these issues in your neighborhood, your church, your home, inside of you?

We recall the history of slavery:

Linnaeus' taxonomy, Jeffersonian reasoning, Phrenology, and IQ testing all served as the scientific foundations upon which the institutions of slavery and racial superiority/inferiority were constructed.... [We recognize that some Europeans] and their descendants have gone to great length to justify the 500 years of trauma and dehumanization they and their institutions produced. The effects of this trauma and dehumanization are observable today, and can be explained by the theory of Post Traumatic Slave Syndrome.[31]

This syndrome is a compilation of and reaction to horrific crimes against humanity inherent to the U.S. institution of slavery, in which many stories of African Americans were left out of the history books. The reality of Middle Passage, or *Maafa*, is neglected, where between ten and fifteen million persons landed here as chattel, while approximately the same number lay on the bottom of the Atlantic.

In bondage, numerous horrific crimes occurred, including rape and so-called scientific experimentation or barbarism inflicted on enslaved bodies. During and following the Emancipation Proclamation, oppression was further institutionalized through black legal codes and other exclusionary acts, the peonage of sharecropping, the convict lease system, Jim Crow laws, and the *Strange Fruit*[32] of lynching. Crimes also include the decimation of towns such as Greenwood, or "Black Wall Street," and Tulsa, Oklahoma; Rosewood, Florida; and Wilmington, North Carolina. The horrific Tuskegee syphilis experiment (1932–1972) was another example of systematic oppression, followed by the post–civil rights and Vietnam War era where some people, because of gender, class, race, age, and sexual orientation experienced various types of systematic oppression. This reality continues today through the new prison industrial complex, the proliferation of drugs, and the destruction of historic black communities. Most recently, problems related to poor school funding, overcrowded classrooms, and publicly funded vouchers for private schools continue to assure a ghettoization of the poor and a growing underclass. Thus, 180 years of the Middle Passage and 246 years of oppression continue to plague our country.

What happened then is the foundation for what is happening now. This legacy has created Leary's Post Traumatic Slave

Syndrome. That is **M + A = P**: Multigenerational trauma together with continued oppression and **A**bsence of opportunity to access the benefits available in the society leads to **P**ost **T**raumatic **S**lave Syndrome, or **PTSS**.

PTSS produces several pathologies. Vacant esteem[33] is the state of believing you have little or no worth, exacerbated by pronouncements of inferiority (from our society, community, and family). Indicators of vacant esteem include:

- First, suicide by police/gangsters and the move to undermine achievements of other black folk reflect a lack of self-worth.
- Second, *ever-present anger* is a huge indicator of PTSS. Anger can be a response to both the fear of failure and of blocked goals. A major trigger of this anger and violence in black folk, particularly young black males, is disrespect. Anger and violence were hallmarks of slavery and the enslaved needed key ingredients to make sure their survival needs were met. Leary notes, "Much of the anger is a reaction to our hopes and dreams being continuously undermined by the institutions which govern us and the racism that permeates [U.S.] society"[34]
- Third, an ironic, insidious, and pervasive indicator of PTSS concerns our adopting the slave master's value system. Such behavior is particularly pathological when dominant culture's standards of beauty, material success, consumerism, violence, and brutality become normative for black communities.
- In sum, African Americans in the United States have been socialized to believe we are spiritually, emotionally, physically, and intellectually inferior. Otherwise, why would black kids think today that to study and learn and excel at school is to be white?[35] Thus, after centuries of being portrayed as inferior and ineffectual, sadly, some of us believe failure is inevitable.

Black people need schools, colleges, universities, seminaries, churches, and other social empowerment groups working together with families to create positive race, class, and gender socialization and the possibility of realized eschatological justice: justice now! As a society, we need to do research and create intergenerational training modules to teach our youth and entire communities about systemic oppression and to teach them the coping skills and mechanisms they need to survive and thrive despite this environment. We need to listen to one another and learn to communicate so that we can engage in intergenerational dialogue. In order to speak with youth, then, it is critical that we understand Hip Hop culture.

When we shift from a denial about reality in order to embrace a determined spirituality, we can begin to address PTSS and help move the souls of black folk to wholeness. By framing this kind of work as a justice-based ministry of relationality, we can provide the context in which people can creatively deal with their anger and their pain without guilt and shame. We, then, have the room to support our youth and young adults in listening to Hip Hop music critically, to help them build their self-esteem, and to be discerning participants in this cultural and musical genre. This awareness will allow them to be present and authentic, to be able to think critically, to grasp that they have a right to express themselves, and to access fair and equal rights in the larger society.

Empowerment—through education around music, culture, and life, in which we all listen with empathy and compassion, rather than condemnation and judgment—helps the Hip Hop generation come to know and love their authentic selves, which then allows them to respect themselves and others. Ultimately, we can then engage majority culture to help all persons become sensitive to their own responsibilities in a patriarchal, hegemonic, oppressive society.

The Sacred and Rage

In traditional African and many African diasporan communities, there is no separation between sacred and secular. Many black folk hold closely to their relationship with the Divine and are able to experience that which is sacred in much of what some deem secular. Part of having an intimate relationship with a greater being, with God, is having a capacity to feel highs and lows with deep contrasts.

Rage may be a response to outrageous acts of oppression and disrespect. The notion of "killing rage,"[36] articulated by bell hooks, is a powerful metaphor of critical analysis that can help us explore individual and communal hypocrisy, betrayal, and miseducation amid our complicity in violence, our lack of integrity, and our capacity to require of others that which we cannot do ourselves. If we pretend subjugation and coercion do not exist, that we do not see or know how to change them, then the oppression remains in perpetuity and never *has* to disappear. Change requires disruption. Denial allows us to be complicit in oppression and violence.

For hooks, to transform denial requires "killing rage," or radical resistance. Killing rage, anger, and fury that bubble up as a result of violation are agonizing. Such rage can evolve into intense grief and destruction if there is no outlet. This rage is a place of aliveness, of immediacy, of subjectivity.[37] Killing rage, a source for empowerment and metamorphosis, helps one name, unmask, and engage the self and others in profound politicization and self-recovery. Such rage, a catalyst for courageous action and resistance, helps one grow and change.

Pathological, addictive, and dysfunctional behaviors dull the pain and the rage. In those moments, we become complicit with white-supremacist patriarchy. Thandeka, a Unitarian Universalist minister, scholar, professor, and Emmy Award–winning journalist and television producer, reminds us that no one is born white; they learn to be white, to embrace white privilege.[38] Killing rage, which can be a destructive or a creative force, provides an opportunity to comply or resist, to be pessimistic or hopeful, to be just or unjust. The consuming nature of rage must be tempered "by an engagement with a full range of emotional responses" to employ one in self-determination.[39] Sharing rage spawns communication and facilitates connections. Squashing rage leads to assimilation and amnesia.

The antithesis of engaged rage is victimhood. "To counter the rhetoric of victimhood," we must engage in a discourse of self-determination, as we struggle to end racist, sexist, classist, and heterosexist domination.[40] Killing rage is an electrifying tool for change, a catalyst viable for public and private sectors. Working with Hip Hop artists to channel their rage can heighten their awareness and move them to a healthier, more balanced life.

Killing rage can energize and encourage. A creative use of killing rage can sensitize artists to their use of language and invite them to be creative and profound without being vulgar. Killing rage embodies irony as it thwarts violence; it instigates yet incriminates apathy, dominance, misery, and complicit behaviors, thoughts, and processes that affect teaching and learning. Killing rage empowers and helps us appreciate God, our realities, and ourselves; it helps black folk love ourselves and one another and not be persuaded by stereotypes that make us hate and demonize ourselves.

Demonization of Blackness

There are many myths regarding white/black relationships. These include magnetism of color, fear, alleged black sexual prowess, signaling brood mares and studs, and white violent resistance against blacks. Notions of blackness exact pleasurable curiosity and negative images, tinged with allure and repulsion. Language and imagery in the West continues to equate blackness with words of doom, gloom, dread, evil, pain, terror, annihilation, and inferiority, while whiteness suggests notions of beauty, purity, innocence, good, delight, joy, light, and superiority.

Most Eastern, including Middle Eastern, cultures negate blackness, including the Arabs who initially did not have these sensibilities until after Islam emerged and engaged in African conquest. From a sense of ambiguity and uncertainty in European and Arabic culture about blackness to cosmic chaos to natural inferiority, dominant culture has used biblical texts and rule of law to foster sociocultural and social action against blacks. The same negation couched in racist, classist terms today was present in the cultural imaginations of European colonialism and nationalism.[41]

Negativity regarding blackness in the Christian tradition began with early patristic understandings of biblical texts, which equated blackness with immorality, the demonic, sin, chaos, evil, and corruption, and personified blackness as the devil. Early church leaders did vary on their views of blackness. Origen saw blackness as a divine good, while Jerome saw blackness as evil and sin, carnal lust, and sexual prowess. The church connected the carnal sense of beauty and viewed things deemed sinful and evil as black. That is, black and blackness were metaphors for the ills of society and faith, as the church portrayed the devil as a black and sometimes red monster with cloven hooves, fiery eyes, donkey-type ears, the smell of sulfur, and a gigantic penis. Ultimately, the control of images of black people and culture dominated and shaped personal and communal identity. Such control of black imagery (and white imagery) was prolific in Western civilization, notwithstanding attempts by black people to shift the thinking and awareness around blackness and the perception of black bodies.

Even with recent corrective language around race by such groups as the National Council of Churches and the World Council of Churches, the baggage continues to permeate our culture.[42] Black artists, including Hip Hop artists, have long felt this tension. Music is one medium that spans the various categories that can separate us. Music is an opportunity to express spirituality in a way that helps us interact and better connect with one another. Music as a presenter of spirituality pertains to its theomusicology.

Music as Spiritual Practice: Theomusicology

Theomusicology is a "theologically informed discipline" that studies sacred and secular actualities and musics, including their therapeutic values (theomusicotherapy).[43] Theomusicological analysis involves decoding music that illumines archetypes of meaning and takes a holistic view of human spirituality, effecting healing and accord. In theomusicology, the Divine speaks through people to reveal the divine self through the grace, the aesthetic, the incredulities, and the hopeful imagination in secular life in which Ultimate Being discloses itself through finite beings.[44]

When one listens critically, one can hear the challenges and evils in the church and the world as the music reveals "hidden cracks beneath the social surface."[45] These fissures occur amid and despite the desire for hopeful change. African music in the United States, from the Spirituals to Hip Hop, sees the cracks, lessens the incongruous vision, and creates a new, transforming music. Theomusicology supports the quest for liberation, seeks to erase intellectual arrogance, and invites an ethics of responsibility.[46] Theomusicology warns against Eurocentric scholarship when such scholarship results in cultural idolatry, noncreative conceit, and negation. Coparticipation in societal and self-rule is the goal.[47] Theomusicology provides insight into theological aesthetics within music and music-making toward healing. By studying the dynamics of theology and spirituality in the music, we can see the theological beauty within the music and can engage music in a way in which people experience healing. God is there within the process of music-making. Where God is, healing can occur.

In musical analysis, I (Cheryl) explore the personal and communal dynamics and the musical and literary rhetoric of sounds and silence to uncover a rich aesthetic vocabulary.[48] Musical style—the complex human action of sound and song and behavior patterns—includes all aspects of musical production, from participation and psychosocial function to formal ambient factors. Songs identify and reinforce cultural structures and practices. Songs respond and react and honor and call for revolution.

My theological aesthetics is grounded in a notion of beauty and of God in dialogue with the beautiful. This aesthetic appreciates all of creation and the human expression in the form of phenomenal art, which radiates that beauty as communal and individual lived reality. Such an aesthetic is participatory, sacred, and essential for healing and holistic health. Music and music-making not only are accessible but also offer such places of vitality and strength for coping with loss and grief. Hip Hop music affords celebration and catharsis, for within this sociocultural dynamic of word and rhythm, artists are heard, if nowhere else. Part of the power that radiates through music comes through its connection with and reflection of our own spirituality.

In spiritual, social, and political communities of the United States, we tend to hold to notions of manifest destiny[49] and a lone-ranger, independent mentality. Such attitudes give credence to navel-gazing and forgetting the gift of being a neighbor. Such minds often embrace a spirit of frontier sensibilities and a Darwinian "survival of the fittest" ethos. Yet we do not listen to *or* for personal and communal pain. We forfeit our accountability for immediate gratification and omit the stewardship of a peaceful, balanced life. Conversely, sometimes we ignore healthy boundaries and tread where it is inappropriate. A healthy, balanced spirituality requires our lived connectedness to God. Connectedness to God affords us a connection with others, so that we can have an intergenerational conversation about life. And a Hip Hop song, alongside scripture, can serve as our text. Studying these texts together can help us more deeply explore the dynamics of salvation.

Salvation, Sin, and the Sacred

Salvation is the way to be saved, ultimately to be free from what torments us most. The journey toward salvation is a response to one of the greatest questions ever: "How do we reconcile sin, a relationship with God, and freedom?" How fallible and finite human beings find freedom from their compulsions, and the consequences of mistakes are the roots of our search for the sacred. This root branches out to bear the fruit of rituals, rites, and spiritual traditions that are as ancient as human experience. The soil of the human soul—its consciousness, thought, and feeling—is nurtured through a rudimentary search for salvation. This anchoring theme is how humanity seeks emotional and mental nourishment beneath the surface of everyday circumstances and choices that follow it.

The Roots and Roots

Music is a journey to make and not just a product to buy. This is the reason buying and listening to a CD for the first time is a ritual for me. When I (Marlon) buy a CD, how I open the CD case, what I play the music on, and where I am when I first listen comprise a ritual. When I heard the first note of *How I Got Over* by The Roots, I knew I had struck Hip Hop gold.

The Roots are a Hip Hop band formed in 1987 by Tariq "Black Thought" Trotter and Ahmir "?uestlove" Thompson in Philadelphia, Pennsylvania. The Roots are a refreshing combination of drums and poetry. They are such music icons that they were asked to be the house band for NBC's *Late Night* with Jimmy Fallon.[50]

When asked by the *Wallstreet Journal* reporter John Jurgensen what this album sounds like, one of the members ?uestlove said, "People keep throwing the word *gospel* up, which is kind of scaring me a bit.... Subject-wise a lot of the issues on the album are dilemmas.... This is as close as we'll ever get to spirituality.... We see suffering that goes on. We're a band that reflects what we see."[51]

This rudimentary, or "root-imentary," Hip Hop band once said that "The Square Roots" does not reflect every person's search for salvation in Rap, but this album has a way of exploring the mistakes, freedom, and sacred nature of life in our time. There are four songs from their latest album, *How I Got Over*, that I will use to illustrate the human search for salvation, freedom, and the sacred.

"How I Got Over" is a gospel hymn composed and published in 1951 by the Reverend W. Herbert Brewster.[52] Many artists have recorded this work, including Mahalia Jackson, who won a Grammy for Best Soul Gospel Performance in 1976. While ?uestlove is uncomfortable with this latest album being called "gospel," the title and the issues raised in the music's lyrics have roots that stem from a lineage of spiritual music. Such music is a vessel through which artists can reflect what they see in their present reality and project divine possibility because of or in spite of it. These songs demonstrate a search for authentic humanity, the Divine, and divine manifestation, such as grace and salvation.

Salvation

The album begins with a beautifully arranged a cappella solo voice. The ethereal voice sounds like a light and fluffy cloud formation made for ears to appreciate, and it is free from the pretension and heaviness that instruments can sometimes add. The first song on the album, titled "Peace of Light," is a song that says a lot. The group seems to want to provoke listeners to unpack the weight of prior experiences and predetermined outcomes before hearing a single word.

To me, this first song is a musical metaphor for salvation because it clears clutter the way salvation should. Salvation cleans the stain of past failure. "Peace of Light" is a metaphor for a generation's desire to be set free from the boundaries of consequence and the borders of personal and peer pressure and punishment. It speaks to Hip Hop's beginning as a way to relieve tensions among rival gangs whose cyclical retribution destroyed communities.

To illustrate how Hip Hop broke through tension, recall the story about Afrika Bambaataa, one of the founding fathers of Hip

Hop. One summer night, Afrika Bambaataa used music to bring peace between neighbors divided by grudges. Before Bambaataa played the first song, he asked rival gangs to forgive each other so that peace could inspire unity and not gang violence.[53] "Peace of Light" reminds us that salvation is a remedy for sin, and it lightens the load for past transgression.

Sin

"Walk Alone," another cut from The Roots's *How I Got Over* album, continues in the lineage of biblical psalms of lamentation. "Walk Alone" explores the journey from poor choice to impending punishment. Black Thought raps about the weight of sin while he aspires to the wings he hopes will support him in this verse.

> The longest walk I'll probably ever be on
> The Road to Perdition, guess I'm finna get my plea on.[54]

This prayer, which is an earnest plea to God, sheds light on the reality of sin for a generation labeled as dark and valueless. Black Thought laments his behavior and cries out for reconciliation and renewal. "Walk Alone" includes guest rappers on the album who are a part of a growing collective of artists featured on OkayPlayer.com, a website developed by The Roots to give peripheral rap artists a chance to be heard. One of these fringe artists, P.O.R.N., talks about the power and imprisonment of sin with supreme clarity that concludes a preacher's third point. While some preachers have termed the style "three points and a celebration," three points and a poem is the composition and delivery style of a sermon during which the preacher makes three points and then ends with excerpts from a work of popular prose. This song is like one of those closing poems.

The song has a poetic way of processing the consequences of past decisions and the possibility of moving beyond them. P.O.R.N., in an OkayPlayer.com interview, talks about the origins of his name, saying, "They've been calling me P.O.R.N. for years, because of some crazy episode with some chick when we were teenagers."[55] P.O.R.N., whose name stems from teenage debauchery, confesses,

There ain't no hell like the hell I raise I'd die in the bed I made 'fore I lay with a love I loathe I'm a snake in the garden of bones.[56]

A man who uses the concept of pornography to identify himself confesses the makings of his own mistakes or the hell he raises, while, at the same time, refusing to allow it to define him. As if to say, "I may have done wrong, but I am not wrong. I have made bad decisions, but I am not bad." This struggle between indiscretion and identity communicates the conscience of the Hip Hop culture when it comes to its own mistakes. Many older adults view Hip Hop artists as young and reckless people who do not care about good decisions or the consequences of bad ones, but this song says otherwise.

This song sees redemption beyond indiscretion and possibility beyond poor decision-making. Hip Hop has a hope that allows it to see consequences as a means to a profitable end and not simply to a dead end. The song openly admits fault but nevertheless hopes to find the faith to believe that some good can come.

Life of the Community, Prophetic Voice, and Hip Hop

The Wu-Tang Clan is the poster family for community and prophetic voice in Hip Hop. There is a mystic and familial thread woven into its fabric. The word *Clan* in their name communicates the kindred nature of the group's approach to life and music. The *Wu-Tang* part of the name reveals an eastern aesthetic and with it, a mystic movement of sound and spirit.

Wu-Tang Clan is a New York City–based Hip Hop group. The founders of the Wu-Tang Clan were cousins Robert Diggs, Gary Grice, and Russell Jones (RZA, GZA, and Ol' Dirty Bastard). This beginning inspired the spirit of family when inviting other members to the group, which consisted of Method Man, Raekwon, Ghostface Killah, Inspectah Deck, U-God, and Masta Killa. In 2007, MTV ranked Wu-Tang Clan the fifth greatest Hip Hop group of all time.[57]

The clan is made up of nine distinct members, and each member embraces individuality and a genuine voice. With their diversity, the Wu-Tang Clan is more than progressive; they are compulsively driven by authenticity. While some rap is becoming a cookie-cutter and formulaic art form with no voices of truth or prophetic hope, this nine-member fraternal order has a way of antagonizing one another to be authentic. They are not content with a uniform sound in which it is hard to distinguish one person's voice from another. They each have a voice that is different not only from other members in the group but also from every other lyricist alive. They are encouraged to have voices that stand out and do not just fit in. Like a Hip Hop crossword puzzle of sound, they each have a piece of the puzzle with its own shape and imagery but come together to create a larger picture.

Wu-Tang Clan was assembled in late 1992 with RZA as the de facto leader and the group's producer. RZA and Ol' Dirty Bastard adopted the name for the group after the film *Shaolin and Wu Tang*.[58] Loud/RCA released their debut album, *Enter the Wu-Tang (36 Chambers)*, in late 1993. The success of *Enter the Wu-Tang (36 Chambers)* established the group as a creative and influential force in mid-1990s Hip Hop, allowing Ol' Dirty Bastard, GZA, RZA, Raekwon, Method Man, and Ghostface Killah to negotiate solo contracts. These individual solo contracts made them a multifaceted group who reached many different rap audiences. They were a synergy of a group, and their influence was greater together than individually.

There is something for every kind of rap listener. From straight-up lyricism to chaotic ramblings, the Wu-Tang Clan served virtually any palette when it came to emceeing. The group covered a varied spectrum from underground to pop sensibilities. This laid the blueprint for Hip Hop collectives for years to come. I believe the newness of these unexplored belief structures was an exciting escape from the familiar of the West.[59]

Spiritually speaking, the Wu-Tang Clan has an ancient aesthetic to their union. Like many latchkey kids raised in the 1980s, these boys have become men who incorporate the mysticism of Eastern traditions experienced while watching Saturday morning kung fu flicks. They destroy the divide between sacred and secular. They, like ancient traditions, have developed a sound that effortlessly incorporates belief systems from Buddhism to the 5 percent religion without ifs, ands, or buts. They are spiritual and not relatively religious. They do not need a religion to relate to, because they see themselves as an embodiment of mystical life in the hood. RZA is not a Christian who goes to church to be spiritually charged; RZA is a walking and rapping sanctuary of spiritual energy and imagination. He raps spirit, makes everyday situations mystical, and does not need a spiritual setting or building to activate his spirituality. For RZA, there is no division between a religious idea and a rap statement. They all use their stories and experiences from the streets as a poetic way to promote life, sacred and secular. They have an ancient-future approach to indigenous cultures. There is no difference between the sacred life and the secular life in older African cultures. There is a spiritual value ascribed to even the most mundane task.

Like indigenous communities, God and spiritual conversations are not divided from everyday life in the urban village, but they are discerned in the villages of Staten Island, Brooklyn, and Queens, New York. A walk to the store is an opportunity to discover spiritual truths at work. The Clan has a sacred appreciation that transcends music and business; it is spiritual. From music to clothing to writing materials to the way they refer to their New York neighborhood as "Shaolin," they are both spiritual and communal.

> RZA has mixed world religion, music, chess, superhero comics, and kung-fu movies into his own idiosyncratic worldview, and he's dead serious about a spiritual quest that began with the Twelve Jewels of the Five Percent Nation of Islam, trekked to the far side of Shaolin, and hasn't ended yet.[60]

In a time when regional tensions divided Hip Hop, the Wu-Tang Clan ascended to speak prophetically. They had a way of speaking with unity and spiritual imagination in a time when they were needed most. Like prophets of old, they spoke in the right time with a voice that was timeless. Their work positively signifies the beauty of Hip Hop, creating an aesthetic that is powerful and prophetic. Listening with discernment, understanding the context, awareness of the spiritual amidst culture itself, and a commitment to our youth provide a novel opportunity for an intergenerational ministry to be planted, if God calls a congregation in this direction.

Prophecy is often understood as a prediction of the future. However, a prophet is one who speaks for God; and while that may entail the future, it can also include speaking to the present and past. Hip Hop, then, is a prophetic voice in the fullest sense of the word because it is three-dimensional. Prophetic Hip Hop not only speaks about the future, but it also has a way of speaking from the past and to the present. The Wu-Tang Clan is an example of this prophetic dimension.

The story of the Wu-Tang Clan is compelling. The wounds of negative energy inspired by East Coast and West Coast rap wars needed to be healed, but this healing would not come easily. The Wu-Tang Clan came with a voice of healing that had a way of honoring what was ancient, speaking to what was present, and projecting their voice into the future. They forgot about the divide between regions and together as a Hip Hop nation focused on the creativity and unity these distinct rappers shared on stage and on CDs. They took us to another space and another time through lyrics that talked about things as disparate as chess, kung fu, and ancient philosophy. Coastal competition was replaced by collective creativity. As a consequence, we can forget about the difference between the coasts and can focus on our favorite Wu-Tang member. With over twenty people on stage at one time, the group visually and verbally gives contemporary voice the ancient desires for truth connection and camaraderie. They have a spiritual curiosity that genuinely bonds their connection. Wu-Tang sewed up the wounds of coastal divides by using a threefold thread bound by the mystical, the ancient, and the future. This is how they became the prophetic voice of Hip Hop. They healed a nation by unifying the past, the present, and the future. This group did what the movement of Jesus did in the first century and what the Spirit of God is moving it (the movement of Jesus) to do in the twenty-first century, to heal a present world with ancient wisdom and hope. Hip Hop is a voice that may use insipid language but has a deep desire to inspire a generation.

Conclusion

Hip Hop has been known by some as a negative voice that makes no room for spiritual dialogue and themes, but it does. This wild and wayward voice is really a paradoxical conversation with a loving God who allows insipid monologues to become inspiring dialogues between broken people and a healing God. It is a paradox with insipid language and inspiring possibilities for spiritual discourse. The immorality and irreligious themes of Hip Hop are not confirmation that there is no relationship among God, Hip Hop, and spirituality; they are evidence of the conversation between the three. It may be an uncomfortable conversation that does not use the best language, but *it is a conversation*. No matter the language, the subject is spiritual comfort and healing truth. Unless it wears a cross and deliberately uses Christian language and premises, we demonize Hip Hop as spiritual dysfunction, but in this guise, so was Jesus. He talked to the dregs of society, spoke in their language, and put himself in the position to be known as an ordinary member of a cult that protested the very essence of Jewish morality and spiritual purity. Jesus was a paradox to the religious and spiritual standard of the day. He had a way of using the commonplace to inspire the disenfranchised.

In the Gospel of John chapter 4, Jesus connected with a Samaritan woman at a well and challenged her to take life-giving water that would quench her soul's thirst forever. This sounds good from our cultural context as citizens of a melting pot for a world and as members of a generation where women's rights are more recognized, but Jesus' conversation was set in a different time and cultural context. In His time, this conversation was an degraded and Godless act of moral decay. As a Jewish man he should not have even been speaking to a woman from Samaria and certainly not one who had been known to have many husbands and to be living with a man who was not her husband.

Looking from the outside in, it appears that Jesus was talking to a lewd woman, therefore his words had to have been lewd. A young Jewish man having a conversation with a known Samaritan harlot must have seemed lewd, but through the lens of scripture, we discover something different. Being there with Jesus, we learn that He was not having an immoral monologue, He was nurturing a divine dialogue. Even though they candidly and uncomfortably talked about her lewd lifestyle, the subject of their chat was not insipid, it was an inspiring message of "worship...spirit and truth" (John 4:24).

We treat young people like the woman at the well and discard them because of the known poor decisions and immorality they discuss in their music. If Jesus were alive today, however, Hip Hop would be the proverbial well he pulled words from, and his message would be to the morally disconnected. These words would not sound so pretty on the outside, but beneath the surface we would find a divine dialogue teeming with living water possibility and healing potential. Jesus would be an underground Hip Hop artist who connected with the disconnected to have gritty spiritual conversations about worship and truth. He would use ordinary words to inspire spiritual conversations.

The relationship among Hip Hop, God, and Spirituality is a conversation that uses commonplace words that can lead to a well of inspiration when we dare to see the conversation through the lens of scripture. When we go with Jesus to the public well that Hip Hop has become we discover a conversation between broken human beings and a healing God.

CHAPTER FOUR

G.O.D. (Gaining One's Definition)

Black Church and Black Culture

Sometimes we experience confusion and distraction because we are not in balance with God, our neighbors, the universe, or ourselves. We are restless and unsure. We experience miseducation and misinformation and become distracted by obsessing over our ego, instead of being our divinely created selves. We can get trapped into addictive desire for stuff. Being one's true self emerges in Common's song "G.O.D (Gaining One's Definition)" and in the Mary and Martha story found in Luke 10:38-42. To "gain one's definition" is to be intimately involved with God, to know God, and to be godly in our being and doing. Gaining ourselves requires an honesty and openness, and being open to inclusivity, education, and salvation rather than to enslavement. What we need is transformation.

God calls us to a full life of witness, embracing the divinely given goodness pronounced at creation. Ultimately, we are meant to be happy with ourselves, with our true being. In the story of Mary and Martha, Mary is clear about her true self and the divine self in whose presence she sits. Martha gets distracted. The story is about embracing a balanced God-focused life, of *diakonia*. The word *diakonia* is Greek and means "care and service." Its original meaning was "to walk urgently through the evil, to bring about change." A balanced, God-focused life involves *diakonia* through Word (Jesus incarnated within preaching and teaching) and sacraments. The Eucharist, for example (also known as Holy Communion or the Lord's Supper), is realized *diakonia*, the divine table service where all are equal.

Our quest for our true self always leads us to the best of ourselves in relation with God and others. This chapter explores how within the black church and black culture together, we become our true, healthy selves. After exploring Common's song and reflecting on lived theology, in which we review black and womanist theologies, the present chapter explores the role of music. This chapter then examines the spiritual and sociocultural imagination of black folk and selected denominations of black churches; it reviews issues around justice and liberation in which Hip Hop is a vehicle that provides a voice for the voiceless; and it closes with generational tensions that frame our life expectations and faith.

"G.O.D. (Gaining One's Definition)" is on rapper Common's second album, *One Day It'll All Make Sense,* released September 30, 1997, on Relativity Records. Lonnie Rashied Lynn Jr. was born March 13, 1972, and is better known by his present stage name, Common (previously Common Sense). This American rapper-turned-actor was a member of Trinity United Church of Christ in Chicago, formerly led by the Reverend Dr. Jeremiah Wright. Common strayed away from his religious convictions until the birth of his daughter, Omoye Assata Lynn, in 1997 during the recording of *One Day It'll All Make Sense.* The album's recording was postponed for almost a year because Common was focused on his new role as a father. Common returned to the studio to finish the album with a new sense of responsibility. This responsibility was the fuel for songs like "G.O.D."

Fatherhood not only took Common physically out of the studio to address the needs of his child but also took him out of immaturity, so that he could return as an architect able to envision a new album and to address deeper issues. An architect is typically someone who designs spaces and places while advising engineers on their construction. Common is not a designer of buildings and physical spaces but an architect of culture.

If culture is the beliefs, social roles, and systems of a group, then cultural architectures open up new places and spaces for thought, emotion, customs, and even social roles like fatherhood. The term *cultural architect* was first used by noted author, speaker, visionary, and filmmaker Erwin McManus.[1] McManus has been referred to as a cultural architect because of his ability to shape and influence culture in such a way that he earns the right to be heard by some of the most influential mavens of art, the humanities, and business. As founder of the Mosaic Church in Los Angeles, he is an evangelist for Christ who speaks with a capacity to shape new thoughts and reimagine old beliefs about God through film, fashion, and faith. The term *cultural architect* soon became McManus's title as the visionary leader and navigator of Mosaic, where he is pastor.

As a cultural architect of Hip Hop, Common is in the lineage of other great cultural architects in music such as classical composer Wolfgang Amadeus Mozart, who shaped the classical era, and jazz great Dizzy Gillespie, who helped form the blueprint of the Harlem Renaissance. Both Mozart and Gillespie used music as their primary tool to create artistry and new moments in culture. Common became a cultural architect when fatherhood challenged him to redefine what it meant to be a man, and this redefinition, in turn, shaped his music and the lives of the people who listened to it. He had to attain a new definition that transcended the typical lifestyle of a young rap star. Fatherhood became a new purpose for his life, and his musical decision to do a song like "G.O.D" was the result.

Common opened up a space where fatherhood and responsibility became a refreshing topic of discussion. "Gaining One's Definition" made Common an architect who designed a new space in Hip Hop to address issues of truth and depth. As architects, musicians are designers who inspire the vision to build a culture and a people. Hip Hop, like all good music, continues to be a place where musical architects of urban life design new spaces to address ever-growing emotions and subject matter, such as fatherhood and God.

Lived Theology: An Overview of Black and Womanist Theologies

Black Theology, Then and Now

Black theology, founded by James H. Cone in 1968, locates its emergence within black religious thought. Shaped by African and Christian traditions, black religious thought developed particular themes that permeate black theology: God's justice, liberation, hope, love, and suffering. Eurocentric Christian thought used its sociocultural and religious worldview to dominate others and ignore the effect of enslaved oppression on black folk. In dialogue with modern and postmodern Eurocentric thought, black Christian thought used its sociocultural and religious worldview to bolster its morale and to struggle for justice and liberation amid contradictions of enslavement and a loving God. The enslaved identified with the Hebrew children, and they believed that God was on their side and would deliver them. Even with a strong faith, they lived with the contradiction of their enslavement and the goodness of God. How could a good God allow them to be so oppressed? Scripture provided them with hope that God was a liberator who promised to redeem Africa (Ethiopia).

Cone notes that over time the church became less radical, which in part prompted the civil rights movement in the 1960s. During that time, thinkers such as Adam Clayton Powell Jr., Benjamin Mays, Howard Thurman, and Martin Luther King, Jr. had a significant effect on the black religious experience. Within the quest for freedom, some activists advocated for integration, and others supported black nationalism (including Bishop Henry McNeal Turner, Marcus Garvey, and Malcolm X). The emergence of Black Power called into question the relationship between black faith and Eurocentric religion. King advocated for integration, nonviolence, and love; Malcolm advocated for self-defense, self-love, and black unity. Struggles of the oppressed, affirmation of black history and culture, rejection of Eurocentric metaphysics, and an ongoing call for liberation are central to the work of black theology.[2]

Black theology is a theology of liberation. By definition, then, black theology must respond and address the needs of the black poor, of the oppressed. Following the model of Jesus, black theology must also support the church in carrying out this revolutionary dictate, pressing the struggle for justice. Since its inception, black theology, particularly as viewed by Cone, has expanded to be open to interreligious dialogue, acknowledging that God can reveal God's self in many forms, in addition to Jesus Christ, that we must engage at the local and global level, and that the black church is black theology incarnated. Initially steeped in race, black theology must now engage in gender justice, poverty as economic justice, and justice around sexual orientation.[3]

The possibility of concretized engagement of black theology in the black church depends upon four types of locales: geographical, psychological, cultural, and theological. Geographical location of pastor and congregants determines access to ideas and ideologies from those in higher education, including universities and seminaries. Psychological location determines a congregation's identity related to blackness or its denial. Cultural location determines one's centeredness, an awareness of one's roots and communal stories of beginnings. Theological location pertains to having access to studying and learning from black theology, that is, understanding how God acts in history regarding the oppressed and how, in concert, society interacts with God and those who are less fortunate.

Doing black theology requires engaging in theoretical study as one prepares to do the transformative work.[4] As one does black theology, it becomes important to yoke the political struggle for liberation with justice to one's Christian identity. To continue a liberationist stance that can engage an intergenerational church, along with rallying for justice, we can and must continue to affirm God's freely given dignity of all persons, connecting ourselves with who we are, whose we are, and our call to be disciples in the world.

The black church needs to continue to signal a clarion call that connects Christianity with social justice and God's encounter with human existence. The black church must continue its work to liberate all and to call a halt to its people's marginalized existence. As we continue to work for the liberation of all people, of God's poor, we must work with the poor, find out where they are, and enter respectful, thoughtful dialogue with them in order to empower all of us to experience true liberation.[5] This type of openness is critically important if we are to engage the Hip Hop generation so they feel we are listening, and they can know liberation.

Womanist Theory and Theologies

Womanist scholars have challenged the original narrow focus of black theology for problematizing race and white feminists for singularly focusing on gender. The term *womanist* arises from the use of the term *womanish* in African American communities and refers to a black feminist who takes seriously experiences and oppressions because of gender, age, race, sexual orientation, class, and ability. Womanist thought is complex and fertile as a contextual rubric for doing critical analysis. With components of survival, of loving, of taking charge, the term *womanist* also conveys a vitality of life, a quest for knowledge, and the paradox of youthful wisdom. Womanist sensibilities foster the freedom of being able to love all people, sexually and nonsexually, and to find credible the manifestation of woman's culture and life. To be womanist means to invite holistic living, loving, and health. Womanist theory is aesthetic, physical, spiritual, emotional, and creative.[6] *Womanist* evokes a cornucopia of multihued reality, yielding compassion, delight, love, hope, and change. Womanist theory, framed by a faith-based curiosity, seeks to uncover, examine, and celebrate the lives and gifts of the forgotten and dismissed. Womanists, committed to unmasking, naming, and exposing inhumane evils committed against all peoples, work for justice and the alleviation of all oppression against all people.

Womanist theorists help us focus the eyes of black women on and toward the transformation of themselves, other persons of African descent, and all persons in society. They focus on the complex, violent, and pathological institutions and communities that are sick and wounded, seeking empowerment rather than negation and annihilation. Cloaked by oppression, my (Cheryl) Christian womanist stance involves: theology (dialogue, identity, sacrality, spirituality, and power), Bible and narratives (authority, characters, rituals, language, and history), ethics (value, behavior, visibility, integrity, and praxis), and context (autobiography, culture, aesthetics, ecology, and community). This interdisciplinary, relational system embodies a God who cares and a God who is deeply concerned when anyone dismisses a person, made in the divine image, with disdain and arrogance.

Womanist theology intentionally creates spaces in which one makes visible African diasporan women's experience. Womanists expose cruelty while offering serious critique and committing to the survival, wholeness, and health of all people. Such a stance affords a deep appreciation for the richness of God's revelation through many faiths, allowing for new avenues of possibility and communal solidarity. Consequently, womanist theology embodies reformation.

Such reformation confronts complex issues of individual and communal daily life within God's grace and social justice, and champions immediacy and inclusivity. My womanist vision searches for a way to champion the freedom, dignity, and justice of *all* people. It is like a dance of morality—a prelude set to the music of life itself, to the rhythm of words, of poetics. Some womanists have Christian, humanist, or other faith traditions, and there are womanist collectives, or women who confess an allegiance to this way of thinking across the world. Womanist religious scholars explore a plethora of topics, often from an interdisciplinary perspective, always aware of theory and its related praxis, for concretized, carefully constructed action, which always has a spiritual component.

Womanist spirituality is a vital, expressive, revolutionary, resistance-based way of life and theoretical discourse. Womanist spirituality emerges out of the rich yet oppressive experience of African Diasporan women, who live as individuals and as communal, social beings in relationship with the Divine, in a way that celebrates life and exposes injustice and malaise.

Injustice stems from all oppressions of racism, classism, sexism, homophobia, ecological pollution, ageism, ableism, and the misuse of power, moving toward change, balance, and promise. Womanist emancipatory spirituality embraces hope and transformation toward engendering mutuality and community, and it honors the *Imago Dei* in all persons, regardless. Womanist spirituality builds on the essential goodness of humanity and focuses on liberation amid personal and societal fragmentation in general and theological discourse in particular. Womanist spirituality calls for living, embodied, vital meditation, thought, and action toward renaming and claiming self and society as social witness. Therefore it is prophetic and not afraid of addressing wrong and organizing for righteousness, pressing toward a healthy mind, body, heart, and soul. This justice-based spirituality is vibrant, profound, beautiful, and relational; and it has the qualities of being righteous, just, impartial, or fair, with attitudes, rules, standards, or ideals regarding right action. With this type of spirituality, one conforms to this principle or ideal of righteousness; conforming to just law, truth, fact, or reason. Committed to social justice, womanist spirituality nurtures equity and joy in humility and moves covenantal relationships to infuse change, balance, and promise.

The Role of Music

The role of music is like the role of architecture. While architects design blueprints that become physical addresses, musicians take on the role of blueprinting mental, artistic places where culture can address life and process its meaning. Music develops addresses of two kinds. First, music designs emotional spaces to address the crucial human values of love, peace, and imagination; second, music designs mental places where people can, for example, retreat. Legendary architect Frank Lloyd Wright (born Frank Lincoln Wright, June 8, 1867–April 9, 1959) was an American architect who designed more than a thousand projects, which resulted in more than five hundred completed works. Wright once said, "All fine architectural values are human values, else not valuable."[7] Architectural values are distinctly human. Therefore, architecture and music share a familial bond to protect human life and human values, which includes protecting life from physical elements and emotional ones as well. Architecture gives us physical places, and music provides emotional spaces to honor what humanity values most: life. Our beliefs, thoughts, emotions, and systems as living beings are protected by architecture and by music.

Mahalia Jackson: The Architect of Good Stories in a Bad Time

The word *gospel* is derived from the Old English expression *god spell*, which is a translation of the Latin word *evangelion*, meaning "good spell." Here, the word *good* refers to "God" and the word *spell* refers to a "tale." So, quite literally, the word *gospel*, when mentioned as a classification of music, means music that contains lyrics that tell a good story, vocally arranged and set to a composition of musical instrumentation. The life, death, burial, and miraculous resurrection of Jesus Christ is typically referred to as "the gospel." Gospel music, as we know it today, is composed music that is usually either a testimony or a request for divine intervention, as it witnesses to the power of a relationship with God.

The twentieth century was a time in which conflict was often the rule, and peace was the exception. The years following the Great Depression and World War II found this nation's citizens striving to recover, and the American dream was not a reality for many Americans. Wars, strikes, civil unrest, and political instability created an uneasy culture, and the headlines were likely more proclamations of what the country was used to hearing—bad news.

Enter Mahalia Jackson (October 26, 1911–January 27, 1972). From her childhood until her death, Mahalia Jackson traveled all over the world singing gospel music. Her gift for gospel became so well known, that even today she is hailed as the "Queen of Gospel." A gifted singer, she was asked why she never strayed from gospel, perhaps to sing the blues. "Blues are the songs of despair," she liked to say. "Gospel songs are the songs of hope. When you sing gospel you have the feeling there is a cure for what's wrong."[8]

In a country in which many citizens experienced more despair than hope, and more calamity than misfortune, Jackson's songs about God's attention and care for the world became a retreat for the listener. Lyric by lyric, she took her audience from their current place of unending defeat away to a place of bravery, confidence, and victory. During one of her most popular songs, "How I Got Over," audience members swayed and smiled, tears streaming from their eyes shut tight, traveled to another space as she confidently sang:

I'm gonna to sing (hallelujah),
you know I'm gonna shout (troubles over).[9]

Her "good stories" transcended cultures, genres, occasions, and disciplines to soothe and comfort all types of people. She became the first gospel singer to perform at the Newport Jazz Festival in 1958, the first gospel singer to give a concert at Carnegie Hall, and the first gospel singer to win a prestigious Grammy award. Her singing provided the emotional climax to Douglas Sirk's remake of *Imitation of Life*, singing *Trouble of the World*. She sang at President John F. Kennedy's inauguration, appeared on *The Ed Sullivan Show*, and her voice was the prologue to Dr. Martin Luther King, Jr.'s "I Have a Dream" speech in Washington.[10]

Through her gift of gospel music, she guided listeners from their current addresses in a tumultuous country to a safe, peaceful place to find their heart's desire. This gift made her a sought-after, unstoppable musical force and gained her world fame.

Ella Fitzgerald: Architect of Image

In a more "secular" venue, Ella Fitzgerald reigned supreme just as Mahalia Jackson was queen in the genre of gospel music. "The

First Lady of Song," Ella Fitzgerald was arguably the finest female jazz singer of all time.[11]

During the height of her career, Ella Fitzgerald (April 25, 1917–June 15, 1996) was a shining exception to the social rules of the United States of the time. Her career, beginning in the 1930s and lasting until 1993, endured a hostile time for two groups she obviously represented: women and African Americans. Ella's gift was unmistakable. While she grew to become one of the most influential singers of her time, critics alternately praised and criticized her for being too upbeat, too hopeful; she even made sad songs seem happy.

Ella played an interesting role during the civil rights era in the United States that directly addressed the country's ills. People of all races invited and sought after her, so she appeared in many national and international venues. Even though her face was synonymous with jazz, there was another image of African American women that was dominant in the United States at the time. It was an accepted stereotype of black women. It was "Mammy." David Pilgrim describes the character of Mammy and what she represented:

> The mammy caricature implied that black women were only fit to be domestic workers; thus, the stereotype became a rationalization for economic discrimination. During the Jim Crow period, approximately 1877 to 1966, America's race-based, race-segregated job economy limited most blacks to menial, low paying, low status jobs. Black women found themselves forced into one job category, house servant.[12]

Ella and "Mammy" looked similar to the public. They were both plus-sized, brown-skinned, smiling women. However, Ella created a new image of what black women could do. She changed perceptions and helped do away with the old stereotypes. Jo Ann Gibson Robinson, a biographer of the civil rights movement, reveals what normal opportunities existed for most black women in the 1950s:

> Jobs for clerks in dime stores, cashiers in markets, and telephone operators were numerous, but were not open to black women. A fifty-dollar-a-week worker could employ a black domestic to

clean her home, cook the food, wash and iron clothes, and nurse the baby for as little as twenty dollars per week.[13]

Ella's life was different. As she became more recognized, she eventually began to interpret the songbooks of great composers such as Duke Ellington and Cole Porter (see her album *Great American Songbook*). In response, Ira Gershwin[14] noted, "I never knew how good our songs were until I heard Ella Fitzgerald sing them."[15]

The nation's leading artists, including Mel Tormé, Tony Bennett, and especially Frank Sinatra, respected and loved Fitzgerald dearly. In fact, Frank Sinatra deferred to her whenever she was present. His love for her even inspired him to give her his dressing room when they performed together, and the opportunity to sing together inspired him to emerge from his retirement.[16] Tony Bennett claimed, "She was the lady who taught us all how to sing."[17]

Ella Fitzgerald's music literally opened the door for people like her: female and black. At a time when she normally would have been forced to enter through the back door, only to disappear upstairs as a servant, she was welcomed through the front door into parlors and concert halls as a desired guest. In places where racial and gender-related tensions ran high, her music created a delightful refuge. Not only was it a space where music lovers could enjoy her perfectly pitched vocals, distinct diction, and inventive scatting; but it was also a space where they could think differently about who and how to love. Long before Hip Hop, Ella Fitzgerald showed us all how to love and not be defined by the place society shaped for us, that is, how to live the existence God called us to embrace. Her music helped set the stage for greater self-expression of black artists.

Social and Spiritual Imagination of Black Folk

Music: Religious Imagination of the Souls of Black Folk

In twentieth- and early twenty-first-century liturgical drama, African Americans have used a variety of music to do a variety of things. From an old "one hundred,"[18] to a Hip Hop praise song, music may become a gesture of hospitality that welcomes a visitor. Music may indicate a church's socioeconomic class based upon the type of music, number of choirs, role of the minister of music, sense of community outreach, and the immediate accessibility of tape and CD recordings of the individual worship service.

A continuing tension exists in black churches regarding style, taste, and function of music in their services. Though it is commonplace for black churches to have gospel choirs, this was not the norm fifty years ago. Many churches, especially so-called mainline African American Baptist and Methodist churches, looked askance at gospel music replacing the traditional Spirituals and hymns, the same way their parents viewed the blues as the devil's music. Similarly, some congregants no longer wish to hear the Spirituals in the church services, harkening back to a time that they wanted to forget the shame of slavery and Jim Crow. Along with such aesthetic tensions are the issues around the balance between inspiring worship and secular entertainment motifs to attract worshipers who would otherwise forgo attendance at formal church services, that is, drawing the line between encouragement to worship and the worship itself. The job of music is to enhance the worship event, not to overwhelm the service and anesthetize the audience in their faith. The integrity and the meaning of worship are to praise God, to gather as community, to share the sacraments, and to embrace the preached word toward daily praxis. When the music unfolds for music's sake,[19] the integrity and the meaning of worship is lost. Such issues, relating to the use of music, are pertinent to those concerned with worship and liturgy that meaningfully engage congregants.

While the vernacular mass remains central in the Roman Catholic liturgy, those Roman churches geared to an African American ministry pride themselves in having a vital gospel choir to engage the congregation and make worship relevant to the cultural realities of the parish. Similarly, most Protestant churches make music a priority. Music, integrated into and within the communal worship service, is vital for helping congregations feel the presence of God. Music is an evangelism tool. Most students of black church growth suggest that the central elements pertinent to increased participating membership numbers are pastoral charisma, leadership, preaching capabilities, and an inspiring ministry of music.

Sociologist W. E. B. DuBois constructed a socioanthropological review of black faith, life, and religious experience, particularly the rural church life of black religion with the preacher, music, and frenzy during slavery and emancipation into the early twentieth century. The preacher was leader, boss, politician, spokesperson, bard or poet, priest, judge, and physician, though the preacher's role varied from place to place. The music was plaintive, moving, often in minor, soulful keys, and came out of the African tradition. It recounted slave experience; it was rhythmic, beautiful.

The frenzy or shouting activity demonstrated the outpouring of the Spirit, which affected people in many ways, including through silence, being spellbound, arrested activity, jumping, hollering, and frantic body movement. These roots extended into gospel hymns, black theology, and philosophy. During this time, most black people belonged to the black church, the social, intellectual, economic center, the clubhouse—the major center of social interaction.

Slavery had caused a breach in the lives of black folk and social upheaval in family systems. Wealthier and more established churches had their own government, financial system, meetings, and laws. Religion was part of African life, so it is not surprising that the church came to be central to African American life. Significantly, the church (1) became Methodist and Baptist, with some Episcopalians, Presbyterians, and Catholics; and (2) predates the black monogamous home because of slave masters using black women as broodmares and black men as studs.

Contrary to DuBois, black people did not lose the joy of this world during enslavement to the present, but they did experience less joy in their present and had some thoughts of joy in heaven. The souls of black folk then and now continue to desire freedom in the present tense, rather than at some later eschatological moment. DuBois argues that some of the bad behaviors and characteristics of black people evolved on the plantation (i.e., a lax moral life, laziness, indulgence, and crime), which DuBois also puts at the foot of religious fatalism. He argues that shiftlessness and other debased attitudes developed during this era and that change happens with the rise of free persons of color and the abolition movement.

101

Because of the allegiance to religion and the quest for freedom, as abolition materialized, many enslaved persons thought that emancipation was literally the coming of the Lord.

Questions emerged before and after emancipation regarding civil, political, and economic status along with problems of the inner life, women, home, child development, wealth, and prevention of crime. These questions came in the form of ethical and religious searching and intellectual unrest. For DuBois, black people live the life of double consciousness—that is, the twoness, within and without the veil of color, having a double life, double thoughts, double duties, double social classes, double ideals, and double words. This double consciousness places blacks in a peculiar ethical dilemma. One possible response is to curse God and die; the other is to be a traitor and coward. DuBois divides them between North and South, one radical, the other hypocritical compromiser. He denigrates the Southern voices and claims they used deception as a natural defense, while he views Northerners as those who tend to emphasize radicalness. DuBois posited that the criminal and sensualist leave the church and go gambling and to brothels. Although he despises Southern submission and subservience, he provides no options for newly emancipated poor blacks to exist alongside their masters. He believes that given the religious fervor of blacks, someday the awakening will come, achieving liberty, justice, and rights for all.[20]

Understanding the context for a black religious ethos in these United States provides the framework for seeing the power of our religious imagination. From the African philosophical context and the early-lived experiences of black folk, enslaved and free in the United States, faith and belief in a divine being, in the supernatural, has been central to ontological and existential blackness. Those brought to this country in shackles and others who managed to come here already liberated knew of a sense of the Divine through African indigenous religions, Christianity, and Islam. Because there was no bifurcation or separation between the so-called sacred and secular, a sense of the Divine would be in music expressly designed for worship and music as cultural expression. So often, artists and musicians, as cultural critics and keen observers of life, deal with the concerns of life in a more timely fashion than the church or the academy.

Many kinds of music express the religious imagination with issues related to supernatural power, the human-God relationship, and the human community experience. Artists create instrumental and vocal music that extols, celebrates, and calls into question life's situations. Music explicitly or implicitly expresses a sense of relationship with God, God's love and power, and how God connects with and shapes human lives. Some music focuses on worship and adoration of God. Other music deals with people's lives and their struggles that are sometimes personal and other times communal. Ultimately, the personal affects the communal, and both interrelate to a sense of the divine. Artists may focus on the presence of God, an absence of that presence, or a sense of disorientation when one is "going through trials and tribulations."

Hip Hop music deals with people's lived reality and how they work to make sense of the world. Part of making sense of the world pertains to their relationships with the supernatural, with God, and with the unexplainable. Sometimes Hip Hop is ironic and comedic, and other times it is social commentary; and still other times the music has distinct spiritual overtones and deals with matters of values and ethics.

Christian Hip Hop or rap artists use language that is explicitly religious and biblical. Like authors of the hymns, Spirituals, gospels, anthems, and other praise songs, authors of Christian Hip Hop work from inspiration, scripture, and lived reality. The songs offer testimony and seek to empower. Each generation works out its understanding of God and its relationship to God and one another. Throughout history, church and religious musicians have incorporated styles, themes, and techniques from popular culture. Artists may adapt a tune and change the words or take particular phrases and reinterpret them. Artists most often take a holistic approach and embrace beauty from myriad, dynamic perspectives. Some musicians have come out of the church; others have never been affiliated with the church because they experienced a disconnect between institutionalized religious practice and their personal experience of faith and spirituality. From the time of the Middle Passage, through enslavement, Reconstruction, and Jim/Jane Crow, to the twenty-first century, in which some want to imagine the end of racism, churches have played a critical role in the development of black music and black life.

Overview of Denominations

The black church is a multiform, diverse institution called such because the leadership and membership are now and have always been predominantly black. Historical, doctrinal differences between African American sects have always been ancillary to the unifying force engendered by a common ethnicity and a shared oppression. Ida Mukenge in *The Black Church in Urban America: A Case Study in Political Economy* notes that historically, the black church has been both a reactionary and a radical black institution since her focus has been sociopolitical and cultural advocacy for her flock. This proud, independent, and divisive collective serves the needs of people and embraces cooperative groups that share similar history and doctrines, including black denominations as subgroups within white denominations and non-Christian bodies. Three types of churches coexisted during the slavery era: (1) white churches with black people as restricted members of the congregation; (2) separate black churches under white leadership and supervision (independent after the Revolutionary War); and (3) separate black churches with black leadership.[21]

In his book *Black Church in America*, Michael Battle argues that the black church is a complex, multifaceted organism that has a primary directive to seek relationality and to embody community. He challenges a monolithic, stereotypical reading of the black church. Battle uses this text to explicate a core essential of African American spirituality: the moving experience of community. Such communal spirituality, in addition to being interior and personal, is also a lived praxis of the relational and the communal, capable of dealing with contemporary global issues in collaboration. This communitarian spirituality avoids becoming absorbed in a fixation on the self as in philosophies of Western enlightenment.[22]

African American churches emerged out of a context of oppression, racism, miseducation, misunderstandings, mythologies, a quest for meaning, and a need for transformation. They emphasized justice and hearing a word from the Lord. African American religion and the church helped people maintain hope, in spite of harsh reality; it was the social advocate and the galvanizing force for black folk. Like their ancestors who had gone before, African Americans experienced religious life as an anchoring force and the

organized hinge for the community, enabling sociocultural artifacts of art, music, philosophy, and literature to blossom.

Although there are many African American persons of faith in
predominantly Euro-American churches, here the focus is on the
ministries, witness, work, worship, and lives of black folk in predominantly African diasporan churches in the United States. Many
predominantly African diasporan churches have missions and
ministries in Africa, South America, the Caribbean, Haiti, and
Santo Domingo. Such churches in the United States incorporate
black folk from across the world with their congregations of people in a so-called first-world, U.S. context. Too often, the results of
systemic oppression means the newly incorporated persons
become a domestically colonized people. One such church is the
African Methodist Episcopal Church (AME). This church was
founded in 1787 by Richard Allen, in Philadelphia, when Blacks
were no longer allowed worship privileges at St. George's
Methodist Church. Currently the AME Church has a membership
of about 3.7 million. The African Methodist Episcopal Zion Church
(AMEZ) was founded in New York City in 1793, when members of
John Street Methodist Episcopal Church needed to break away
because of discrimination in worship and the denial of full ordina-
tion to African American preachers. Of note: the AMEZ was the
first Methodist denomination to ordain women, and they have
about 1.5 million members. Founded in 1870, the Christian
Methodist Episcopal Church (CME) separated from Methodist
Church South when Bishop James O. Andrews of the Methodist
Church South had two slaves: one was male; the other, female.
Bishop Andrews was willing to release the man but would not let
the woman slave go in 1844. Today, CME membership numbers
just under a million.

While Methodists make up the oldest black denominations,
Baptists make up the oldest black congregations. The two oldest
black Baptist churches are the African Baptist in Mecklenberg,
Virginia (founded in 1758), and Silver Bluff Baptist Church in
Silver Bluff, South Carolina, founded by George Liele between
1753 and 1755. Black Baptists and Methodists both experienced
racism and an oppressive gospel, in which slaves had to obey their
masters. Black Baptists organized into groups after the Civil War.
These groups, cited here with their founding dates and their

present-day membership include National Baptist Convention, USA, founded in 1895, with 7.5 million members; the National Baptist Convention of America, made up of mostly rural congregations and founded in 1915, with 3.5 million members; and the Progressive National Baptist Convention, founded in 1961, viewed as a reformist group, with 1.2 million members. Pentecostal churches emerged out of the legacy of William Seymour at Azusa Street (1906–9). These churches include Church of God in Christ, founded by Bishop Charles Mason, who had a spiritual experience in 1893; the church was incorporated in 1906.[23] This rich legacy of African American/diasporan churches created an incubator for a wealth of new music, a music that afforded solace, joy, and inspiration to many. The music is one way that believers and others can experience ultimate intimacy with God daily.

Encountering the Sacred Daily

Scripture provides possible options to have intimacy daily with God. Biblical texts tell about the closeness of God to nature and God's care for the birds of the air and the lilies of the field that signals the deep care God has for all of creation and humanity (Matt. 6:25-28). God's deep concern for all creation—honored and celebrated in a variety of texts, from Genesis and the Psalms to the Gospels—makes apparent the great possibilities of a daily encounter of the sacred, if one does not place God within an institutional box. The manifestation and incarnation of the sacred in the world has such a power that with prayerful discernment, empathy, and focus, one can encounter the sacred daily. While many experience the sacred through prayer, meditation, and corporate worship, one can also experience the sacred through nature and art.

A glimpse of a rainbow, butterflies, sunrises, and sunsets reveals the Divine. Landscapes, mountain ranges, and fields of flowers reflect glimmers of God. Such manifestations of God in nature often inspire artists when they create their paintings, sculptures, films, dance, and music. From hymns to Hip Hop, music is a marvelous vehicle for talking about God and about the interface of God and humanity in daily life. Tones, rhythms, and tempos help frame lyrics in powerful ways. Hip Hop artists illumine their observations and stories, to engage in protest, culture critique, self-expression and to speak for justice.

Justice, Liberation, and Hip Hop

Theories of Justice

Not a day goes by that we do not hear about bad things happening to good people—both systemic and personal evil. As believers in God, we wonder about the existence of a good God in a world created by this God with the reality of sin and evil. Traditionally, scholars discuss the contradiction of evil and good, questions of justice, by questioning God's existence. The technical term for this discussion is *theodicy* (from the Greek: *theos* = God and *dike* = justice). Some theories suggest that evil is a possibility and only imaginary, therefore it cannot exist; some argue that evil is a theological mystery that we cannot understand; other theories make evil coequal with a good God. Other theories limit God based upon our own limited imagination. In short, these theories of evil either find that God is powerless or do not honor God's power or freedom.[24] Some scholars argue that we decide how we define "good" and "evil," making such concepts subjective, and that ultimately neither one exists absolutely. Ironically, many philosophers deliberate the question of evil and fail to see the injustice and contradiction involved in using categories such as race, gender, class, and reason to defend racial, gender, heterosexist, or class inferiority, which deprives particular groups of their humanity.[25]

When crises emerge and bad things happen, believers want and need clear logic and reason to make sense of why God allows evil to exist. Often they stop pondering why things happen, usually still believing that the God they know must have an ethical, solid reason for allowing evil. Interestingly, most Christian religious scholars and thinkers have failed to wrestle with this question in concert with the teachings of Jesus whose preaching was antithetical to greed, poverty, hate, injustice, and disrespect for the neighbor. How can one reconcile God and the historical facts of myriad forms of evil?

Most Anglo-Western analytic philosophers build a theodicy on Irenaeus's (c. 130–c. 202) progressive human perfection theory or

St. Augustine's (354–430) free will defense.[26] Irenaeus posits soul-making and the spiritual and moral development of immature creatures, shaped by divinely appointed good and evil toward God's perfection and good purpose. Augustine's theory engages the so-called fall doctrine (when in reality the first couple did not fall out of anything; they were put out, expelled) with a corrupted humanity. Such theories are problematic, not satisfying, and ultimately not helpful to those who are hurting while their advocates cry out for justice.

Several contemporary key thinkers on justice also have theories. John Rawls sees justice as fairness,[27] Michael Walzer sees justice as spheres when dealing with distributive or shared justice,[28] and Robert Nozick talks about justice as distribution, as long as the distribution occurs through free exchanges by consenting adults and is made from a just starting position, even if large inequalities emerge from the process.[29] These three theories also seem unsatisfactory, for their premises are hypothetical or require particular assumptions that often do not occur in society.

Justice is the antithesis of violence. Justice concerns thought and action, whereas individuals or societies maintain, direct, or manage what is right, what is just, especially by impartially modifying conflicting claims or the assignment of merited rewards or punishments. Justice embodies, albeit imperfectly in this world, divine grace. Justice intensifies love to honor human relationships and to make them more meaningful and reconciles the relational use of power with the loving gospel of Jesus Christ. Justice energizes our lives in ways that allow us to work for the good of all; to be merciful and offer compassion wherever we are, to don the garb of humility without fear.

Injustices Personified

In the twenty-first century, violence and the reality of evil are ever-present dangers. There is no place on the planet where people are safe from heinous acts. As we become more technologically advanced, people have developed more ways of sophisticatedly hurting other people, society, and themselves. Harm emerges in systemic and personal ways, fueled by a variety of reasons; there is no reason for insane acts of terror. Systemically, through laws, cultural mores, and stereotypes, certain groups of people receive the brunt of oppression.

Laws privilege one group and shortchange another, either through limiting its power or disavowing its needs. Cultural mores make it an acceptable practice to respect some and disrespect others. Stereotypes crystallize into belief systems that shape behavioral norms, allowing certain people to experience harm and to be ignored and devalued. During the Clinton administration, for example, the quest to cut the national budget allowed welfare recipients to be demonized and their funding cut. Notwithstanding that, while some reform was needed, the welfare budget was only 1 percent of the total national budget. Black women on welfare became the scapegoats, as the well-placed lie of alleged welfare queens accused of having babies in order to collect more government money resulted in black women's devaluation. Black women could not possibly be receiving an inordinate amount of the funding given that black people make up only 13 percent of the total population and many of them are not on welfare. No one, however, is above experiencing or causing evil.

Greed allows people to manipulate power and to control others; greed takes from some so that others are allowed to have. Whether self-indulgence, avarice, or desire, greed makes the perpetrator less humane and causes those perpetrated against angst and pain. Poverty is one outcome of greed, particularly when those with power decide to assure that those without remain in their circumstances by refusing to allow a particular group of people access to education and opportunity. Hate of individuals or groups because of class, gender, race, sexual orientation, age, and ability allows some individuals to do unspeakable things to others. Such behaviors result in injustice. Fairness, righteousness, and respect disappear, as manipulation and power over others are put in place. The realities of these behaviors locally and globally serve as catalysts for Hip Hop artists. Many use music, rhyming, MCing, rapping, and break dancing to signify against injustice.

Protest through Hip Hop Music

Persons bought, sold, and packed like sardines in the bowels of slave ships traveling from Africa to the United States brought many cultural artifacts and customs with them, including music. Artists and other participants have used music, then and now, for many purposes, particularly as protest against injustice. Like the singers of Spirituals, blues, jazz, and gospel music before them, Hip Hop artists have critiqued and offered commentary on society through their music. They have talked about pain, grief, and loss. Premature death, materialism, mediocrity, and hypocrisy have all been fodder for their music. They have signified about the indifference that has been shown toward the poor, the downtrodden, those who live on the street.

For the church to continue to grow and embrace youth and young adults, we must become aware of their social commentary. Rather than decry interest in Hip Hop, we need to listen to how youth protest and to reflect on how black folk historically engaged in protest before landing on the shores of the United States. While the language may be a bit harsh and vulgar in gangsta rap, not all rap music includes vulgarity. To educate ourselves fully, it becomes important to see how protest emerges even in coarse language. Sensing how others see, listen, hear, and process information affords us an opportunity to communicate better and to support them in their growth. To follow Jesus' command to love our neighbors as ourselves, we need to have a capacity to be empathetic, to walk in their shoes. This process begins when we learn more about our neighbor, while suspending judgment, recognizing that Hip Hop artists are not ogres, but they are expressing their own reality in their own way.

Generational Tensions

Generational Tensions, Rubber Bands, and Possibility

There are tensions between the Hip Hop generation and other generations, but in this section we reorient the *problems* of tension to become the *possibility* of tension. The generational gaps may be as wide as ever, but like a rubber band pulled in opposite directions, perhaps the wider the distance between generations, the greater the possibility for a hard and fast snap back into intergenerational harmony.

The tension of an object pulled in opposite directions creates an intensity that strengthens the core. This phenomenon gives stringed instruments their vibratory tone. A string pulled from two opposite ends, from the top of the instrument to the base, gives the instrument its sound. The beautiful sound produced from a guitar plucked with a finger or a cello strummed with a bow is the sonic testimony of tension's possibility. There is a beautiful side to the ugliness we know when two generations pull in opposite directions.

Generational tension, when explored properly, can produce a symphony of possibilities that become the soundtrack of change. Generational tension is a gift that can build strength from one generation to the next. When generations have intergenerational dialogue, they come to see how much they are alike, as well as how much they are different. When each generation shares their multifaceted stories, with openness and commitment to engage with each other fully, they become a symphony with tremendous options for appreciating each other, for building bridges and mending fences, and for being able to experience the rubric of accountability shared by Jesus, love of God, neighbor, and self. Such love frames and mediates tensions, rubber bands, and possibilities toward communal empowerment.

Life Expectations and the "Poverty of Ambition"

Focusing your life solely on making a buck shows a certain poverty of ambition. It asks too little of yourself. Because it's only when you hitch your wagon to something larger than yourself that you realize your true potential.
—Barack Obama[30]

In 2008, then-Senator Barack Obama paid homage to Senator Ted Kennedy by speaking in his stead at the Wesleyan College commencement in Middletown, Connecticut. In front of fifteen thousand people, Obama not only represented Kennedy, who could not appear because of health reasons, but also represented one generation speaking to another. He was charged to translate lasting ideals for a new generation. Obama shared many inspiring ideals as he spoke as an older political leader addressing a neophyte community. In his speech, he communicated a generational admission of guilt. As a member of a generation who "came of age" during the peace corps era, the civil rights movement, and John F. Kennedy's presidency, Obama admitted that his generation had managed to develop a culture that focused on the wrong kind of ambition, what he called the "Poverty of Ambition."[31]

This commencement speech was a transformative moment for me (Marlon) because it communicated the heart of what separates two generations from each other and what separates those generations from their collective destiny. I believe the Poverty of Ambition is an ambition for all the wrong things. This kind of ambition chases three goals that keep a nation, a community, and a soul in poverty. When there is Poverty of Ambition

- affluence becomes more important than influence;
- success more important than significance; and
- celebrity status more valuable than character.

The Poverty of Ambition is a major tension between younger and older generations. The weird part is that this displaced ambition is an intergenerational problem that both generations share. This shared problem only looks adversarial when seen from different vantage points, driven by the difference in life expectations. The older generation knows discipline but lacks ambition, and the younger has ambition but lacks discipline.

The Working Parent and the Latchkey Kid

The Baby Boom generation is the generation that was born following World War II from about 1946 up to approximately 1964, a time that was marked by an increase in birth rates. The subsequent generation, also known as Generation X, is generally defined as those born from 1961 to 1981. Even though living in the same homes, at some point, these two generations have different expectations of life, discipline, and ambition.

The life expectations of black modern culture were shaped by the struggle of the twentieth-century civil rights movement, culminating in the events of the 1950s through early 1970s. The political, social, and emotional hardships this generation endured shaped its ambition for a better life, an affluent life absent of pain and strife.

So they committed their lives to a disciplined pursuit of the American dream, complete with a two-car garage. Hard work paid off for many who ascended corporate ladders and others who gained academic degrees that made them the first in their family to attain such a pedigree. These well-meaning sojourners of the 1960s, struggle did not want their children to suffer as they did, so they worked hard, believing that their disciplined hard work would be a living example of true ambition. This discipline-focused life provided affluent homes and environments for some who were supposed to replace the time lost while parents pursued a better life. Affluence was to stand in for the parental relationships that could only be developed by time spent and shared together.

While trying to translate the power of discipline by using affluence as an object lesson, some baby boomers lost absolute influence in their children's lives. Their influence was only determined by the objects they bought, rather than by connecting through shared experience.

This left their children to be raised by televisions that babysat them while their civil rights–liberated parents exercised their right to excel vocationally. Many kids were left without adequate supervision and walked themselves home from school, prepared their own evening snacks, did homework alone, and watched *The Cosby Show* before bed while their parents worked hard to provide "a better life." The Poverty of Ambition became the sole expectation of a generation that simply wanted to come out of the struggle of the past more powerful and affluent than those before them. However, in exchange for that better life, many soon lost a significant connection with their kids.

Biggie Smalls and Tupac Shakur are two iconic Generation X rappers. In many ways, they have designed the blueprint for the liturgical cadence in Hip Hop that worships money and affluence. Both of them were latchkey kids with busy mommas who did not have as much time to spend with their boys as they would have liked.

Tupac Shakur's mother's name was Afeni Shakur Davis, who was born Alice Faye Williams on January 22, 1947. She is presently a music businesswoman and a philanthropist, but she was once a political activist and an active member of the Black Panther Party. Her allegiance to the Panthers went so far that in 1971, she got arrested for her participation in Panther activities while she was expecting her son. Her disciplined efforts for the Black Panther Party put her son in jeopardy before he was even born. She was so committed to the struggle that she decided to name her son Tupac. The name means "warrior" and "messenger." She wanted her son to represent the strength and the ideals of a people moving toward social and political affluence. Her life as a freedom fighter continued to challenge Tupac's life beyond the womb. He was left to fend for himself many a day while his mother fought for the power she believed every black person was entitled to experience.[32]

Voletta Wallace (born February 3, 1950) is the mother of the late rapper and icon The Notorious B.I.G. Wallace was born in Jamaica and was estranged from her parents when she left home to get more out of life. She immigrated to the United States and moved to New York City. There she gave birth on May 21, 1972, to an eight-pound baby, Christopher.

Wallace raised Christopher in Brooklyn, New York, while teaching preschool. She had a passion for education and a love for her son that drove her to have a full-time job, work on a master's degree, and raise her son alone. She worked hard to provide a better life for her son so he would not have to live a challenging life like she had lived growing up in Jamaica. She even managed to provide private school education for her son, who had a special way with words. This meant that she spent a lot of time away from the home that she worked hard to provide, leaving Christopher alone often. Even though he had everything he needed and much of what he wanted, his ambition led him to the streets, believing that he was entitled to more than his hard-working mother could provide.

The decadent, materialistic, and violent themes in the music of artists such as Biggie Smalls and Tupac Shakur are evidence of poor ambition, but their stories are also evidence of lives characterized by a deep sense of entitlement. Both artists were the children of mothers who worked hard in give their children lives that kept them from the struggles they grew up knowing; yet their boys turned to lives of crime and excess. They were ambitious about money and material assets, but they lacked discipline. This lack of discipline nurtured by a sense of entitlement led them to believe they could take shortcuts to attain wealth, freedom, and status, at all costs.

Some of the older generation sees rap as a snake that seduces listeners to trade character for celebrity without discipline as in albums like G-Unit's *Get Rich or Die Trying*, which is on a continuum with Tupac and Biggie's materialist lyrics. As members of a generation who were vocationally and organizationally disciplined, they wonder how their sons and daughters could be so lacking. One possibility is that there was too much emphasis on seeking affluence and too little on family time. Often, one generation has an ambition that lacks discipline, and the other has a discipline that lacks ambition.

A Poverty of Ambition pulls two generations in opposite directions: one pole toward entitled ambition and the other toward discipline. Obama's phrase "Poverty of Ambition" reveals some of these problems of generational tensions and the opportunities they offer. But the generations can come together and rise out of the poverty of ambition to inspire a rich faith that shapes the future of what it means to follow God.

Faith Possibility in the Tension

In generational tension driven by different values and goals, the faith of both generations has been skewed. A Poverty of Ambition in the Baby Boom generation makes discipline and commitment demigods while faith becomes systemic. For Gen Xers, at least, ambition and personal desire become demigods and faith is romantic. There is a possibility for progression in the tension, and that possibility is Renaissance!

Renaissance Possibilities

When discipline tempers postmodern ambition and ambition fuels modern discipline, something amazing happens. Hip Hop becomes the platform for new possibilities in faith, church, and life. In fact, it becomes the possibility for a renaissance for church and the world it serves. Hip Hop allows an older generation's desire for discipline to become one with a younger generation's ambition. Soon, like the intersection of a flame to kerosene, an explosion of possibility happens. The future belongs to those who can create a cross section in which the passion of ambition and the anchor of discipline become one. With one generation specializing in ambition and the other in discipline, we can experience a future of infinite possibilities that include:

- open discussions that synergize life philosophies and worldviews
- an exchange of life stories that inspire both present generations and ones to come
- a cross-pollination of resources in which technological and social media resources of a younger generation connect with the financial resources and asset bases of an older generation
- older faith expressions that embrace spiritual discipline become contextualized by young ambitious social gospel efforts
- younger evangelical missions that have ambitious goals to reach the world for Christ that will become fortified by the spiritual disciplines shared by an older generation.

Practically speaking, social gospel efforts (community service–focused faith) of rappers (such as Sean "Puffy" Combs, who started a blog and "the Love Movement,"[33] which has the subtitle "dream, believe, do, then repeat") will be unified with the spiritual discipline of an older generation who highly value the scripture and spiritual disciplines of prayer and meditation. This intersection will foster the possibility for renaissance. Ambitious and risqué musical efforts that are designed by younger people such as Kanye West (who features his faith in Jesus in many songs) and that reach the edge of the church and beyond will intersect with the spiritual discipline of scripture study promoted by an older generation to create a renaissance in what artists say and why. Ultimately, engaging the Hip Hop generation through a purposeful intersection of discussions, shared values, and collective projects will create a "Medici effect" in the church and in the world it serves.

Author and businessman Franz Johansson wrote a book called *The Medici Effect* that uses the Medici family of Italy as a model for innovation. The Medici family was a wealthy family who fostered interdisciplinary connections among artists, bankers, architects, educators, and business owners. They hosted parties and meetings where people of different backgrounds and interests stretched one another beyond their comfort zones on opposite poles of society to inspire a creative tension. This tension created an intersection at which a catalytic conversion of different kinds of people and life passions ultimately changed the history of a continent. The Medici family dynamically brought together what is today known as the Italian Renaissance. This kind of renaissance is waiting for us to discover it in the tension between modern and postmodern generations through Hip Hop music. A renaissance will follow when we have open discussions, worldviews, personal stories, and resources shared by the life, liturgy, and faith of the Hip Hop generation and its mothers and fathers of faith.

CHAPTER FIVE

Put Down the Pimp Stick to Pick Up the Pulpit

The Impact of Hip Hop on the Black Church

Communication, attitude, and relationships affect everything we do. These three elements affect our experience of God, our lives, and ourselves. Communication pertains to how we make contact, interact, and how we grasp the message or stories. Attitude concerns our approach, outlook, feelings, opinions, and ways of thinking. Relationships pertain to associations and dealings with God, self, and others. When done with honesty, integrity, love, and mutual respect, relationships can be powerful; we can communicate out of empathy toward understanding, with openness and hope.

But too often abuse arises in our relationships, particularly in our homes. Statistics show that one in four people are victims of domestic violence. That means if a congregation or organization has one hundred members, twenty-five of them have experienced abuse. Abusers may use belts, switches, sticks. Some pinch. Some abuse because their parents did the same. Some well-meaning parents spank and punish their children out of love and out of their understanding of scripture, particularly Proverbs 13:24: "Those who spare the rod hate their children, / but those who love them are diligent to discipline them."

Sparing the rod and spoiling the child is not about punishment. The rod was not a kind of "board of education"; rather, in the Bible, the rod is the staff a shepherd used to bring the sheep to him. Sheep are dumb animals that will drown if left in a watering hole. First, we need to understand the use and meaning of a rod, then we can move to the second part where the proverb tells us to spend time with our children, to hold them close. The latest toys and gadgets, no matter how expensive, can never take the place of time with loved ones and having ongoing support by a "village" of people, like the church. But we have become nomadic people, in that many of us do not live in the communities in which we were born. So now, it is even more important for the church to reach out to the young people in its congregation and in communities surrounding the church.

In order to reach the Hip Hop generation, the church needs to put down all sticks and not be a pimp or pusher of punishment. Rather the church needs to fill itself with love for our youth; a love with acceptance, not condemnation; a gift of compassion, not a font of fear. "Put down the pimp stick to pick up the pulpit" is the church's invitation to be relevant.[1] This chapter explores the dynamics and effects of Hip Hop on the black church. After examining the Church's response (or nonresponse) to youth reality, youth ministries, and prophetic understandings, the chapter reflects on power and intricacies of liturgy, music, and evangelism and explores the implications of paradoxes, challenges, and problems. This chapter also addresses wrestling with tensions when doing ministry in dialogue with Hip Hop culture and concludes by deconstructing the dynamics of judgment and pondering Paul's use of syncretism.

What effect does Hip Hop have on the church? Hip Hop makes the church face its commission to reach the unreached and connect with the disconnected. In a changing world, the church is learning that it must deal with Hip Hop in a way that allows the church to discover a new sense of what the Great Commission of Jesus (Matt. 28:19-20) is for itself, in the service of others. Hip Hop challenges the church to look risqué when reaching out to such people as former pimps, the way that Jesus and the apostle Paul reached out to sinners two thousand years ago.

Don "Magic" Juan (born Donald Campbell) is known in Hip Hop as a mentor and elder who is celebrated for his sensitivity and trusted leadership among Hip Hop artists and celebrities alike. Juan met West Coast rapper Snoop Dogg backstage at one of his concerts, and Snoop adopted him as an uncle and spiritual advisor. Campbell was formerly a pimp in Chicago and was known for his decadent lifestyle and charismatic flare. In 1985, he had what he calls "a moment of clarity" inspired by God during which he received a vision from the "Most High" that led him to retire from the "pimpin' game" and plant a church and a community assistance program in Chicago. He literally "put down the pimp stick to pick up the pulpit." His approach to the movement of Jesus is interesting because he uses resources as risqué as Christian pornography for married couples and the International Players

Ball featuring women in bathing suits competing for the title of "The Best of the Best."[2]

Many leaders in the Christian community have challenged Juan's methods and theology since he appointed himself Archbishop Don "Magic" Juan, but what is unchallenged is his paternal leadership in a community of mostly young men who grew up in homes without fathers and very few positive male influences. The greatest travesty is not who Don Juan is, but what the church is not in the lives of impressionable young people seeking fathers, reconciliation with God, and leadership. The travesty is that the church is not an impressive source of innovation, inspiration, and interest. Although the church has access to the most relevant and creative resource known to humanity, the Holy Spirit, it nevertheless refuses to allow the Spirit to lead us in a sensitivity training that equips us to reach innovatively those who are reaching a nation through their music.

The church's unwillingness to risk being seen with and connecting with a wayward generation is the real travesty, not a former pimp's risqué approach to evangelism. Juan is immersed in Hip Hop culture and has found a way to intrigue, inspire, and innovate where most people are traditionally irritated, insulted, and repulsed. Though he dresses like a person who quantum-leaped out of the 1970s and into the present, he turns irresponsibility into innovation through his affirmation to a community that many others have rejected. To turn irresponsibility into innovation means to use what frustrates you about the world as a cue to do something about it. This concept is a response to Mahatma Gandhi's words when he challenged the world to "be the change you want to see." Don Juan may be a bad model for discipleship and a nuisance to the church, but he is also a motivation for the church, which must get past its fears to reach younger generations. Juan may irresponsibly represent the gospel of Jesus, but he also has the ears of thousands of young people the church is unable to reach for lack of sensitivity.

Sensitivity (or Not) to Youth Reality

The Awkward and the Awesome

The church's call is to be in mission for Jesus. It is called to put its finger on the pulse of the world and sensitively listen for God's heartbeat. The Matthew 28:19 commission to go into the world and make disciples of all nations is directive. This commission is bold enough to touch, sensitive enough to feel, and quiet enough to hear the heart of God pulsating underneath our world's pain.

Georgia Tom and Christ

"Unintelligible" wiles of young folk unnerve traditional communities. The differences between the generations often leave a bad taste in the mouths of the young and old. For example, gospel music is the standard for modern and traditional music in the black church today, but it was once rejected as music that lacked taste. Gospel music was considered a nuisance to the traditional worship services led with tasteful and holy hymns. But today, gospel songs are known as the hallowed standards from heaven that bless worship experiences, despite the fact they were once known as bar tunes that came from the bowels of society.

Thomas Dorsey, a young blues musician, introduced gospel music to the church. Dorsey used blues arrangements to chart a new course for spiritual music. Before being known as Thomas Dorsey, the founder of gospel, he was "Georgia Tom," the blues artist. When he first played his neohymns set to the rhythm of blues music, he was deemed a demon of sound; but today he is known as a deliverer of souls. A musical genre once known as morally awkward for the church is now considered awesome. Likewise, there are youth in our midst who may appear to be awkward demons, who will eventually become deliverers when given the right support and sensitivity.

To be sensitive to the reality of youth, we must be willing to embrace what is awkward at first and to provide a safe environment for it to become awesome and even anointed. We must help them know what is appropriate and affirm their lived experience. We must help them think critically about what they do, sing, and engage in when exploring their creativity. Hip Hop is like a teenager learning to navigate his or her way around. It is like a clumsy teen learning to redefine space and distance with growing limbs. The differences between development of the mind and the body make some youth clumsy. Misjudging steps and boundaries are part of their natural development. In response, adults can provide a safe and consistent environment of encouragement where youth can grow more sure and confident in themselves and in their faith. This is the work of the church with respect to Hip Hop. The language, ideology, and trends of the Hip Hop movement may seem socially, politically, and spiritually clumsy to an onlooking establishment such as the church, but the church must be sensitive to this developing movement, for this is the future.

Jesus did not put down a pimp stick to minister to others, but he did leave his lofty place in heaven to deal sensitively with human folk who were clumsy, irritating, insulting, and totally irresponsible with the life and purpose that God had given them. Creating a nurturing space for youth to become awesome means following the way of Jesus. Here is John 3:16 rearticulated, "The ancient God so loved an immature and irritating humanity that God sent this phenomenal son to create a space for the clumsy to find clarity." That was Jesus' "missio," his mission, and it is ours. God sends us to those around us to touch, feel, and listen for the pulse and possibility of life everlasting.

Resistance from the Establishment, Grandma's Couch, and Mission

The church is an ancient and beautiful establishment: the bride of a regal and dynamic groom (Jesus) who wants to save the world. But Jesus wants an outdoorsy kind of bride, not one who is staid or artificial. We often misunderstand the kind of beauty that the bride is. We treat her (the church) like grandmother's plastic-wrapped white (now kind of pearl) couch that no one can sit on. As a teenager, you dare not even set foot in the room where the couch is, let alone attempt to sit on those plastic seat cushions. The church is not that kind of beauty. The church is that rugged kind of beauty who can take the dirt, grime, accidents, and mistakes of a young person and wipe them clean.

The church should create a space in which those who are in between awkward and awesome can experiment with the love and grace of God. The beauty of the church is not to be protected from the socially, politically, and even spiritually clumsy, because it can handle any stain or smudge or damage. God designed the church to be a place where the people have opportunities to choose and make mistakes. Allowing and forgiving mistakes are parts of making disciples for Jesus.

We do not have the right to use our personal irritations as motivation to promote a plastic-covered faith. As missionaries, God calls us to respond to who and what irritates us with the love and grace of a grit-proof God. A missionary is one who knows that he or she is uniquely responsible to influence what irritates them about a culture in which they live. At the core, a missionary is an anthropologist and an archeologist. Like an anthropologist, the missionary becomes a participant observer of the culture he or she wants to connect with in order to learn the practices, language, and music of that culture. Missionaries are also like archeologists in that they excavate what is ancient and precious when it is buried beneath the dirt of the present. They do not bring God to people; missionaries, like archeologists, discover and excavate God wherever God can be found because God is already there through prevenient grace.

Acts 17 tells the story of how Paul was left alone in the city of Athens. Athens was a cultured, educated city that had a rich political tradition. It was an intellectual mecca, where innovative thought and expansive philosophy found expression, much like Kemet or ancient Egypt. Similarly, Hip Hop is a foreign culture few missionaries dare to explore for redemptive potential. The daring missionaries who do explore Hip Hop are usually demonized for their interest; the music is teeming with divine potential and possibilities masked in heretical and irreverent trends that seem countersacred.

Sunlight and Insecurity

Missiology is practical theology that processes the mandate, message, and work of Christian mission. This process must not exclude anthropology for fear of rejection. The truth may be that Hip Hop practitioners are not as countersacred as the church is "plain old scared." Approaching what is different with an already different message can be scary, but putting our personal feelings before the prophetic power of the message that sets us free from our insecurities is harmful. Like a person standing in the sunlight, we stand in the way of Jesus (the Son of God), and the shadows of our insecurities get projected onto the folks we deem irreverent and disreputable. We must get our insecurities and fears out of the way of Jesus' light and let his light shine on the secular while we gaze in awe at the human beauty and divine possibility his light reveals. Our irritation is an indication that we are in the way of the light.

Paul was more called than scared. He not only explored the missiological commission to share the good news of Jesus but also knew how to reach God in the persons to whom he evangelized. Jesus was the Divine wrapped in the flesh. He was flesh and divine on the outside and on the inside. He was a complete package of divinity and humanity. This is true of those whom the church seeks to reach as well; they live completely human and divine, but we allow what is human and flawed to impair our sight of what is divine. The flesh we inhabit externally and the soul, or spirit, on the inside are both divinely made. Sometimes our negative views of the external and our ungodly behavior keep us from seeing God's glory inside and out.

Strawberry Blow Pop Dropped in the Dirt

Strawberry Charms Blow Pops are my favorite childhood candy. Blow Pops are lollipops with bubble gum centers surrounded by a hard candy shell. I love the fact that what you see is not all you get. Eating a strawberry Blow Pop is not about what the lollipop is as much as it is about what the sweet treat is becoming. The Blow Pop becomes chewing gum with a sweet and sour crunch! Once opened, a one-dimensional lollipop becomes a multisensory explosion of fun with a bubble-gum center you can blow with your mouth until the pop is heard with your ears and a strawberry scent can be smelled with your nose.

Question: What happens to a strawberry Blow Pop when it is dropped in the dirt while no one is looking? Answer: It is eaten! One sensitively and patiently takes it to the nearest source of water to wash it off. What a travesty of all things sweet and savory, if one has to destroy it just because of a mishap. One can look past an irritating dirty patch to discover an intriguing way to redeem the pop. The focus is not about what the strawberry delight is when it is dirty; the focus is on all that it can become when it is clean. Seeing the possibility of a taste, sound, and smell beyond the dirt is akin to the goal of an anthropologist. The anthropologist must become more intrigued with what a culture is becoming for her or him and the world than be personally irritated by what the culture appears to be now. She or he must see an opportunity to bring a larger truth to the world through what is uniquely human and special about the taste, sound, and sight of a people.

Good missionaries are also good cultural anthropologists. They become participant-observers of the people they want to serve and share Jesus with. As anthropologists, missionaries stand with the people to observe what is meaningful about their culture. They look for trends that communicate deeper human trends that they are exploring. In essence, anthropologists look for what human trends they can identify.

What do the trends in music, dress, and language say about the humanity of a people? While in Děčín, Czech Republic, a small city outside of Prague, I (Marlon) did an anthropological study on a segregated ethnic group in central Europe known popularly as "the Gypsies." Some believe they are an immigrant ethnic group living mostly in Europe, who trace their origins to medieval India. Others believe they are Balkans who originated in Egypt and, in one narrative, were exiled as punishment for allegedly harboring the infant Jesus. When I asked one of the so-called Gypsies he said, "We are from where we are, so deal with it." His coarse response communicated the general disposition of this fringe people who are treated like black folk in a 1950s United States: segregated, discredited, and identified as criminal derelicts. Popular society tells them their best contributions to a society are their low-paying vocations that require minimum intellect and discipline. Dominant society calls them the dregs of the community, and they are, not surprisingly, angry because of it.

They openly accepted me as a brother because they believed I was a disenfranchised African American survivor of a journey they were still moving through—from oppression to opportunity. Because I was young and a black male, I soon became known as the Hip Hop ambassador from a liberated people in America. My interpreter, Marco, however, was the whitest Czech in the whole town, which made it hard for him to move fluidly with me through the ghettos of what was called Gypsy Town. Some of the places in

Gypsy Town where my new friends hung out were threatening for Marco, so we did as much interviewing and observing in the daytime as possible. I had to spend thirty minutes communicating that he was "cool" before every single interview.

Marco insisted every day that the Gypsies were "bad . . . very bad people," and from their trends and surface behavior, you might have said the same. The young men and women were excessive cursers, drinkers, and tobacco and marijuana smokers who listened to Tupac nonstop. This was annoying mostly because they acted like *All Eyes on Me* was Tupac's only album. Most of them could not speak much English, but they knew the English in that album from start to finish. They played it all day while I was around, and it kind of insulted me because they assumed I liked Tupac because I was young, black, and from the United States. The fact that I did like that album did not matter. They did not know that, and I was subtly offended; but what should have completely turned me off intrigued me instead.

By moving through my irritation, I discovered intrigue, brothers, and friendship. Their weed-smoking was a self-medicating behavior used to mask the true rejection that was their way of life. Their cursing was a reflection of the true curse they felt in their hearts as a disenfranchised people. All the Tupac music was a way to connect with the deep longing for freedom, and the hunger for meaning they sensed in Shakur's voice was deeper than language. I was given an audience of the biggest dope-dealing pimp of the region. He had heard about me and wanted to meet me. This made me scared and excited. He wanted to meet at an after-hours club that he owned that opened at 2 A.M. Marco and I walked through the doors of the club and saw a few friends who escorted me to my host's table. As I walked toward the table, my heart began to beat so fast, I could hear it. Looking in the direction of the table, all I saw were strobe lights reflecting erratic beams of light through the thick, blue smoke. The smoke cleared as I approached the table, and I was able to see my heavyset host who had a woman underneath each arm and who wore a button-down shirt exposing chest hairs and several gold chains.

He removed his arm from the neck of one of the women and extended his hand toward me. When I looked in his hand, I saw the biggest bag of marijuana I had ever seen. This irritated my religious sense because I am a former drug abuser, and my deliverance is a daily walk. That night made it a hard walk. I sat down, and he motioned to one of the women to sit next to me. She smiled, as did I, but I was embarrassed, wondering what in the world my pastor would say if he saw me sitting next to a known prostitute in a club. I wore an uncomfortable grin that may have looked like a satisfied smile depending on where one was sitting in the club. After all, men have gone to war for mistaking uncomfortable grins for satisfied smiles.

After politely letting him know that I was not interested in the drugs or the women, he asked why I was in Europe. I asked Marco to let him know that I had traveled thousands of miles around the world to learn more about the Gypsy culture. He asked why I would do a thing like that, considering the Gypsy culture is not that important. I told him that I stand with the Creator of the world, and through God's eyes, there is beauty and power in what some see as "meaningless." He then asked who this creator was, and I almost jumped out of my seat. A bigwig in the culture I had come to love was asking me about Jesus!

I leaned forward, stared him in the eye, and responded to his question by saying, "Jesus, the Son of God who sees beauty in what others call ugly, calls us all to live a life of purpose." Then this scary-looking man asked me a precious and timeless question, "Can you introduce him to me, and may I live for him?"

That drug-dealing pimp accepted Jesus that night and asked for a round of drink from the bar afterward to celebrate. We talked about what the "new life" looked like until the sun came up. By my digging beneath the surface of the dirt around a drug dealer who insulted my religious sensibilities, together we discovered God anew. By pushing through my irritation, I learned to love a rowdy bunch of the most innovative, fun-loving, funny, and sincere people I have ever met. They were a mess, but the Messiah was at work in that mess; and as a missionary anthropologist, I had to change my perspective and join forces with people to help them see what I sensed: the Divine at work.

The irritation that turned into intrigue led to my discovering God in new ways. We must be daring enough to go where others dare not go and be present for the lost who others dare not be around; we must be missionaries who turn insult into inspiration.

Liturgy, Music, and Evangelism

Hip Hop in Worship

On a recent humid summer evening, I (Cheryl) participated in a Hip Hop worship event unfolded to a packed intergenerational house. The MC, or presiding liturgist, for the event, Rev. Phil Brickle—who operates a homeless ministry and feeding program in Raleigh, North Carolina—set the context for our time together: we had come to praise and worship. As Brickle announced the performing groups for the evening's program, he used the language of offering. All were clear that this was not entertainment or performance but worship. Throughout the evening, the worshipful expressions by youth from early teens to early twenties were powerful outpourings of praise as they offered their gifts to the Lord. A variety of performers praised God with honesty, integrity, and exuberance. The youth ministries included spoken word, Hip Hop, liturgical dance, and step.

The themes of the music, spoken word, and lyrics that accompanied the liturgical dance were words of encouragement *and* critique. The songs told people's life stories and how success often requires sacrifice, and they offered critique of a dead gospel and personal connection with scripture, saying that one knows the world is full of crime and evil, yet one can still identify with Peter walking on the water and Jonah being swallowed by the big fish.

One performer, doing a gospel rap sermon, shared his experience of the Christian walk, and he admonished listeners to read the Word, focus on exposing hypocrisy, and remember that God is not pleased when we misbehave. Other songs focused on family issues, living with disabilities, the importance of keeping it real, and understanding the reality that if persons cannot find heaven on earth, it is hard for them to maintain hope. He went on to say that despite this reality, one must try not to be pessimistic, recognizing that life is complex and offers many important opportunities for forgiveness. Other offerings focused on the need to be kind even when this experience is not reciprocated, over a background beat, while inviting the audience to create additional rhythm by chanting, "Jesus, Jesus, Jesus." A sister and brother team noted that their vocation is to compel young people to live for Christ. They

129

signified about the presence of the devil as intruder. The step team used a type of dancing that involved clapping, stomping, and using their hands to slap their bodies to make a beat. Sometimes the highly coordinated movements involved one stepper connecting with another by slapping each other's hands in precision movement. An intergenerational vocal quartet sang a few contemporary gospel/praise songs. The last group to perform prior to the featured artists was an ensemble of teens who signed the words of the music and used gentle liturgical dance movements. Their dance signified faith and inspiration.

All of the Hip Hop music and spoken word had an accompanying sound track. Some of the sounds were more lyrical, while others were mostly percussive beat. The culminating act was an inspirational Hip Hop quartet, Leviticus. This group comes out of the Young Missionary Temple Christian Methodist Church in Raleigh, North Carolina. The members of this group have grown up together in Sunday school, church choir, the youth mentoring program, and usher board.

In just seven years, the members of Leviticus (Timothy Caldwell, Jared Caldwell, Joseph Ragland, and Ashton Howard) have grown in wisdom and faith. They began working together in 2003; and in addition to offering praise at the church I (Cheryl) minister, they have made numerous regional appearances. They made their Apollo Theater debut in August 2010 on Amateur Night.[3] Their performance was dynamic, with great energy, high praise, and a passion for worship. Their articulation was sharp, and their dance movements had the audience up on their feet. Leviticus took the house down with their Hip Hop version of "Now I Lay Me Down to Sleep." Just as youth are participants in Hip Hop ministries, there are adults working with them and offering guidance. In Leviticus's case, their mentor is Reginald Caldwell, father of two singers and father-mentor to countless young people.

In Austin, Texas, a man who grew up with Hip Hop uses this music in teen ministries. Reverend Kevin White, pastor for youth ministries at Greater Mount Zion Baptist Church, finds Hip Hop music a powerful tool when used appropriately and with balance. Reading material related to Hip Hop, knowing the culture, and hanging out with youth, he brought Hip Hop music to Greater Mount Zion. His interest in Hip Hop emerged as he was growing up when it was coming on the scene from the East Coast. He knows the power of music. So when Hip Hop came around, it emerged as a voice for the voiceless; it tells stories on the street. He knows how Hip Hop allows people to bond and "kick it" with one another. This is how culture operates. We can use the same kind of feel and put the gospel into it.

Hip Hop, as a tool for ministry, is another vehicle to communicate the gospel, the Word of God. In fact, some rappers who are really walking with Jesus and studying the Word are now going to seminary. When they come out, they will be modern-day street preachers, communicating in everyday language. People connect with the beat and the gospel. This music and culture can be used together instead of them pushing each other away.

Reverend White posits that kids are listening to Hip Hop and that we may as well use it and change the message. The music has beats kids recognize, but the message is changed. White noted that to him, as Tommy Kyllonen says, Hip Hop is like the new Roman road. When the apostles set out to communicate the gospel, the Roman Empire already had established a vast network of roads; this allowed the gospel to flow. Culture is at a point at which Hip Hop crosses gender, race, and geographical areas; it is another road on which the good news of Jesus can be proclaimed.[4] Using liturgy and music to engage and educate provides an opportunity for evangelism. Before reviewing the use of Hip Hop as a tool of evangelism, first we turn to the function of music.

Music, Sounds, and Spirituality

Music provides the appropriate mystery and silence to human language, gestures, and sounds required by prayers offered to God. Music—made of sounds and silence by nature, the human voice, and instruments—exudes "vitality and ... doxology. This natural language of praise is found in the fusion of ordered sound, ruled kinetic participation, and a communal sense of shared narrative.... The body remembers shared music making long after the mind may be dimmed."[5]

Music has the tremendous capacity to instruct and communicate memory with influential connections. The experience of music has a deep relationship with our spiritual selves, our temperaments, wants, and desires. Music helps us tell our human, experiential stories, as we deal with symbols through time. It is also a means to elicit bodily, sensory memory. All of our senses, as well as our entire body, can be engaged when making music. When we worship and sing praise songs, sorrow songs, words of thanksgiving, and intercession to God, that experience of singing can confer special esteem and dignity upon our own human needs and desires. The experience of music engages our senses, particularly as we experience spiritual, divine presence. The role of the spirit allows our experience to transcend what we hear with melody and lyrics. As we embrace the experience of making music, the movement of sound connects with beliefs, attitudes, and sustained ways of seeing the world, because music expresses what cannot be stated verbally. Making music is phenomenal and dynamic: it is a practice, a living practice that involves our physical reality and the world in which we live; its powers resonate within our bodies; and music's deep connection with us moves our soul.[6]

Music, Worship, and Empowerment

From Genesis to Revelation, scripture requires us to worship, to make a joyful noise unto the Lord, but we see this especially in the psalms. Psalm 150 commands that everything that has breath praise the Lord. The psalm tells us where, when, and how to praise God, and it closes with specific instrumentation regarding corporate praise and worship: with trumpet sound; lute and harp; tambourine and dance; strings and pipe; and loud, clanging cymbals.

The New Testament is also full of worship references. In Luke 1, Mary's Magnificat reflects personal worship, as she petitions the Lord for God's divine favor. In the passion narratives of all four Gospels, Jesus commands the disciples to remember him. While he did not tell them (or us) to remember his death per se, he admonished them to remember him for who he is, for all that he has done, and his edict to them: to heal the sick, raise the dead, and preach good news to the captives. Worship as praise involves music to honor and adore God, as Trinity: Creator, Son, and Holy Spirit.

Over the years, the church has developed a means to celebrate and worship throughout the year using a liturgical calendar. The liturgical calendar begins with Advent, during which time we prepare for Christmas, for the birth of the Christ Child, and prepare to receive Jesus as he comes again, the *parousia*, symbolized by the color violet (or sometimes now, blue). The third Sunday in Advent, termed *Gaudete* Sunday (rose color), signals to us to rejoice in the Lord always. Christmastide, symbolized by the color white (joy and purity), is the celebration of the Word made flesh, the birth of the incarnated Jesus, who emptied himself to come into the world (Phil. 2:6). Lent, a time of penance, begins with Ash Wednesday and lasts for forty weekdays, in recognition of the forty days and nights that Christ fasted in the desert while being tempted by Satan. (When counting the forty days, skip all Sundays.) Lent ends with Holy Week, which begins with Palm Sunday. The week also includes Holy Thursday, Good Friday, and Holy Saturday, and it ends with Easter Sunday. The color of Lent is violet, and the color for Easter is white. Fifty days following Easter is Pentecost, symbolized by the color red, which celebrates the outpouring of the Holy Spirit (Acts 2). After Pentecost is ordinary time, also known as Kingdomtide. This season pertains to God's rule over us. The color is green.

Although many Protestant churches are not liturgical churches, an awareness of the different senses of time in the Christian life can help give us a better sense of spiritual seasons. Having an awareness of spiritual seasons offers a different focus on the type of music that we use, as well as offering a variety of scriptures for proclamation. Worship is a dynamic event during which we honor and adore God as a corporate community.

Music is essential for such a powerful celebration and witness. Music is part of an energetic, moving witness in the church, particularly in worship. Following the New Testament church, African American liturgical traditions center on how we live the life that God calls us to embrace, how we desire and prayerfully engage in ultimate intimacy with God, recognizing the importance of personal and corporate worship, confessing wrongdoing, receiving forgiveness or pardon, and experiencing transforming renewal. In gathering together for the worship event, we can experience empowerment. Melva Costen, specialist in liturgy and music, reminds us that when gathered in such empowerment events, we remember the importance of us going out into the world to serve and love, even if the world and people in the world are hostile and abusive.

Songs, sermons, and prayer provide opportunities for empowerment and engagement that can be life changing. Singing communicates our faith experience. The preaching event is a celebratory affirmation, during which the preacher has the authority to proclaim the good news in a way that both listener and preacher can experience the Word. The preacher challenges the congregation to embody the testimony in a holy manner toward transcendent transformation, nurturing the total individual and communal self.

The congregation utters prayers of gratitude, thanksgiving, and joy because God affords us the freedom to do so. God saves us so that the church can worship and be Jesus in the world. In worship, the church comes forth regardless of life circumstances and even amid systemic, heinous oppression. Such salvific freedom to respond, framed by creativity, spontaneity, openness, and vulnerability to *diakonia*, service, and proclamation, undergirds all forms of African American worship.[7] Such salvific freedom gives opportunities for improvisation, creativity, and joy in trying new things and exercising God's gifts to celebrate and honor God. This is also the desire of the Hip Hop generation, as they praise God in dance, spoken word, and song.

Such gifts, graces, and offerings are tools for the service of God. Serving God includes participating in evangelism, making disciples of all generations, including children of the Hip Hop culture who are outside of the church. Ralph C. Watkins reminds us that the call to evangelize will yield intergenerational churches. We need churches with all age groups to give us balance. Diversity is not to be feared but to be embraced. For the same folk who are in the world are also in the church. To evangelize those steeped in Hip Hop culture, we must be mindful of their need to self-express and to have meaningful dialogue. The church needs to engage them well rather than just preach at them.

Preachers must be creative, be able to tell stories and create word pictures, and be versatile and socially relevant; sermon delivery must have flow—cadence and syncopation. Pastors must discover their own unique voice, have a vocal presence, and use story, metaphor, or simile when talking about the text. Hip Hop participants want to be free, to know what Jesus has to offer, to be allowed to come to Jesus in their own way, and to be able to ask questions, where the church community is loving but firm, real and relational. With evangelism, we are to meet people where they are, let culture be our friend, not our enemy. As we build community within the church, we will find that we all need our Hip Hop sisters and brothers, just as we need our infants and retirees. God calls us to help the Hip Hop generation release emptiness and stuff and embrace love. God calls us to go out into the highways and the byways to praise God.

Paradoxes, Challenges, Problems, Opportunities

The gift of life is blessing. Some days the blessedness seems to be dwarfed because of the stuff of life, the challenges, problems, and paradoxes that unfold at home, at work, in the community, or at the church. There are many things we do not understand. Sometimes we misread a situation and fail to grasp fully what is transpiring. Much of the African diasporan history of abuse and oppression colors who we are today, how we process information, what we value, and how we contribute in the world. Perhaps paradoxically, the music and culture of Hip Hop is more about a mind-set than a particular locale.

Traditional African philosophy did not envision a separation of secular and sacred, for all is part of the sacred. But in today's world, the separation is very apparent, even in the church. So while the church becomes more secular, the church must, like Jesus, speak the language that modern people can understand. In worship, the congregation reflects on God's acts of grace and mercy, as God responds to sociocultural, theological, and political concerns. Then the congregation responds in word, act, and song.[8] But just as many black congregations rejected gospel music early on, we find ourselves again at a crossroads where some churches embrace Hip Hop and others are adamant that there is nothing redemptive about Hip Hop culture, including its music.

Kevin White says that if it is allowed, Hip Hop can have an effect. His congregation, for which he serves as a youth minister, welcomes rappers and even changes in the music beat. The challenge with many black churches is that they are not ready to embrace Hip Hop, because it is viewed in such a negative light in the secular arena. White says that when his congregation first started worship services with students, they used Hip Hop heavily. But he soon recognized that there is a generational gap even in Hip Hop; there is old-school and new-school Hip Hop. The messages they communicate are totally different.

For some parents, including Hip Hop in worship means perpetuating something that they disapprove of because they do not understand that the church is trying to communicate a different message to youth. Parents really have to understand the context and culture of town (society), gown (academy), and church and then seek a balance. In the church or in the world; on Wall Street (big business), or Main Street (everyday folk), if we cannot talk in the same language, we cannot communicate. If we cannot communicate, we will lose our integrity, our values, and our souls. There has never been a time in these United States when we have not had drugs, guns, and gang warfare. Just as a rose by any other name is still a rose, whether we call it heroin, Mrs. Pinkham's Laudanum, crack cocaine, or ju-ju dust, drugs are drugs. All individuals have the potential to become thugs, whether we dub them Mafia, gangsters, militia, or a crew given an intent to do harm. The challenge of working with youth doing Hip Hop is getting out of our comfort zones and remembering the church's reason for being—to bring Jesus' salvation to the world. With prayerful communication, open doors, and open hearts, the church can learn to let go and let God.

In White's church, they use Hip Hop videos, or they may use a DJ during praise and worship. Even the preacher's message is delivered differently. Messages or sermons are shorter, with a lot of interaction and, for example, group discussion. This Hip Hop generation likes to talk, so everyone has an opportunity to use the mike. Back in the day, only the preacher had a mike; now you have to understand and incorporate students. After the sermon, students are given a chance to dialogue and to act out what they heard through rap, skit, song, and poetry. But many black churches are still hesitant to use Christian Hip Hop, which is about Jesus and getting connected to Jesus, the one who can help those who are oppressed in the community.[9]

Hip Hop Meets a Need

Hip Hop is good for reaching the younger crowd, although it is not fully embraced because of the negative stereotypes surrounding this genre. Although the church needs to use this music, it must be used with wisdom. A challenge is not letting Hip Hop become just another gimmick. Kevin White notes that if the church tries to use Hip Hop as a gimmick, then people will always look for the next trick, just like in the music industry. Understanding that it is a culture, the church needs to engage by letting people be and share themselves in a loving way.[10]

This is the import of speaking the language of the youthful souls of black folk in the twenty-first century. Everyone in the church needs God, not only the adults. In addition to youth, young adults and even forty-somethings can relate to Hip Hop. One of the challenges that the church faces is that many in the twenty-to-forty age group are unchurched. If the church wants to create disciples as Jesus taught, then the church needs to be able to communicate to people wherever they are. People do not always mature at the same rate, nor do they tend to change their style in music to appease someone else. Tommy Kyllonen, like the apostle Paul, reminds us that the church must meet the needs of others. In meeting these needs, it is also important that the Great Commission is central to daily Christian living. If the church is to meet the challenge of engaging Hip Hop aficionados, it must be prayerful, open, and authentic in its approach and witness.[11]

Tensions and Messages Given and Received

If we do not take seriously the needs and cares of our youth, the church will continue to experience loss, unbearable pain, grief, angst, and confusion. The church cannot continue to be the church if it has no children, youth, and young adults. Perhaps if the church had been a better witness, Tupac Shakur, one of Hip Hop's icons, would not have met such a tragic death. Leona Welch, author and minister, views Tupac Shakur as emblematic of many young black males whose nurture is stymied through great pain and deprivation.

For all of his success, Shakur was failed by the church and society. Somehow, the church did not provide access, programming, or mentoring that would or could reach out to a young, bright black male child before his life was so disconnected and dysfunctional, to a point of no return. The church and society at large created a system that forced him and his mother to move eleven times by the time he was nine. This contributed to him feeling alienated and broken in spirit, heart, and soul. Welch sees in him a hard, street-language outer self and a softer, gentle true self who cried out for help. Shakur's cries paralleled those of any persons sick and tired of being sick and tired. Some of his work even shows incredible similarities to the prayers of King David recorded in the Psalms. That he was a street prophet who could call us on our hypocrisy, that he could pray in one moment and blast our hypocrisy in another, makes his case even more tragic. He indicted us with our sins of omission, such as not taking time out to help another parent's child who may be lost.[12] How many more Tupac Shakurs must die in the streets before the church is willing to be disciples and invite "who so ever will, let them come"? Can the church work to make those who find Hip Hop persuasive feel like they belong? Beyond the graphic sexism and heterosexism in Hip Hop and rap songs, can the church see other issues of race, class, and ability emerging?

Some do not see a lot of tension in society. Rather, they see a lack of respect and self-love and Hip Hop as just another vehicle that allows one to disrespect others: men and women disrespecting one another, women not respecting themselves, and men not respecting other men. Hip Hop too often measures the pulse of access, acquisition, and accumulation. What you drive, how many people you sleep with, and how hard you appear to be are key values. Hip Hop culture tends to be antiauthority, so an opportunity emerges for the church when Hip Hop can be used to talk about submission to the ultimate authority of God.[13]

Insult into Inspiration: Archeology and Mission

Archeology is the scientific study of ancient cultures through the examination of their material remains. These remains include buildings, graves, tools, and other artifacts, usually dug up with careful methods and sensitive processes that involve instruments as small as a toothbrush to exhume sites buried as deep as twenty feet. The archaeologist digs up the ruins in order to excavate precious antiquity lying beneath. The work of a missionary is like the work of an archeologist. Archeologists do not bring what is ancient to an archeological dig with the hope of putting it in the ground; they discover it where it already is. To be sensitive to youth reality, the church must mobilize missionaries who refuse to bring God to people, but who passionately discover God where God already is and has been in the lives of those they want to reach for Christ.

Missionaries realize that being sensitive to those they want to reach means journeying with people to reveal the divine. These life-sensitive missionaries work with indigenous people slowly and patiently, to excavate the ancient, knowing that mission is a process and not an event. There is a process for pulling precious artifacts of God's love (God's prevenient grace) that is at work beneath the ruins of present pain.

Missionaries do not bring God to the mission field any more than archeologists bring artifacts to a dig; such an act would be unprofessional and insane. It is not productive or helpful to force dogma, doctrine, or theological ideals down a person's throat under the assumption that mission means thrusting Jesus on others. Missionaries do not begin a work of God in people's lives. They partner with people to help them discover where God has been at work. They do not begin conversations about God; they continue conversations that God has already been having in the events and experiences of a person's life.

Because Athens was a progressive city with some of the foremost philosophers living there, some threw insults Paul's way, declaring that his message was weird and ignorant. A well-educated and cultured man himself, Paul used the slanderous insults directed toward him as inspiration. The apostle Paul did not strike the people of Athens who insulted his intelligence with a proverbial shovel. He listened to the people, experienced the culture, and then continued a conversation that God was already having in the lives of those he called "extremely religious" people (Acts 17:22).

Speaking to people about God does not activate God's work, for God has already been speaking through their lives. God is already in conversation with the "Godless." The church must simply join the conversation. Some may say that the Athenians' conversation with God lacked some key communication dynamics. Although they did not know God's name or know much about God, they did have a relationship with God. They had a divine reality that Paul could not ignore. God was at work in the lives of Athenians, and Paul decided to see God's work as a process and not an event, a journey and not a destination.

Jerome's Journey

Be patient my son for the Journey will be more clear. I was like, can you be clearer?
—Jerome Washington[14]

Mission is not a destination but a journey. It does not happen in a day; it happens daily. Overestimating the event of transformation and underestimating the process of planting seeds of change is easy. Mission work is not like a stagnant pond where mosquitoes breed but more like a stream that flows out of the river waters of God's plan.

I (Marlon) learned this lesson through my relationship with Jerome Washington, a prolific poet in Houston. Through poetry, I was able to hear the cries and queries in a new way. Jerome's words ask real questions that are often silenced by the church. Jerome's poems felt like sermons that had a finger on the pulse of the culture. A sea of head-nods and a symphony of finger-snaps were the choreography and sound track that affirmed his intuitive wisdom.

The blue lines resembled a cross, I was afraid of the cross
'Cause positive equals accountability and responsibility.
—Jerome Washington

One day Jerome joined me for catfish and conversation. During our lunch, I asked him about his story, and he openly shared. As I listened, his story reminded me of the story of the prophet Jeremiah. I told Jerome that like Jeremiah, he was consecrated before being formed in his mother's womb, to speak his words to the nations. Trying to stop the tears in my eyes, I saw a vision of Jerome's unique ability to infuse uncommon and absolute poetic truth. I gripped my napkin and told him his journey as a poet and prophet was stuck in the womb of his potential. I invited him into a discipleship relationship and a journey to be birthed into God's purpose.

I knew this was to be his dramatic soul-saving event. He was going to cry with me as I led him in the Sinner's Prayer, but Jerome took another bite, furrowed his brow, and with a blank stare said, "Hmm." I was hurt and a bit insulted. How is this dude going to eat the fish I paid for and not acknowledge my tear-stained "Jesus speech"?

> *It was the eleventh day when I found out I will soon be a father*
> *Not only a father, but a follower, walking into the unknown blind*
> *Like three mice; me, myself, and I.*
> —Jerome Washington

Months of silence passed; then Jerome called out of the blue to tell me he and his girlfriend were having a baby. He wanted to begin a journey with God and did not know where to start. He had already named their unborn child Journey. Our discipleship relationship began that night on the phone. His commitment would soon be tested though, and after a series of hard times, Jerome grew distant.

> *I held my daughter Journey close and held my faith closer.*
> *We both were born that day, to fulfill God's purpose."*
> —Jerome Washington

I tried to keep in touch with Jerome, but sometimes he would not answer my calls, so I just prayed and talked when he did. A year went by, and he reappeared. He wanted to tell me something important, that he wanted to receive the life and way of Christ. He asked if I would help him finally come out of the womb, and I could not believe he remembered our conversation about Jeremiah. For this great prophet, it was always about the influent stream of God's plan. Today Jerome and his group, The Global Movement, are leaders in a musical community of artists we call Influent Stream Artists. Among others, Jerome tours the city sharing his original written and arranged words of freedom and truth that mirror the heart of Christ.

The Unreligious Are Not Always Irreligious

Religious people are sometimes so insulted by the unreligious that they cannot see a divine stream flowing in the lives of the so-called secular. This attitude devalues and secludes potential followers of Jesus from the sacred places of our minds, daily schedules, and buildings. Just because someone is not religious does not mean that they are irreligious or antireligious.

Detroit underground rapper MosEL on a recently released song said, "I don't find God and peace in organized religions so I find God in other visions...follow me."[15] This emerging artist responds to the rejection he experienced in established religion by finding his own way and then challenging his listeners to follow him in doing the same. Rapper Jay Electronica on his 2009 mix tape, *Victory*, says rappers "Tupac and Biggie Smalls were the last pastors." In that one sentence, he says that there is no pastor alive who can lead him with sensitivity. Electronica also underscores the Church's irrelevance by giving pastoral authority to two men who were in no way sanctioned or ordained by the church.

Paul was different because he embraced culture in order to transform it. He never forgot that although God found him guilty, he was blinded, not as a punishment, but as an act of God's grace (see Acts 9 and Acts 7:57–8:3).

After embracing the people who insulted him, Paul began to preach the good news of Jesus. He moved from insult to inspiration by deciding to love the people who insulted him. The insults were only a surface response to what he believed was lying dormant beneath their hunger for "the unknown God." Their resistance to the gospel authenticated their need for Christ. Paul knew that he could not authentically share the good news with an attitude, so first he had to love those very ones who hurt him. Through Paul's action, we can see the core of the gospel message. The ones who inflicted the wounds are now the ones healed, as we are healed by the stripes of Jesus that our sins caused.

Paul reoriented the syncretism of a polytheistic Roman Empire by communicating good news about the heart of the true and living God revealed in Jesus. Using Paul's example, we must meet the syncretism of our time. Syncretism in the twenty-first century may seem like a nuisance to the established church, but it is quite the opposite. As a nation we have shifted from being mostly Christian to many being not Christian or other-than-Christian, and syncretism drives much of the spiritual reality of the day. But for the church, our time in history can be an opportunity.

Human 2.0 and Youth Ministry

The Hip Hop generation is a great place to begin to understand the needs of the future church better; they are the 2.0 version of human life. The term 2.0 is computer speak for a version of a product. Likewise, we have new versions of the Bible, including the NIV (New International Version), NKJV (New King James Version), and NRSV (New Revised Standard Version), among many others.

Hardware is the mainframe of a computer. The motherboard, the keyboard, and the monitor are all components of the computer's hardware. Software drives the programs that a computer uses. Microsoft Word, PowerPoint, and iTunes are all software programs that work inside the hardware of a computer. When a computer is in need of a newer version of the software, the maker of the existing program usually presents an opportunity for computer users to receive the newer version. It typically goes from a 1.0 version to a 2.0 version. If the church is sensitive to God, it will not be content to create some other place for youth to experience God in new buildings, gymnasiums, and summer camps. A church sensitive to the spirit of God will see youth as a community of consultants for framing and shaping the future of the church, because ths generation is a newer version of humanity.

God is the master programmer who provides hardware and software for human life. Human hardware is the human body. God includes the human body and all of its natural senses of touch, taste, and sound in a relationship with God as hardware, amidst divine compassion and love. Practices such as communion and rituals such as prayer invite hands, mouths, and minds to participate with God to be at work in the world. Part of our human software is the soul. This soul is the way we experience the grace of salvation and the love of God. God is the master programmer, and God is giving humanity a genuine opportunity through our youth and their perspectives to upgrade our capacity to reach the lost. Their experiences and grassroots knowledge can equip the church to do more than youth ministry; they can equip the church to do ministry, period, in a new human context.

Peter Drucker, a 2002 Presidential Medal of Freedom honoree, declares that, "Every few hundred years in Western history there occurs a sharp transformation.... Within a few decades, society rearranges itself, its worldview, values, and its arts."[16] We are experiencing this transformation in these times. The context of life as we know is changing. In this transition, Gen Yers and the church should not miss a great opportunity. Currently, the vast majority of Generation-Y culture is missing an opportunity to maximize potential in life through the mission of Jesus Christ. The church (as an institution), however, is missing an opportunity for Gen Yers to assist it in maximizing its potential.

Just as this generation is younger, they are also newer. They are the newest version of human beings equipped with many upgrades. As with downloading new software into an old processing unit, there are bound to be glitches, and the older hardware may not be able to process the newer software; the computer may freeze and shut down. This is the metaphor that drives the relationship between the church as a representative of an older culture and young culture (human 2.0). While there are some nonnegotiable practices and spiritual disciplines that are a must in the church, the "hardware" structures of the church that we give preference must be updated constantly to process the new "software" that comes with human 2.0.

Japanese cultural anthropologists have a great understanding of this new generation's identity. The Japanese term for Generation Y is *Shin Jin Rui*, which means a new kind of human being raised in a new world. We must collaborate with this new generation that has an understanding of the new sense of life. The church must let its irritation, defenses, and resistances go. Hip Hop has unveiled a new human reality that the church can explore. This is not a generation that the church *has to* deal with; it is a generation that the church *gets to* partner with to bring the power and love of Christ into a fuller reality.

This is a *got to* moment in the history of a church if it is to survive. This is a moment in human history in which the church can live out its mandate to be a community of faithful followers of Jesus Christ.

CHAPTER SIX

Jesus Walks

Youth, the Church, and the Need for Transformation

Lights fade stage left, and a spotlight hits the shiny bald head and gray beard of Bishop T. D. Jakes. Then light pierces the stained-glass windows of a well-made life-size church prop on stage right as Jakes passionately says, "We are at war; we are at war with terrorism, racism, but most of all, we at war with ourselves." Then a young Kanye West appears from behind a pew on stage and runs toward the front of the stage. And with this he begins his hit "Jesus Walks" on the 2004 BET Awards.

With friends and family piled into our television room, we all leaned forward with mouths wide open to watch. And soon it became apparent that Kanye West cared more about his personal conviction and need for transformation than he did his personal image as a decadent and indecent rapper. This presentation on the awards show also revealed a seasoned preacher's passion for young people and their pilgrimage toward Christ. Bishop Jakes did not have to risk being seen with and associated with Kanye but he did associate with Kanye because he evidently cared. Together, Jakes and Kanye represented youth, church, and the need for transformation that a walk with Jesus can inspire.

The young and the old need Jesus, but youth need the old to translate Jesus in a modern context. Without this translation, the hustlers, killers, murderers, drug dealers, and even the strippers will never know the glory and strength of God in this life and mission that Jesus may have for them. Proverbs 20:29 reminds us that "the glory of youths is their strength, / but the beauty of the aged is their gray hair." Youthful vitality and the wisdom of our elders (parents, grandparents, and great grandparents) can live together to the benefit of both because they need each other.

Too often adults forget they were ever youth, and youth frequently cannot imagine being that old. Many youth live for the moment in such ways that longevity is impossible. Others are stellar students and will become stellar adults, involved in the life of

145

the church. Some youth wrestle with demons (thoughts, past hurts, current challenges, propensities to self-destruct, low self-esteem, poor body image, temptations to use addictive substances, and confusion over identity) and feel they have no one who truly cares or who even has the capacity to listen. Some youth, trapped in a cyclical generational tragedy, transcend while others acquiesce.

In 2004, the success of "Jesus Walks," from the album *College Dropout*, was not just because of Kanye West's conviction to find Jesus. The song, released by hardcore rap label Roc-A-Fella Records, was successful despite West's religious conviction. This song had both street credibility and Christian consciousness. I (Marlon) witnessed people with alcoholic drinks in one hand and marijuana cigarettes in another publicly declaring a desire for Jesus to walk with them. These were people who may have never said the name of Jesus, let alone hungered for his companionship. But through this transparent and vulnerable letter to God, they felt validated in the eyes of Christ.

> To the hustlers, killers, murderers, drug dealers even the strippers,
> Jesus walks with them!
> — Kanye West[1]

That Kanye invited T. D. Jakes to join him onstage to share this Jesus message is not surprising, because Kanye was inspired by church leadership to be a rapper. He says, "All my songs are about something that was negative and how God can help you through it. Like how a minister will bring up problems in [a church] service; I try to do that lyrically. I have a responsibility to other Black men around me to help us make sane decisions and use our heads instead of always trying to look cool."[2]

Theologian and church planter Diallo Smith says, "New religious thought and spiritual expressions are beginning to emerge from unconventional sources. I believe that it will be imperative, in order to evaluate critically these new religious modes with equity and justice, to embrace post-modern theories that serve to democratize culture."[3] The democratization of the church allows young rappers like Kanye West to be schooled and nurtured by older leaders like Bishop Jakes. This brings value and hope to youth and the church alike. Proverbs 20:29 speaks from an ancient time and space to affirm the need for cross-pollination between the old and the new. Both young and old share a need for intersection that integrates the strength of the young and the splendor of the old.

Facing Challenges: School, Home, Society, and Church

When examining Hip Hop culture and the church's vocation as a community called to love neighbor and disciple the unsaved, we cannot afford to romanticize the contexts of black church(es), Christianity, or Hip Hop. With keen powers of observation, we can engage in an analysis of our sociohistorical legacies of oppression and make sure it is not prejudiced by a bias toward victimhood. In the twenty-first century, for example, African Americans do not have to be defensive against an alleged racist backlash, have a need to display being "really black," or have to present a solid, united front to the predominant culture. Hip Hop encourages this because it is not monolithic but diverse.

Not all Hip Hop music and performance is about rage; some is not offensive or confrontational. The music of spoken word, for example, focuses less on rhyme and more on powerful cascades of words juxtaposed against echoing operatic cadenzas. Hip Hop and spoken word often critique the U.S. status quo.

> I am stronger than struggle.
> —The Fort Lauderdale, Florida, Slam Team from Brave New Voices

Founded in 1996, Youth Speaks[4] uses spoken-word perform-ance, education, and youth development programs. The organiza-tion is designed to provide a voice for the voiceless youth in inner-city settings through poetry. Their vision is to "shift percep-tions of youth by combating illiteracy, alienation, and silence to create a global movement of brave new voices bringing the noise from the margins to the core." With a mission to "empower the next generation of leaders,"[5] Youth Speaks works with forty-five thousand teens each year in the Bay Area alone and has created partner programs in thirty-six cities across the United States. Performer, dancer, and community organizer Marc Bismuthic Joseph is one of the founders of Youth Speaks.

Youth Speaks has a worldwide poetry competition for youth every year that includes more than seven hundred students from fifty states. Youth poetry teams gather in Los Angeles for a three-day battle with words that concludes with a final competition, narrowing fifty teams to four, who compete on this night for the title of Brave New Voices team of the year. HBO heard about Youth Speaks and decided to film a documentary featuring the stories behind the teams and the final competition with celebrity judges and hosts that include Rosario Dawson, Common, Sanaa Lathan, and Talib Kweli, to name a few.

Marc invited me (Marlon) to the thirteenth annual Brave New Voices International Youth Poetry Slam Festival to share in this night of word and wonder, and I was so glad he did. I was so inspired by these young poets, who beautifully communicated the pain and possibility of youth life that I slept better that night than I ever had knowing that our future rests in the hands of such social sculptors of love and imagination.

Hearing the pure passion in their poetry moved me to cry, laugh out loud, and stand on my seat roaring my support. This poetic passion vocalized themes ranging from ecological responsibility to domestic abuse to mental illness sensitivity to a nostalgic journey through old video games. "I am stronger than struggle," performed by the Ft. Lauderdale, Florida Slam Team, opened the competition and set the pace for a rollercoaster ride of pure, unadulterated young folk passion! It gave me hope to know that not all young passion is poisoned.

Poisoned passion is the biggest problem for youth, and it limits the power, progress, and voice of a generation that longs to change the world. Youth Speaks gives youth the opportunity to put their passion in a good place to produce lives of greatness. This greatness was revealed in the passionate stories and truths that rang in this night of poetry and power. Among all of the teams that shared that night, the Denver team communicated so much about what happens when youth angst becomes pure passion. They were a team made up of many different races and cultural backgrounds, but they had a unified exuberance about them. They looked like an international delegation of determination, drive, and passion.

John H. McWhorter, a linguist and political commentator, thinks things are changing for the better in that most African Americans no longer assume victimhood, thus they are better equipped to meet challenges. Some Hip Hop and spoken-word music is more formulaic and vaudevillian in presentation, which is not about the authentic black soul in the United States, nor has it ever been.[6] In the minds of some, before dealing with self-expression, there are critical, internal, structural, familial problems that must be faced when working with young people, if they are to become their authentic selves. One issue is absentee fathers.

Youth minister Kevin White contends that fatherlessness is the primary challenge that leads to many others. Other issues that the church needs to address when working with male youth, in particular, include degrading women and not knowing how to be a man. Some Hip Hop artists have become virtual daddies. Some kids think, "This person is making all of this money and has all of this status, so he has to be a man. Let me look to him." This negative effect of Hip Hop encourages violence, a lack of discipline, and a lack of respect for authority. And when male youth lack a father in the home, it is much more difficult to know what a father actually does or how a marriage commitment works.

In her work with adolescent girls, Christian educator Evelyn L. Parker gleans four critical concepts for nurturing healthy spirituality in adolescent girls: realization, resistance, resilience, and ritual. Realization pertains to one's heightened awareness to experience critical consciousness and critical thinking, so that when she knows something has gone wrong she can name the impetus and space of the wrong of systems and uses of power, rather than first personalizing the wrong. Practicing resistance means to resist any dehumanizing powers, particularly by defying stereotypes, oppression, and restrictions society works to instill. After coming to critical consciousness and defiance of societal punitive manipulation, one comes to resilience. Resilience produces spiritual stamina, which allows one to refocus, regroup, and reform oneself toward self-actualization. Rituals help refuel and renew, and to express one's heart sense in ceremony and in liturgy.[7] These concepts all speak to wellness and a spirituality that embraces sociocultural realities, the personal, and the communal in concert with one's relationship with a power greater than oneself, with God. Perhaps these themes could even be used to help adolescents and the adults who care about them discern how best to use Hip Hop culture.

Hip Hop Theology

All persons experience the sacred and the profane: with deep, hallowed spirituality and ordinary, common social realities. And underneath the hype, Hip Hop also has its theology, which is within the values it promotes. Not only that, but Hip Hop culture has the potential to meet the spiritual within the ordinary; and it can seek ways to channel nihilism, rage against oppression, and disillusionment by focusing on spirituality. From this perspective, Hip Hop can critique hypocrisy within itself and the church.

Daniel White Hodge, a Hip Hop scholar who focuses on culture, faith, and spirituality, discerns five elements in Hip Hop's understanding of the profane. It unmasks hypocrisy and double standards, uses four-letter words to make a stronger point, uses humor as a coping tool, avoids imposing perfection and idealism, and does not trust institutions. We can find parallels for Hip Hop theology in some biblical stories, especially those in which God deals with the messiness of human lives. In the psalms we can see that the writers used everyday language to address their complaints and laments to God. In the New Testament, we see how Jesus ministers to sinners and loves people wherever they are. Jesus even used profane language to offer social commentary.[8] Although Hip Hop can help the church reach out, it can also be a dangerous and ruthless enemy.

Hip Hop's Code of Ethics

Carl Kenney, a blogger "committed to engaging readers into a meaningful discussion related to matters that impact faith and society," notes how in Hip Hop culture, the motto and code of ethics of "Do not snitch" is decimating many in inner cities. The requirement to "stop snitching," not to tell police or any authority about violence as a way of establishing street credibility (street cred), is being celebrated by some in Hip Hop culture through song, on T-shirts and album covers, and in videos, murals, and websites. Granted, there have been times when police brutality showed police to be untrustworthy, but this code requires that even if one personally witnesses a crime, he or she should never tell—no crime is heinous enough to make a person come forward.

For many in those communities, the disparities in treatment and sentences between black people and white people are so great that "stopping snitching" is a way to level the playing field and bring some balance into the criminal justice system. That this is a rule of the streets many are unwilling to break supports the continuation of insanity, of more crime and violence on the streets. Dealing with street rules and the accompanying injustices create a challenge for those who do ministry in urban settings and take the Great Commission seriously.[9] What does it mean for a young person to practice his or her faith? How does one engage in ministry and discipleship with youth?

Because Hip Hop is a diverse phenomenon, the church must be discerning about what to embrace from Hip Hop culture and what to discard.[10] How do we help young people and adults who are so heavily influenced by Hip Hop understand that they have choices? How can the church deal with the muddy places and spaces that keep Hip Hop culture and the church separate? Should the church adopt a "separate but equal" policy, that is, a policy that says that the church is "not of this world." Perhaps there is a middle place in which the church and Hip Hop culture, especially in its negative aspects, meet.

Hodge posits that the spaces between the profane (Hip Hop culture) and the sacred (the church) are the neo-secular sacred. Within the neo-secular sacred, messy things occur, and we can approach God in distinct, new ways. This space lets us be who we are in our everyday living. From the Hip Hop side, the neo-secular sacred has three key elements: it is panentheistic, which sees God in all things; finds bad and good in all life; and rejects religionism (practice of dogmatic traditions) as the only way to find God.

Hip Hop's stance toward organized religion makes it difficult for the church to be in ministry to those who subscribe to Hip Hop culture. The connections with the Nation of Islam, the attitudes of Holy Hip enthusiasts from fanaticism and rigidity to ultravulnerability regarding self-worth, and the graphic, sex-infused, violent language are obstacles for many in the church. How does one do evangelism, outreach, and mission with followers of Hip Hop? Hodge says that although this work can be difficult, challenging, and scary, the church can do missions with Hip Hop followers.

- First, the church must let go of old models and paradigms of God, mission, church, salvation, evangelism, and culture.
- Second, the church must move to engage in open, authentic, nonjudgmental dialogue, recognizing that salvation is a journey.
- Third, the church must recognize that this is an involved process, which does not always engender consensus.
- Fourth, the church needs to let go of religionism, which alienates people.
- Fifth, the church must move toward faith practices and theologies that make room and time for all to grow in discipleship in Christ Jesus.
- Sixth, the church can use stories and music from Hip Hop culture to reinterpret scripture, understanding that Hip Hop is not satanic.

All of this will be required if the church wants to create a space where Gen Xers and the Millennial Generation can come with us to Christ.

Hodge provides six steps for moving in this direction. Missions involve preparing the way so that people can release their mistrust of the church.

- First, the church must share the good news of Jesus (Jesuz in Hip Hop language) and identify with sinners, knowing that the church is made up of sinners, but without legitimizing sin.
- Second, to connect with the Hip Hop generation, the church must face and deal with social injustices in our neighborhoods, particularly those with inner-city challenges.
- Third, mission by the church requires operating within the Holy Spirit, which provides discernment to know when, what, where, and how we are to engage which issues.
- Fourth, when the church truly accepts and engages the true nature and realities of "the hood," which has different mores and a set of values, so that we understand

the context without being judgmental, the church can engage in mission and ministry.

- Fifth, such ministry requires transparency of all, including church leaders.
- Sixth, the church must encourage small-group study of scripture for mutual accountability.[11]

In New Wave evangelical and Christian Hip Hop music, small-group Bible study is important for helping people experience different types of liturgy, rituals, and silence, in which one listens for God. The silence (even in Hip Hop music) can allow people to bring out hidden things, and learning to embrace silence shows how a love of truth can be framed by sound.[12]

If the church desires to build ministries that involve Hip Hop culture, then it must understand the full complexity of such a venture. If it is true that all people really desire God, then it becomes expedient for us to move in a direction of faithful transparency with an acute attentiveness to training and programming. Such a spiritual journey of Christian discernment and education moves the church to do the training and the questioning that help it translate the Christian faith into twenty-first-century language, images, and music. Who is Jesus today? Who is the church, really?

Programming for Hip Hop Worship

Like blues, jazz, and R&B previously, Hip Hop initiated by African Americans has profoundly shaped popular culture; thus, other youth have adopted a black sensibility or aesthetic.[13] Popular culture, particularly music, transcends the realm of society to enter church sanctuaries. Poets, musical lyricists, and composers do not stop becoming who they are when they enter the doors of the church. They bring themselves and their gifts of creativity when they worship and as they practice their faith daily.

Creativity is inside all of us and is of God; thus it is a gift given by God. Creativity happens in ordinary and extraordinary ways, expressive of our imagination and capacity to invent. God's initial acts of creation set the capacity for all creation into motion. Creativity involves divine authenticity and activity. We often have creative moments when we experience our vast range of emotions:

anger, joy, sadness, elation, fear, worry, curiosity, envy, excitement, but also hate, desperation, and rage. Creativity is not always orderly; sometimes it is messy. In Hip Hop culture and its variety of expressions, some of the language and the themes are offensive. Sometimes they feel good, and sometimes they trigger ugly thoughts and feelings.

From practicing creativity comes hope.[14] When the church speaks in hope with one another about who God is and what God wants us to do, the faith community can deal with the messiness and work together for the good of all, even those beyond the immediate community. Hip Hop is diverse language, a language of music that invites intergenerational dialogue, a necessity for the church to continue to live and thrive.

Music, a divinely bestowed gift, involves mind, body, and spirit. Making music involves using sound and silence; and in worship, music brings the community together, as it helps us connect with God, in praise, across cultures, ideologies, and distances—even the distances of diseases that ravage our mental capacities, such as Alzheimer's disease. The depth, breadth, and transcendent power of music allow us to experience God, as we share and engage in music-making. Just as some physicists believe that the tiniest particles of the universe are strings, which vibrate, all creation sings the glory of God.

Music-making allows us to work for justice and peace, as music has galvanized many to do this work across time and space. Music motivates and helps mold and shape us, thus we must be careful about what music we listen to and participate in making. Music, as God's gift to us, provides opportunities for us to become who God created us to be as we become fully human and able to praise the glory of God.[15] As we pray, praise, and question whether we are ready to embrace Hip Hop as a tool of our ministry, we must again remember that in some places and spaces, Hip Hop is already engaged in ministry.

Transcending geography, class, race, and gender, Christian Hip Hop is alive and well. William Brown and Benson Fraser note that Christian Hip Hop artists focus on the deadliness of life without Christ, as opposed to rhyming about chaos, misogyny, and money. The ten-thousand-member Without Walls International Church in Tampa, Florida, has such a ministry, Club X, where young people rap based on scripture. Club Life and Metro Ministries in New York City engage dance and song to Hip Hop music that has Christian lyrics. These two ministries reflect the growing interest in youth ministries, intentionally embracing Hip Hop, engaging in discipleship to spread the kingdom of God, and bringing street smarts to the evangelistic tasks of spreading the message of Christ.

While Hip Hop culture signifies the voice of Generation X and the Millennial Generation, it is not all about joy and religion. Simultaneously, Hip Hop culture continues to produce music that celebrates violence, misogyny, or degradation of women and sensationalizes sexuality. Atlanta pastor and social activist Gerald Durley reminds young people of the negative stereotypical messages that harm both the black community and the larger society. This social commentary invites them not to be deceived but to be aware of subliminal messages that can stunt their spiritual growth even when they claim that they listen to the beat and not the words. Problematically, much of Hip Hop promotes materialism and hedonism, violent power and control—subjects the church has wrestled with since its inception.

Parents, ministers, and Christian educators question if Hip Hop can be redemptive given its glorification of violence, vice, and sex. According to Bobby Hill, creator of Vanguard Ministries in Chesapeake, Virginia, one should not confuse content and context. He calls for conservatism regarding content and liberalism regarding context: the containers and the medium. For those youth who feel disconnected and disenfranchised and who are trying to fit in, in a world of fragmentation, Hip Hop offers a point of contact. Youth want to keep it real, and the adults who care about them need to connect with their values, learn their language, and be open and honest about adult realities, shortcomings, and mistakes—notably the failings of social institutions and systems.

Some Hip Hop artists, unchurched persons, and cultural critiques see no difference between the church, particularly preachers collecting money, and artists' appeal to materialism on videos. They see no difference in the notorious extramarital liaisons of prominent clergy and the pleasure-seeking self-gratification of some Hip Hop artists. Brown and Fraser remind us that just as ministries nurtured the hippie-driven Jesus Movement in the early 1970s, letting youth and young adults express their relationship with God through street drama, music, communes, coffeehouses, and flower-power fashions—the mores and style of the time—today Hip Hop culture may be the current venue. Just as Paul deliberated with first-century Greeks at Mars Hill, ministries can engage youth and young adults through Hip Hop culture and music as a venue, a stepping-stone to connection, so that lives may be transformed through the gospel message.[16]

Kevin White has been a leader in student ministry for about eight years. In this time, many young people have been transformed. This mission helped foster a new level of expectation and accountability in the community. After the word of God is poured out, there is always someone walking with the students to help them. There must be some application with the information students receive. As they become more involved in community and in serving people in community, young people go walk and go do what Jesus is doing in the community. White notes that their mission is to connect students to Jesus and then to capture opportunities for following him. Just as Jesus provided encouragement wherever he was, these students then serve as cheerleaders for others. Sometimes that is intimidating because they look different and do not want to be outcasts or go against their culture. So they have to have people around them to let them know that it is OK to stand out and be different.

If the church does not give youth an opportunity to follow Jesus through service, then it is doing an incomplete job and not truly following the Great Commission. Evangelizing, teaching, doing what Jesus commanded them to do—to serve and disciple others—this is only a part. But Jesus does not call anyone to do all this alone. Jesus promises that "I will be with you always." This is where fellowship and accountability from the church community counts. It is the opportunity for the church to be with you always. Being with, not against or over in a pejorative sense, opens the door to possibilities for transformation, even of hard-core gangsta rappers. Such change is not only about the church reaching out but about those who have adopted the thug life, turning to Christ.

Transformed by God's grace, T-Bone went from the thug life to being a youth evangelist with good intentions, despite some lingering rough edges. In his *The Last Street Preacha*, T-Bone works to shift Hip Hop machismo into a gospel genre. He sings about demons as opposed to rival street gangs. Like other contemporary Christian music artists, T-Bone's songs focus on faith and loyalty steeped in affection, as opposed to violence. He also professes a love for his dad, while many Hip Hop singers honor their mothers.[17] Scripture teaches a "whosoever will" gospel, but the question remains. Is the church willing to be a part of such a gospel for such a time as this?

Creating an Intergenerational Church

Can Hip Hop reflect the sacred? Stacey Jones, a senior pastor at Urban Jerusalem Church in central Minneapolis, answers with an unequivocal yes. Since music reflects its culture, when a Christian environment produces Hip Hop, it engenders divinely based or Godly attitudes. In fact, many Hip Hop artists today record under the umbrella of Christian Hip Hop, as they extol the message of Christ. Jones and his wife, Tryenyse, began a Hip Hop church to meet the needs of Gen Xers and the Millennial Generation, which, according to statistics, are the most unchurched generations. Hip Hop and faith have always been connected in the life of the Joneses; they simultaneously participate in Hip Hop and love God. Though Tryenyse leads the music, she shares the mike with other rappers. One rapper, who prefers to be called an MC, noted that MCs offer commentary regarding the wellbeing of the community. Stacey Jones's sermons may be straightforward, or they may contain rap. Their goal is to reach those whom others have not reached out to, walk with, learn from, and support them.[18]

Kevin White reminds us that churches need to pray in order to see whether God wants them to engage in Hip Hop ministry; God will reveal how to engage an intergenerational church if that is the ministry God is calling us to practice. One must be educated about Hip Hop and understand how Hip Hop has influenced culture first before beginning ministry using it.

Using secular music has a long history in the church. Even reformer Martin Luther (1483–1546) used barroom tunes to quote scripture. White prays that as a leader, he will be able to embrace secular music and use Hip Hop. We must remember that we can become so caught up in being nontraditional that we can be traditional in being nontraditional.[19]

Historically, black adolescents and young adults have framed secular music with sacred rhetoric: Thomas Dorsey infused black speech, Spirituals, and blues to create gospel blues; Edwin Hawkins infused rhythm and blues to create contemporary gospel music. Hip Hop culture has produced a spiritual music, sound, and ambience incarnated by gospel notables such as Yolanda Adams, Fred Hammond, Tye Tribbett, and Mary May, who include dance, visual image-making, language or discourse, graphic artistry, and personal message. African American youth build on historical black religious musical traditions to praise God and to focus on religious and everyday concerns, in search of liberation and deliverance from oppression.[20]

God-conscious Hip Hop artists focus on "da world," "da streetz," and "da homies."[21] *Da world* pertains to evil and suffering in the world; *da streetz* relates to urban daily life and survival; and *da homies* concerns the deepest thoughts and feelings of those living an urban life.[22] Theologically, one can locate most Hip Hop artists who explore religious and secular concerns as doing liberation theology: addressing sociopolitical concerns of the poor and oppressed and preaching Jesus the Christ as a liberating force who saves and transforms.

In focus-group interviews, Pamela P. Martin, LaTrese E. Adkins, Tuere A. Bowles, Simone T. Robinson, and Sheretta T. Butler-Barnes explored the understandings of gospel, gangsta, and mainstream rap of thirty-three teens, ages twelve to nineteen; including in their research interactions among female and male teens, their religious customs, and their parental religious practices. In Study 1, three themes emerged. First, as one strengthens one's faith amidst countering forces, one's faith helps in discerning wise action, as opposed to those actions espoused in some gangsta rap. Second, rap music afforded teens opportunities to apply their faith as they think about scriptural implications in the song and think through their own behavior. Third, rappers communicate about their own relationships with God and deal with societal and personal vices.

In Study 2, which focused exclusively on teen girls, two themes emerged. First, female independence indicated girls depended upon their religious socialization for healthy identity models, which they affirmed were also sanctioned by God and scripture.

Second, female teens actively pass on negative stereotypical imagery about themselves.

Aligning with black church values, adolescents stand by their faith and allow rap to help them think through their values and actions. A rapper's street credibility and power of persuasion place her or him in the role of prophetic voice. Youth attest to scripture and history for positive role models, despite rap's negative imagery. Although female Hip Hop artists use pejorative language to address systemic oppression, teen girls in the study did not embrace this language. The findings of these researchers affirm that teens engage in comparative analysis between scripture and rap lyrics, thus it behooves clergy and Christian educators to make sure that sermons and instruction speak to the needs of teens in a culturally relevant manner. This reality is an opportunity for adults involved in teens' lives—from clergy and parents to other leaders—to observe, record, and empathetically find meaning from a teen's viewpoint.[23]

Only by taking youth's needs and concerns seriously can the church become intergenerational and move forward to help youth become their authentic selves. But waiting until they are teens and young adults to give input is, in the vernacular, "a day late and a dollar short." The church needs to provide active, critical, loving support to families prior to birth or adoption, so that we do not unconsciously blame babies for a dysfunctional family situation. If we love them and model before them from birth, while they may stray as they seek to find themselves during and after puberty, they will hopefully remember what they have learned and ultimately return to the church. We cannot, however, model one thing and demand another.

When we explore lived experience around ministerial practice and faith, having analysis of these experiences provides additional information that can help us sort through what is at stake, the values, and the challenges. A project orchestrated by researchers from North Carolina State University—African American Faith Communities Project—"is designed to investigate the many different ways faith communities support families as well as what Christians teach adolescent girls and boys about their Black heritage."[24] Central to this effort is gleaning the values and messages adolescents receive from family and church; determining how this information factors into teen decision-making about friendships, school, and work; and understanding how religion affects their value system. The first two studies in mid- and southeastern Michigan (Lansing and Detroit areas), though limited in scope, attest to the importance of the church, scripture, and a relationship with God for life.[25] In line with these findings is the forthcoming volume by five researchers who place Hip Hop culture at the center of their research on African American adolescents.

Youth: Worldviews, Pain, and Angst

Roses and Concrete

Funny it seems, but by keeping its dreams, it learned to breathe fresh air.
Long live the rose that grew from concrete when no one else ever cared.
—Tupac Shakur (at age 18)

Let us begin this conversation about integrating young strength and old splendor by examining the youth-based pain and angst that shapes youth's worldview. If this discussion about Hip Hop has taught us anything, it has taught us that no matter how concrete the barriers young people face, through Hip Hop they are discovering the strength to grow like "The Rose That Grew from the Concrete," a poem written by rapper, actor, and poet Tupac Shakur (1971–1996).

Shakur is a documentarian of ghetto life and follows in the footsteps of Langston Hughes and Richard Wright. His words give a clear view of the pain and the suffering to be found in many of our urban areas worldwide. In a poem featuring a rose, Shakur seems to have opened the window of his life to write a metaphorical story about flourishing despite suffering. *The Rose That Grew from Concrete* is the title of a collection of poems he wrote when he was eighteen. This was before he used rap as a medium for his poems. This poem is a look at the challenge and adversity that preceded Tupac's career as a rapper. You can hear the purity in these words that personify the "rose" to illustrate its strength to overcome obstacles, pain, and angst, much the way Tupac longed to do in his personal life. This poem quickly became such an inspirational tale of making something of yourself despite adversity that an album was made about the poem in 2000 that featured great musicians, lyricists, and poets such as Mos Def, Talib Kweli, and Sonya Sanchez.

There is a serenity in the imagery and feel of the poem that we do not see later in Shakur's career. The poem simply and poignantly says life is tough but we can make it, but Tupac did not make it. The pain and angst of being young and black and unsupported killed his rose. His pain and angst made him passionate about all the wrong things. He had no one to direct his passion, and he consistently found himself displacing it onto drugs, crime, sex, and a reckless abandonment of self-control in public settings. His life was consumed by fear, sorrow, and low self-esteem. His death was just a tragic waste of talent. Tupac Shakur needed someone to teach him that using fists of fury to fight pain in life was only the way down and not up or out. Tupac was killed by the poison of his own displaced passion before he was shot in Las Vegas in September of 1996.

Discipline Is Passion

The world is tilting but you are standing still...and the consequences are apocalyptic.
—The Denver, Colorado, Slam Team

During breaks at the Youth Speaks worldwide poetry competition, the Denver Slam Team danced with one another and laughed hard, with heads tilted back and chins toward the ceiling, but when it was time to go onstage, they had a focus and intensity that made you a little uncomfortable. Two members of the Denver team were wildly dancing together with big smiles on their faces one minute, and five minutes later as they walked on the stage with composed faces for their shared poem, they respectfully and strategically directed the sound technician about how to place three microphones.

Then a tall, beautiful, and regal teenage African American girl stepped toward the mike, followed by a short, white American teenage boy; they took a unified breath and said together, "This is dedicated to BP." They began an exchange of prose that sounded like a love story. Then it progressively became a brutal and bitter breakup story right before our eyes. As they continued, the audience realized why the poem was dedicated to British Petroleum, the global energy company who was responsible for a massive oil spill in the Gulf of Mexico. The breakup was a metaphor for how humanity has abused the relationship with our earth. The body language of the boy, who represented humanity, went from honorable to dismissive until the girl, representing the Earth, turned to the disinterested boy and said, "The world is tilting, but you are standing still... and the consequences are apocalyptic."

We must identify what it means to have pure passion, and this kind of Youth Speaks event points the way. To be purely passionate is to be intentional and disciplined.

Give Me a Seven

Near the end of the competition, Denver appeared to be in the lead, and in the last round, they decided to end strong They took the stage and faced the judges, looking away from the audience, to share what became one of the most dynamic poems I have ever heard in a competition. The Denver team decided to share as their final poem of the night "Give Me a Seven." In this grand finale, they communicated their passion for poetry and angry resistance to mediocrity.

Young angst creates a worldview that risks big for greatness because it is the angst-filled protest against the mediocrity of the past. Young people refuse to discard their passion for art, ballet, entrepreneurship, and poetry because of a fear of failure. An "almost but not quite" life just will not do.

In the presence of angst and pain, there is hope. Youth Speaks is an example of how elders of a preceding generation create a platform and a place where the next generation can, through their gifts, express their passion and angst in a manner that propels culture and society forward.

Music: A Tool for Communication

Music is a mirror that directly reflects the emotion and heart of a culture. It is a communication tool that listens to the heart of the human condition. As a communication tool, music both listens and speaks. This is why Cornel West, African American philosopher, author, critic, actor, and civil rights activist, says that "music is made to connect, inform, resonate, and motivate."[26] Connecting, informing, resonating, and motivating are all expressions made better by good music.

Talkin' Trash or Communicating

Taking out the trash stinks! Removing the bag without ripping it and walking it outside into the unpredictable weather is a pain for me. At the beginning of my marriage to my beautiful, funny, and caring wife, she got on my nerves asking about the trash and whether or not I had taken it out. I felt that she was the "IRS" (internal refuse service). "When are you going to take out the trash?" she'd say. Or she'd comment, "What is your problem with trash bags?" Or "Are you gonna neglect the care of this house?"

And as you might expect, none of her questions made me take out the trash any quicker, because everything I heard her say didn't sway me from what I already thought about taking out the trash, "It's not that big of a deal." Until one day I came home and found my wife crying uncontrollably and trying to communicate a message to me that I just could not understand. I thought that someone had broken into our home or maybe that a loved one had died. Finally, she calmed down a bit and pointed to the trashcan, whispering, "You didn't take out the trash."

I immediately took out the trash and realized that it meant more to her than I had thought. Something larger was going on that I had not taken the time to listen to. I asked her later why taking the trash out meant so much to her, and I listened to her tell me that when I made sure the trash was never full, it made her feel cared for and loved. I became her "knight in shining armor" when I took out the trash.

Communication is not just about listening to what people are saying, rather it is more about the feeling behind the words. The person we are communicating with couldn't care less about the what, when, where, and how of what you are saying. He or she cares more about why you feel the way you do. Folks respond to communication that shares feelings more readily than they respond to communication that merely gives facts. I was thinking about taking out the trash and frankly reacting to being told what to do, but I didn't really hear what my wife was communicating. She was saying something about our relationship. To her, taking out the trash was about me showing her that I loved her.

This is a parable for music as a communication tool. We are only talking trash if the music we make is not listening to what people are feeling and responding accordingly. This is the work of a good musician: to create harmony and words that effectively respond to what the people are feeling, otherwise we are just talking trash.

True communication spends less time going down a list of words that describe what you have, who you have sex with, where you live, and how you spend your money. True communication focuses on the emotional "why" of human culture. The listener cares less about the capacity to articulate interrogatives and more about the capacity to *communicate* the longings and passion of the human heart. Music is a communication tool because it connects people to one another, their inner being, and God. The words, ideas, and themes are all parts of communication mechanics, but only when music listens to and speaks the heart of culture does it make a difference.

Stax Records founder Estelle Axton once said, "That is how you learn the music business. You talk to the person buying the music and that lets you know what to make." Good music communicates well when it listens to the people well enough to share the emotion and the core concerns of the day.

Stax Records and Cultural Reflection

Stax Records was founded in 1957 as Satellite Records; the new name was adopted in 1961. The label was a major factor in the creation of the Southern soul and Memphis soul music styles, also releasing gospel, funk, jazz, and blues recordings. Although Stax is renowned for its output of African American music, the label was founded by two white businesspeople, Jim Stewart and his sister Estelle Axton, who bought an old movie theater in a black neighborhood in Memphis, Tennessee, with plans to record country albums.

Stewart and Axton, whose names combine to become "Stax," were like anthropologists who could not ignore the voices of the people in the neighborhood where they were. They had an open-door policy that extended beyond the physical door. Their open door allowed what was happening in the neighborhood to come inside. Stewart and Axton were so good at listening and speaking with the people around them that pretty soon the record company was just as much a community center as it was a record label.

The record store connected to the label had the latest and greatest soul albums, and Estelle, who managed the store, placed speakers outside the store so that people from all over the neighborhood would come to hang out, buy albums, and make music.

The business was soon nicknamed "Soulsville" because they wanted to embody the soul of the people making and listening to the music. In Detroit, Motown, or "Hitsville," was known for making hits that allowed people to escape the hardships of ghetto life; Soulsville listened to the pain on the streets and reimagined it with soul and funk. Stax Records recording artist Rufus Thomas once said, "Motown had the sweet, and we had the funk." Stax is a good model for music that communicates from the heart of the people to the heart of the people.

At the time of Stax's inception, Memphis, Tennessee, was a city that was not listening to the heartbeat of a nation that was tired of segregation. Despite the marches and protests nationwide, the powers that be in Memphis resisted the yearnings of the people. They only listened for what they wanted to keep and did not listen to the winds of change that were increasingly inevitable. But at Stax Records, black and white musicians and community members experienced something totally different. They experienced a community, albeit a business, that was communicating with and for the people who spoke of desegregation. The house band, Booker T. & the MG's, was an ethnically integrated band, with two white musicians playing with two black musicians as though they were family. This way Stax Records communicated much more than music: it communicated the pain, promise, hope, and love of the people, with no need to talk trash.

Empowering Disciples: Youth Practices of Faith, Evangelism, and Transformation

In many places, the kingdom of God is not growing. In these places, people shift from church to church, but the number of new people committed to following Christ does not significantly grow. And while God calls the church to reach, inspire, and connect with people, the church is having difficulty reaching youth. This is, in part, because youth practices of faith today are not traditional pathways for spiritual exploration and development. Youth are not sheep seeking a place where they can be led. They are the gifted, irreverent, and deeply troubled "stray cats," who are not easily corralled.

Shepherds' Staffs and Stray Cats

Siegfried Fischbacher and Roy Horn are German-American entertainers known for their long-running show of illusions and exotic animals in Las Vegas, Nevada. On October 3, 2003, during a show, Roy Horn was bitten by a seven-year-old tiger named Montecore. Horn was critically injured in the attack. Sources say that while he was being rushed to the hospital, Horn said, "Don't shoot the cat!"[27]

While he was on a stretcher within an inch of his life, Roy asked that the tiger be spared because it was born to be wild and not perform for audiences. Roy was convicted by his tiger bite and understood that he was bound to get bit for taming cats he should be releasing into the wild. Siegfried and Roy are a parable for how the church is trying to approach evangelism, discipleship, and transformation in a new cultural landscape. The church has been trying to shepherd the wild cats of nonchurch culture with traditional shepherds' staffs.

New church members are tamed just enough to teach them a few tricks in order to showcase them as reformed members of the wild. But no matter how good the church gets at taming lions, tigers, and panthers, they will turn and attack because they were not born to be tamed; they were born to be released as free agents into the jungle of possibility. Like cats, they come to church only when they desire to be fed and caressed. Then they run away for a period and return as if nothing has happened. They believe in Jesus and what he represents, but they must be inspired and initiated for discipleship in ways that will change their lives for good. Disciples of Jesus are transformed so that they can be released and not managed. They want inspiration and not institutionalization. The church must provide a relevant landscape for these lions to roam and freely choose the way of Jesus.

Adaptive Experimentation

What does releasing stray cats into the jungle of God's mission look like? At the Awakenings Movement where I (Marlon) am a pastor and cultural provocateur (explained further below), we asked ourselves how we could expose outlying Houstonians to a daily, weekly, and monthly landscape that gives them permission to roam the city following Jesus and seeking purpose. We also got tired of getting bit while trying to tame cats that we should have been releasing. We decided to experiment and adapt existing practices for a new approach and format for evangelism, discipleship, and transformation.

Wharton School of Business Dean, Jerry Wind, believes adapting and experimenting is a nonnegotiable direction all changing organizations must take. Wind's Adaptive Experimentation is a philosophy for organizational growth that assures continuous learning for optimization over time. The organization must be willing to experiment constantly and adapt the organization to provide new context for old ideas, mission, and products. He believes it is essential to develop a context for communicating the unchanging mission in an ever-changing world.

We decided to empower disciples at Awakenings by developing new sights and new sounds but the same truth in a worship format that was in a different location and context every week. This sounded like a good model for the twenty-first century, but it was also a good model for the first-century and early church as well. Jesus was challenged to communicate a lofty and often difficult-to-understand message of God's kingdom to an ever-changing audience. Jesus used parables to present the same message to a diverse crowd of people. When speaking to a crowd of farmers, he probably experimented with a parable about sowing seeds. Knowing there were housewives in the crowd, he adapted his message to use baking imagery of yeast and bread. Parables were a standard way Jesus adapted his never-changing message to an ever-changing crowd. In fact, Matthew 13:34-35 says that "Jesus told the crowds all these things in parables; without a parable he told them nothing. This was to fulfill what had been spoken through the prophet: 'I will open my mouth to speak in parables; / I will proclaim what has been hidden from the foundation of the world.' "

Jesus communicated the unchanging love of God to an ever-changing audience from city to city and context to context. We knew that if Jesus embraced adaptive experimentation through his teachings, then how could we as followers of Jesus be any different? Wind believes that it is hard to gauge success with a small experiment, so we did a big experiment.

After nine months of study, a series of focus groups, a strategic development plan, and a communication campaign, we became the movement in our name. In January 2010, I resigned as a pastor who shepherds people in and was rehired as a cultural provocateur who provokes people out. Then as a movement and church, we sowed those who attend our worship service into the city in order to grow relationships and community service and to provoke a true, life-changing cultural renaissance. We contextualized the heart of our church, and from week to week our worship ranged from (1) a dynamic worship service of originally arranged music, film, and truth in a reputable live-performance venue in which the likes of Snoop Dogg, the White Stripes, and Corinne Bailey Rae performed, to (2) a community service project that was worship incarnate, to (3) a theological laboratory in a bar to question and dissect the life of Christ, to (4) worshiping in AM Circles—small groups that foster intimate and authentic relationships. We move weekly, inviting stray cats to join us as we explore divine possibility to worship, serve, learn, and laugh with one another.

Our Sunday worship service has become a big moving parable for what it means to follow Jesus dynamically. Stray cats are not seduced into a building only to be set free later. Instead, people can text message a number from their cell phones every week to receive a message about where we are going to be worshiping and how. Each week is a new adventure! Rather than meet in the same place every week doing the same things, we roam the city.

Every church can't adapt and experiment like this, because some churches are too big to make such drastic moves, and some may be too small. Be that as it may, empowering disciples in a changing world to evangelize and transform the world can only be done through adaptive experimentation. We must experiment with practices of faith to reach young Christians who do not presently attend church and people who are not followers of Christ. We must turn the church inside out by focusing our programming and faith practices outward, or else we will continue to get bit by stray cats who long to know Jesus and to be free.

Hip Hop and Christian Faith: A Response to Disruptions in Life

Hip Hop music is finding ways to embrace the Christian faith as a response to the pain and angst of the journey. The life of Christ is a deeper way to process the "booty-full" disruptions of life and to discover beauty lying beneath. It is a way to grow from what seems to be ugly to discover what can be beautiful. From Common's "G.O.D." to Kanye West's "Jesus Walks," Hip Hop is finding ways to discover twenty-first-century potential in the first-century Christian principles of the church.

As mentioned in chapter 5, the role of a missionary who walks with the Hip Hop generations and experience is to be an archeologist who excavates beauty from the lives of those who experience ugly disruptions.

From Booty to Beauty

In the late 1980s, my friends and I (Marlon) always used the word "booty" to describe what we did not like. Recess ends ten minutes early because the teacher has to use the restroom: "Ugh. That's booty." The radio DJ talks in the middle of the song while you are trying to make a slow jam tape: "So booty." We were middle-school students calling every disruptive experience "booty," from Momma's annoying voice calling us to wash the dishes in the middle of the *Cosby Show* to the slow-driving cars passing in the neighborhood making us call a "car time" pause in the middle of a good game of street kickball. Every interruption in our normal sense of life was "booty," until that fateful morning when the female students around us started to develop from little girls to young ladies. Overnight it seemed that the word took on a totally different meaning—meaning that made us feel different about life, love, and romance. "Booty" suddenly took on a positive connotation.

Beauty is when our human senses are minding their own business and God intervenes with a chord progression that reaches us in a place that evokes our awareness of God. That is what makes a great song great, a face gorgeous, a painting intriguing. It reaches you in a place you did not expect, in a good way. Hip Hop has an opportunity to see daily disruptions as beautiful, divine interventions.

But here is the problem. The ugly of our everyday lives makes it hard for us to sense the beautiful manifestations of God. Often we see only unwelcome interruptions to the lives we are trying to manage, rather than the possible beautiful messages from God in these interruptions. Hip Hop longs to manage the unmanageable and manipulate the messy. Hip Hop as a culture is growing to embrace the crucial human need for divine intervention in the life and story of Jesus, because in a disruptive world of chaos and clutter, Jesus is beauty.

As people who feel called to the Hip Hop generation, we must partner with this generation to be "beauty focused" not outcome or expectation focused. We get to walk with a generation facing ecological, academic, and social disruptions to help them discover the Messiah in this mess through the power and love of Jesus. He is the only one who can turn disruption into destiny.

Letters and Love

As a missionary-archeologist in the church, I am learning to write letters of thanks to those who I think I am helping in this mission. I get to do this work of love, and I "dig" the benefits. The work of digging up God where God can be found is its own reward. I'm finding that letters are beautiful tools to express my thanks. The letter below is written to a member of our community at Awakenings who shared her story with me. She is an example of a person on the fringe who could not be reached or discipled through traditional methods and whose transformation had to be understood differently. Time stood still as this twenty-three-year-old woman described the trial and triumph of her life. This young girl experienced disruption on every level, but she inspired me. This is my letter to her:

Dear Immaculately Conceived,

Meeting you was a defining moment in my life. As you revealed your story, I have discovered the essence of Christ's redemptive power that commissions us to find God's beauty in the ugly of life.

It may seem ugly to imagine that you were literally the result of a South African slave raped by her Apartheid master, but you were beautifully crafted as a creation of God before the foundation of the world. It's hard to think that your mom placed you and your brother in an orphanage as mixed-race children to protect you from the prejudice. You were not abandoned by your mother; you were immaculately conceived by God. A random gift of an America-bound plane ticket may have seemed coincidental, but it was no accident. You were destined to make an impact on me—an impact I am compelled to share and live out. You teach me that God calls us all to discover the divine mission in the miserable.

My adventurous friend, you were designed by the Creator of the cosmos before you were orphaned and inspired by the Giver of light before you were abused. You are not a product of your past environment; you are the creation of God's preferred future. The great I AM is God your Father, God the Son, and God the Holy Spirit. I AM is everything your parents were not, and He is doing everything they could not.

Your conception may have been a traumatic experience your mother shamefully endured, but you were born to beautifully embrace peace with arms of grace, walk in dignity with feet of mercy and run in destiny with legs of love.

Your hand may have never swung in your father's, but your life is held in God's hand with each step. You can't fully understand why your father rejected you then, but you must understand that God is fully embracing you now.

You may have been born in the oppressive chains of apartheid, but you were hand-shaped and molded by God's freedom. Yes, you lost your twin brother and best friend to a drive-by shooting, but you inspire me because you choose to lose yourself in Christ, a brother and a friend Who so loved you that He left heaven so that you could live on earth as it is in heaven.

You are a workmanship, intricately created in Christ. You did

not move from home to home seeking the love of others in vain because your life is becoming a movement of love. God knew that your mission was true enough to be discovered in misery. Momma may not have lovingly called your name in the past, but God is lovingly calling you from your future. Please continue to challenge us to find redemptive beauty in the ugly of this world.
Sincerely,
An inspired seeker of beauty

Like the life of the subject of this letter, the lives of Hip Hop generations have been disrupted by abandonment of many kinds, particularly fathers. The stories of Jesus, the young lady in this letter, and Hip Hop are all stories about people who were called bastards by humanity but were called blessed by God. From a girl born in South Africa without a father and living in an orphanage, to Jesus born in a manger without an earthly father, to Hip Hop born in a community disrupted in every way possible, the church must express the love of God, our parent. The church needs to make such expressions in ways that protect, defend, and nurture the creativity of this culture while challenging that culture's character.

This is the culture of our children, and we must not, cannot, abandon them. We have been called to excavate the beauty of God lying beneath the ruins caused by disruption. The church is called to guide a community of seekers in discovering manifestations of a God whom they can sense in a senseless world of pain.

Epilogue

I think people underestimate the power of a musician. . . . They think we're not intellectual, we don't study policy, we don't know law and order. But we sing about it.
—Wyclef Jean[1]

From its inception, Hip Hop moved crowds and shook night-clubs and concert venues. Today it shapes cultures worldwide. Hip Hop is becoming an ever-present reality in which we live, breathe, and have our very being. The run for the Haitian presidency by poet and producer Wyclef Jean proves that reality.

Wyclef Jean is a former member of the 1990s rap group The Fugees. He went on to pursue a solo career, gaining international success and hometown acclaim in his native Haiti. He recently used his standing as a musician to champion the recovery effort of helping Haiti rise from the debris of earthquake devastation. Riding on the wave of his ambassadorship for Haiti, he decided to run for president with no formal experience or political training, and this decision was being met with celebration and criticism alike.

Wyclef released *Welcome to Haiti: Creole 101* in 2004 to honor the native love and naïve hopes he has for his country. The album included a song, "President," in which Jean talked about the poverty of Haiti and what he would do to resolve it if he were elected president. This song has proven to be prophetic because large groups of young people are gathering all around the Caribbean nation to support Wyclef, not only despite his political naïveté, but also because of it. These are the same reasons traditional political voices do not accept him—they find the management of his nonprofit corporation, Yele Haiti (that feeds thousands), questionable. His lack of political experience limits his potential to lead such a volatile nation, but the young people of Haiti support him. Young voters in Haiti do not trust traditional politics, mostly because the political powers that be do not trust them. Traditional criticism of Wyclef is not a deterrent for young voters; it is, rather, motivation to support him and an indirect confirmation of the notion that powerful institutions do not support or believe in young people.

In a nation in which half the population is under twenty-one, Wyclef has a distinct advantage. He told *Time* magazine in an interview that he understood the momentum that would drive his campaign: the "enormous youth population doesn't believe in politicians anymore."[2] Traditional institutions such as governments and the church are losing credibility because they don't live out their own belief systems and ideals. The intent of the church, as led by the Holy Spirit, is to engender trust and belief, but the distrust of youth and their lack of belief in both institutions are difficult to overcome. Democracy, as a political institution, was born out of a belief in protecting the rights of the least and last (like young people), while the church was born out of the belief in a young, questionable radical named Jesus. Both institutions not only are failing young people by not embracing and directing their emerging idealism, but also are failing themselves by not upholding their own core beliefs. Believing the unbelievable and supporting the unsupported are central to democratic and Christian thought.

Wyclef's presidential ambitions,[3] his widespread support from youth, and youth's resistance to traditional government all speak to a larger opportunity for the church to live out its mission. In all the questionable activity of youth, the church is uniquely called to love them; and, because of their naïve ideals, the church is especially called to believe in youth culture. The church can reclaim its inherent design by believing in a generation of rebels and revolutionaries ready for empowering transformation. Believing in a seemingly rebellious young person is how the church got started anyway—remember Jesus? This old institution of the church was once a new movement of young mutineers who dared to believe that the embodied Divine came to earth, wrapped in the flesh of a young, politically inexperienced, and compassionate young leader from Nazareth. Believing in the unbelievable is the church's ancient mission and present opportunity.

As it turns out, this book has been not only the exploration of a young music but also the discovery of the church's ancient responsibility to young culture. In this book we have discovered what can happen when the church trusts its core intuition more than being bound by its institutional values. What we have before us is the possibility of a new reality in which we live, breathe, and have our very being in Jesus' name.

As we conclude this journey, we remind parents, educators, and Hip Hop aficionados themselves that this genre is rich in possibilities for use as pedagogical tools. K-12 teachers across the United States, from East Coast to West, use Hip Hop to teach subjects from algebra to Shakespeare. In Los Angeles, LaMar Queen, a math teacher, uses Hip Hop, particularly rhyme, to help students memorize complex algebra, improving their skills and their grades. Using rap, he presents a math concept and moves through sample problems point by point and follows with traditional instruction. Teachers have always used music to enhance instruction. Just as they used to play rock and roll tunes, they now use Hip Hop. Alan Sitomer experienced an intellectual awakening, when planning to teach the poet Dylan Thomas, and he started to think about Tupac Shakur. Sitomer homed in on Shakur's lyrics about respect and the import of standing up to violence and hostility, finding positive messages about increasing one's mindfulness and challenging adversity. Making the connection between Tupac and Thomas ignited excitement in Sitomer's classroom, helping create incredible improvement in the inner-city school. Queen and Sitomer make significant impacts on their students' lives by using rap music. Herein lies a stellar example for teachers and ministers who participate in religious education.[4]

In addition to pedagogical uses, Hip Hop continues to be a tool for protest, social justice, and community development. Terverius Black, an independent Hip Hop producer in Huntsville, Alabama, told his adviser that he had directed several music videos of the Hip Hop artists he'd recorded, wanted ultimately to produce movies, and had completed his first script, about a Christian Hip Hop group struggling to honor its values in a music industry overflowing with disruption and sin. In a few weeks, Lavon Colman, his financial adviser's aunt, a white Memphis, Tennessee, woman, gave Black $200,000 to fund his venture. Colman's dad had collaborated with a black pastor during the civil rights era in Tennessee. She backed the movie because she wanted to see what she had seen in Memphis: blacks and whites working together. Black hired Courtney "J.R." Peebles and Willie "P-Dub" Moore Jr., two St. Louis musicians to make up the fictional Christian hip hop group "True City," for his movie, *Stand*. Both artists grew up in the church, where they knew Christianity and music. Both artists left their roots for more lucrative venues; both returned to St. Louis, which has a large Christian Hip Hop scene, and their Christian roots. The film concerns three friends struggling to feed their families with low-paying jobs while they simultaneously pursue a music career. When they do have an opportunity for fame, they have to decide between compromising their values or holding on to them.[5]

For those new to this genre of music and its use as a pedagogical tool, three recent works on Hip Hop/rap are excellent resources. *The Anthology of Rap*, edited by Adam Bradley and Andrew DuBois (New Haven: Yale University Press, 2010), lists almost three hundred lyrics from rap's inception to the present day. Shawn Carter's *Decoded Jay-Z* (New York: Spiegel & Grau, 2010), contains a collection of lyrics and their meanings, as it tells the story of Hip Hop culture, its times, and profiles one of the most stellar twenty-first century popular artists. Dan Charnas's *The Big Payback: The History of the Business of Hip Hop* (New York: New American Library, 2010), includes encyclopedic information about producers, agents, label executives, talent scouts, and musicians themselves, explaining how Hip Hop became the music entertainment industry's lucrative gold mine. These texts provide excellent resources for those committed to empowering our youth, to help them help themselves "Wake Up"; and if we are fortunate, we will "Wake Up," to the profound gift our youth are, to the amazing opportunity we have to use this music and culture to make a difference, to praise and luxuriate in the goodness of God, a God who gives such gifts that result in the complex, moving, troubling, phenomenal music and culture called Hip Hop.

> And we sing and dance and worship and praise
> And we write, waxing spiritually, poignantly, reflecting

How spirited, sometimes broken, sometimes hurting,
sometimes protesting souls
scream the body electric.
The nobility and exuberance of youth,
Undaunted
By the tediousness of the lives of their elders,
who may decide to not bend and learn and love,
as their children and grandchildren experiment,
And empower themselves
Through self-expression, communally,
personally, unambiguously:
Graced realities, graced notes
where young turks worry with their spirituality
With their identity, their quest to be, to become,
to know, to live, to soar.
And, like Jesus, they may need to ask their parents,
why were you looking for us
Were we not about our spiritual business
that our Creator calls us to engage
Our gifts, our talents, our realities?
Can we get a witness?
Can we get young and old and in-between
To sit together and reason;
to embrace God in broadest terms
To look for the God within,
that our elders remember that they were once young
And to help our young know they can self-express
without the use of violent, abusive language?
To God be the glory for the things God does, for who God is,
that God has allowed us to birth a book about a generation
who births pictures through rap and rhyme
Wake up, somebody! Wake up![6]

Notes

1. I'm Bound to Wreck Your Body and Say Turn the Party Out

1. From Naughty by Nature, Hip Hop group of the 1990s.

2. Allison Samuels, N'Gai Croal, and David Gates, "Battle for the Soul of Hip Hop," *Newsweek* (October 9, 2000): 62–63.

3. The group Brand Nubian is the leader of the social-conscience movement of Hip Hop that picked up in the early 1990s.

4. Brand Nubian, "Punks Step Up to Get Beat Down." *In God We Trust.* CD. Elektra Records, 1993.

5. Digital Underground was an alternative rap group from Oakland, California. "The Humpty Dance" is a humorous dance number that climbed all the way to number 11 on the pop charts, number 7 on the R&B charts, and number 1 on the Billboard Rap Singles chart.

6. LL Cool J, "I Need Love." *Bigger and Deffer.* Audio Cassette. Def Jam Records, 1987.

7. This film is about an African prince who goes to Queens, New York, to find a wife whom he can respect for her intelligence and will. *Coming to America,* DVD, directed by John Landis (Hollywood: Paramount Pictures, 1988).

8. Brooke Giles, "Stories, Psalms and Psalmists." *Awakenings Movement.* Eldorado Ballroom (2310 Dowling St.). June 2009. Podcast.

9. The B-side of an album is the side of the album that does not have the song that is released for radio play. The B-side has to be discovered by the person who listens to the entire album from start to finish.

10. The Great Depression was a severe worldwide economic depression in the decade preceding World War II, which started around 1929 and lasted until the late 1930s or early 1940s.

11. Afrika Bambaataa is an American DJ from South Bronx, New York, who was instrumental in the early development of Hip Hop throughout the 1980s. He is one of three originators of break-beat deejaying and is known as the Godfather/Grandfather and the Amen Ra of Universal Hip Hop Culture as well as the Father of the Electro Funk Sound.

12. DJ Cool Herc is one of the founding fathers of Hip Hop music, who, as a pioneer, was one of the first DJs to use turntables as an instrument.

13. Alycia Miles, "Stories, Psalms and Psalmists." *Awakenings Movement.*

14. Sugarhill Gang is a foundational Hip Hop group that was founded in the early 1970s and was the first Hip Hop group to record a single that would become a Top 40 hit.

15. Kurtis Blow is one of the first commercially successful Hip Hop artists and the first to sign with a major label, Krush Records, in 1980. "The Breaks," a single from his 1980 debut album, is the first certified gold song for Hip Hop.

16. Q-Tip on *JPeriod Presents Audio Documentary*. Q-Tip is a New York–based American Hip Hop artist, producer, singer, and actor who was part of the critically acclaimed Hip Hop group A Tribe Called Quest. *JPeriod Presents Audio Documentary* is a podcast that features a national DJ's interpretation of resonant voices and songs in Hip Hop.

17. Biz Markie is a humorous rapper and DJ from the 1990s who still travels the world sharing music with fans.

18. *Yo! MTV Raps* was a two-hour-long American television music video program, which ran from August 1988 to August 1995 (and until 1999 with the renamed *Yo!*). The program was the first Hip Hop music show on the network.

19. Biz Markie, "Turn tha Party Out." Written by Marlon Williams and Marcel Hall. *Greatest Hits*. CD. Landspeed Records, 2002.

20. Biz Markie, "Vapors." Written by Marcel Hall, Marlon Wiliams, and Antonio Handy. *Greatest Hits*. CD. Cold Chillin/Warner Bros. Records, 1987.

21. Biz Markie, "Make the Music with Your Mouth, Biz." Written by Marcel Hall and Marlon Williams. *Goin' Off*. CD. Cold Chillin Records/Warner Bros. Records, 1988.

22. Scarface is a Houston-based Hip Hop artist with the group The Geto Boys, signed to Rap-A-Lot Records.

23. Brad Jordan, telephone interview, March 22, 2009.

24. See note 22.

25 Nas is a Queens, New York–based lyricist who released his first album, *Illmatic*, on Columbia Records in 1994, and was also apart of the supergroup The Firm, featuring Jay-Z and Foxy Brown.

26. Freeway, a Philadelphia-based maven of metaphors, best known for his tenure on Roc-A-Fella Records, is a member of the group State Property, and has recently signed to Cash Money Records.

27. Def Jam South is the Southern division of Def Jam Recordings. The label is best known for launching the career of Ludacris and his Disturbing tha Peace group and label. In 2003, Def Jam South shut down but was relaunched in 2005. It also jumpstarted the career of Young Jeezy.

28. Ludacris was formerly an Atlanta DJ called Chris Luva Luva. He would release his debut album, *Incognegro*, independently on his own Disturbing tha Peace record label.

29. The Geto Boys, "Mind Playing Tricks on Me." *We Can't Be Stopped*. CD. Def American/Warner Bros. Records, 1990. This album was selected as one of *The Source*'s 100 Best Rap Albums.

30. The Geto Boys, "Gangsta of Love." *Grip It! On That Other Level*. CD. Rap-A-Lot Records, 1989.

31. James Mercer Langston Hughes (February 1, 1902–May 22, 1967) was an American poet, novelist, playwright, short-story writer, and columnist. He was

one of the earliest innovators of the new literary art form jazz poetry. Hughes is best known for his work during the Harlem Renaissance.

32. Brad Jordan, telephone interview, March 22, 2009.

33. Benedict Anderson, *Imagined Communities: Reflections on the Origin and Spread of Nationalism*, rev. ed. (New York: Verso, 1991).

34. Derek Greenfield, personal interview, October 23, 2009.

35. S. Craig Watkins, *Hip Hop Matters: Politics, Pop Culture, and the Struggle for the Soul of the Movement* (Boston: Beacon Press, 2005), 148–52, 181, 256.

36. Ibid., 119.

37. Ibid., 2–6, 22, 118–20.

38. Jeffrey O. G. Ogbar, *Hip-hop Revolution: The Culture and Politics of Rap* (Lawrence: University Press of Kansas, 2007), 84, 109, 146.

39. William J. Brown and Benson P. Fraser, "Hip Hop Kingdom Come," *Christianity Today* (January 8, 2001): 48–52, 54.

40. Brett Edaki, "Desperately Seeking Silence: Youth Culture's Unspoken Need," *Cross Currents* 57, no. 3 (Fall 2007): 381–85.

41. Mary Timothy Prokes, FSE, *Theology of the Body* (Edinburgh, Scotland: T&T Clark, 1996), 1–20.

42. Christine E. Gudorf, *Body, Sex, and Pleasure: Reconstructing Sexual Ethics* (Cleveland: Pilgrim Press, 1994), 1–28.

43. Nas, "Whose World Is This." *Illmatic.* CD. Columbia Records, 1992.

44. "The world is yours" is the chorus line from "Whose World Is This."

45. *Scarface*, videocassette, directed by Oliver Stone (Universal City, Calif.: Universal Pictures, 1983).

46. Antonio "Tony" Montana is the main character from the film *Scarface* and is portrayed by Al Pacino.

47. Tupac Shakur—known by his stage names, 2Pac (or simply Pac) and Makaveli—was an American rapper. He has sold seventy-five million albums to date and is one of the best-selling music artists in the world. Nas—formerly Nasty Nas—is an American rapper and actor. Outkast is an American Hip Hop duo based in East Point, Georgia, consisting of André "André 3000" Benjamin (formerly known as Dré) and Antwan "Big Boi" Patton. The duo is one of the most successful Hip Hop groups of all time, receiving six Grammy awards and selling more than twenty-five million albums.

48. A sound bite from the Beastie Boys song "Shake Your Rump."

49. Conversation with Danielle Ewing, writer and relationships enthusiast.

50. "Biggie Smalls" is the nickname for the Notorious B.I.G.

51. Notorious B.I.G., "Machine Gun Funk," *Ready to Die.* CD. Arista Records, 1995.

52. From the chorus of "Machine Gun Funk."

53. Chinua Achebe, *Things Fall Apart* (New York: Anchor, 1994). Achebe's novel provides an unremittingly unsentimental rendering of Nigerian tribal life before and after the arrival of colonialism.

54. Ogbar, *Hip-hop Revolution*, 68–72.

55. Bill Wylie-Kellermann, "Resisting Death Incarnate: The Principles of Urban Violence," in *Putting Down Stones: A Faithful Response to Urban Violence* (Washington, DC: Sojourners, 1998), 6.

56. Ibid.

57. Watkins, *Hip-hop Matters*, 50, 95.

58. Greenfield interview.

59. Cheo H. Coker, "Who's Gonna Take the Weight?" *Essence* (August 1994): 63–64.

60. Bernard Braxton, *Sexual, Racial and Political Faces of Corruption* (Washington, D.C.: Verta Press, 1977), 7–8, 13–16, 19–24.

61. Carolyn F. Swift, *Women and Violence: Breaking the Connection*, Work in Progress Series (Wellesley, Mass.: Wellesley College, 1987), 3–15.

62. Greenfield interview.

63. Ibid.

64. Tara Roberts, "Dilemma of a Womanist," in "A Hip Hop Nation Divided," *Essence* (August 1994): 62, 64.

65. Samuels, Croal, and Gates, "Battle for the Soul of Hip Hop," 58–65.

2. Hip Hop Is Dead

1. Christopher Paul, personal interview, April 1, 2010.

2. Stephen Crites, "The Narrative Quality of Experience," *Journal of the American Academy of Religion* (September 1971): 305.

3. Cheryl Kirk-Duggan, *Exorcizing Evil: A Womanist Perspective on the Spirituals* (Maryknoll, N.Y.: Orbis, 1997), 58, 61.

4. Jahnheninz Jahn, *Muntu: The New African Culture* (New York: Grove Press, 1961), 100–106.

5. Peter Paris, *The Spirituality of African Peoples* (Minneapolis: Augsburg Fortress, 1995), vi, 122–23, 130, 146–48, 152.

6. Kirk-Duggan, *Exorcizing Evil*, 62.

7. Dominique Zahan, *The Religion, Spirituality, and Thought of Traditional Africa* (Chicago: University of Chicago Press, 1979), 4–5, 9; John S. Mbiti, *African Religions and Philosophy* (New York: Praeger, 1969), 1–3.

8. The earlier meaning being "a usage well established among African-Americans by the 1960s," according to *The American Heritage Dictionary*, 4th edition.

9. See Howard Johnson and Jim Pines, *Reggae—Deep Roots Music* (New York: Proteus Books, 1984).

10. See http://aalbc.com/authors/thelast.htm; DuEwa M. Frazier, "The Last Poets: Still on a Mission"; http://aalbc.com/authors/thelastpoetsstillonamission.htm (viewed May 25, 2010); http://www.soprupradio.com/?tag=last-poets (viewed May 25, 2010).

11. Paul interview.

12. Ibid.

13. K. Leigh Hamm Forell, "Ideas in Practice: Bringin' Hip Hop to the Basics," *Journal of Developmental Education* 30 (Winter 2006): 28–30.

14. Scott Crossley, "Metaphorical Conceptions in Hip-/Hop Music," *African American Review* 39, no. 4 (Winter 2006): 501–12.

15. See http://www.blackapologetics.com/fivepercentfaq.html (viewed May 31, 2010).

16. Paul interview; Josef Sorett, "Hip Hop Religion and Spiritual Sampling in a 'Post-Racial' Age," March 24, 2010; http://www.religiondispatches.org/books/culture/2281/HipHop_religion_and_spiritual_sampling_in_a_%E2%80%9Cpost-racial%E2%80%9D_age/ (viewed May 31, 2010).

17. Derek Greenfield, "What's the Deal with the White Middle-aged Guy Teaching Hip Hop? Lessons in Popular Culture, Positionality, and Pedagogy" *Pedagogy, Culture & Society*, Vol. 15, No. 2 (July 2007): 230–36, 241–42.

18. Bronwen E. Low, "Hip Hop, Language, and Difference: The N-Word as a Pedagogical Limit-Case" *Journal of Language, Identity, and Education* 6(2) (2007): 147–60.

19. K. Leigh Hamm Forell, "Ideas in Practice: Bringin' Hip Hop to the Basics" *Journal of Developmental Education* Vol. 30 (Winter 2006): 28–33.

20. James Stackhouse, telephone interview, May 2010.

21. Paul Williams, "Twenty-first-century Jeremiad: Contemporary Hip Hop and American Tradition," *European Journal of American Culture* 27, no. 2 (2008): 111–32.

22. Henning Nelms, *Magic and Showmanship: A Handbook for Conjurers* (Mineola, N.Y.: Dover Publications, 2000), 1.

23. David Blaine, Technology Entertainment Design Conference, October 2009.

24. McKenna T, "Where Digital Music Technology and Law Collide—Contemporary Issues of Digital Sampling, Appropriation and Copyright Law," 2000 (1), *The Journal of Information, Law and Technology (JILT)*; http://www.law.warwick.ac.uk/jilt/00-1/mckenna.html.

25. *NY-Z*, Dir. Danny Clinch, Perf. Jay-Z; Viewed March 22, 2010 on http://www.youtube.com/watch?v=cqZJJ_3gDis.

26. "Jay-Z is the best rapper alive," Lil Wayne, November 12, 2007.

27. See www.beatboxbattle.com.

28. Scatting, "American Memory," The Library of Congress; http://rs6.loc.gov/ammem/index.html.

29. David Toop, *Rap Attack 2: African Rap to Global Hip Hop* (New York: Serpent's Tail, 1994).

30. William S. Bouroughs, Sound Piece.

31. Richard Giles, personal interview, April 19, 2010.

32. Ibid.

33. Ibid.

34. Ibid.

35. Paul and Stackhouse interviews.

36. Paul interview.

37. Stackhouse interview.

38. Paul interview.

39. First published in *The Crisis* in 1921, the verse that would become Hughes's signature poem, "The Negro Speaks of Rivers," appeared in his first book of poetry, *The Weary Blues*, in 1926.

40. Paul Edwards, *How to Rap: The Art and Science of the Hip-Hop MC* (Chicago: Chicago Review Press, 2009).

41. Naughty By Nature, "Hip Hop Hooray." *19 Naughty III*. CD. Tommy Boy Records, 1993.

183

42. For a classical understanding of the "black preacher," particularly during the antebellum and postbellum periods, see W.E.B. Dubois, *The Souls of Black Folk* (New York: Penguin Books, 1996).

43. "Griots," http://www.merriam-webster.com/dictionary/griot (viewed May 1, 2010).

44. Edwards, *How to Rap*.

45. See http://www.elijahwald.com/bio.html.

46. Gil Scott Heron, "The Revolution Will Not Be Televised." *Pieces of a Man.* CD. Flying Dutchman, 1971.

47. Adam Krims, *Rap Music and the Poetics of Identity* (Cambridge: Cambridge University Press, 2000), 44.

48. Kool Moe Dee, *There's a God on the Mic: The True 50 Greatest MCs* (New York: Thunder's Mouth Press, 2003), 325.

49. Ibid., 334.

50. Ibid., 325.

51. Malik Yusef, "Crack Music." *Late Registration.* Roc-A-Fella Records, 2005.

52. Lovie Olivia, personal interview, December 2008.

53. Teacher's Guide to "Reflections in Black: Smithsonian African American Photography," 2003, Oakland Museum of California. http://museumca.org/exhibit/exhi_rib.html (viewed May 10, 2010).

54. Ibid.

55. Stephen Thomas, "Biz Markie Biography." *allmusic.com* (viewed May 1, 2010).

56. Olivia Marsaud, "Bakary Soumano," http://www.afrik.com/article4428.html (viewed May 16, 2010).

57. Ibid.

58. Ibid.

59. *The Woodsman* is a 2004 film directed by Nicole Kassell. The movie stars Kevin Bacon as a convicted child molester who must adjust to life after prison.

60. Michael D. Harris, "Color Lines: Mapping Color Consciousness in the Art of Archibald Motley, Jr.," in *Colored Pictures: Race and Visual Representation* (Chapel Hill: University of North Carolina Press, 2003), 157.

61. Archibald Motley Jr., oral history interview with Archibald Motley, Smithsonian Archives of American Art (January 23, 1979).

62. Awaovieyi Agie, "André 3000, Profile of an Artist." Interview. Langfield Entertainment, April 7, 2005. http://www.langfieldentertainment.com/ANDRE3000.htm (viewed January 26, 2011).

63. Matthew Miller, "The Wealthiest Black Americans," May 6, 2009; Forbes.com.

64. See http://ema.mtv.co.uk/artists/jay_z.

65. RIAA-Gold & Platinum, August 8, 2008; see www.riaa.com.

66. "Jay-Z Leaves Def Jam Presidency," Pitchfork.

67. "Jay-Z Beats Elvis for No. 1 Albums Record." *Access Hollywood* (viewed September 16, 2009).

68. DJ Flash Gordon Parks, personal interview, June 25, 2010.

3. I Used to Love Her

1. Title from the Common album *Resurrection* personifying Hip Hop and his relationship with it. See Common, *Resurrection*. CD. Relativity Records, 1994.

2. Parental Advisory is a message affixed by the Recording Industry Association of America (RIAA) to audio recordings in the United States containing excessive use of profane language. *Parental Advisory Label Program (PAL)*. 23 October 2006. Recording Industry Association of America. April 17, 2010; see http://riaa.com/parentaladvisory.php?content_selector.

3. Ice-T, *Rhyme Pays*. CD. Sire/Warner Bros. Records, 1986.

4. Ice-T, "I Love The Ladies." *Rhyme Pays*. CD. Sire/Warner Bros. Records, 1986.

5. The Notorious B.I.G.'s "Juicy," "Big Poppa," and "One More Chance" from the album *Ready to Die* all reached number 1 on the Billboard Charts the year of their release. "Ready to Die—Charts & Awards—Billboard Singles," AllMusic (viewed January 25, 2009), http://www.allmusic.com/artist/the-notorious-big-p44889/biography.

6. The Notorious B.I.G., "Juicy." *Ready to Die*. Bad Boy Records, 1994.

7. "Biggie Saved East Coast Rap Ready to Die" (Explicit) *Tower Records* (Muze data). Viewed on December 10, 2009.

8. Steve Huey, "Notorious B.I.G.—Biography," AllMusic (retrieved October 7, 2006). http://www.allmusic.com/artist/the-notorious-big-p44889/biography.

9. For an in-depth discussion of my view of black aesthetic, see Cheryl Kirk-Duggan, *Exorcizing Evil: A Womanist Perspective on the Spirituals* (Maryknoll, NY: Orbis, 1997), 79–87.

10. Norman Harris, *Connecting Times: The Sixties in Afro-American Fiction* (Jackson, MS: University Press of Mississippi, 1988), 5, 10–12.

11. W. E. B. DuBois, *The Souls of Black Folk* (New York: Simon & Schuster, 2005), 3–6.

12. James Standifer, "Musical Behaviors of Black People in American Society," *Black Music Research Journal* (1980): 57.

13. Michel Foucault, *The Archaeology of Knowledge* (New York: Harper & Row, 1972), 56; see also page 131. Discourse occurs in modes (e.g., economics, history, and music).

14. Vincent Harding, *Hope and History: Why We Must Share the Story of the Movement* (Maryknoll, N.Y.: Orbis Press, 1990), 1–10.

15. Richard Shusterman, "Challenging Conventions in the Fine Art of Rap," in *That's the Joint: The Hip Hop Studies Reader*, ed. Murray Forman and Mark Anthony Neal (New York: Routledge, 2004), 463–69.

16. Henry Louis Gates Jr., *Figures in Black: Words, Signs, and the "Racial" Self* (New York: Oxford University Press, 1987), xxxi; Houston Baker, *Blues, Ideology, and Afro-American Literature: A Vernacular Theory* (Chicago: University of Chicago Press, 1984), 60; Henry Louis Gates Jr., *The Signifying Monkey: A Theory of Afro-American Literary Criticism* (New York: Oxford University Press, 1988), xxiii, 45, 50–51.

17. Gates, *Signifying Monkey*, xi, xix.

18. Ibid., xxi.

19. Victor Anderson, *Beyond Ontological Blackness: An Essay on African American Religious and Cultural Criticism* (New York: Continuum, 1995), 11–17, 87.

20. Flora Wilson Bridges, *Resurrection Song: African-American Spirituality* (Maryknoll, N.Y.: Orbis Books, 2001), 1–5.

21. Karen Baker-Fletcher and Garth Kasimu Baker-Fletcher, *My Sister, My Brother: Womanist and Xodus God-Talk* (Maryknoll, N.Y.: Orbis Books, 1997), 227–30.

22. Barbara A. Holmes, *Joy Unspeakable: Contemplative Practices of the Black Church* (Minneapolis: Fortress Press, 2004), vii–xi, 2, 31.

23. Ibid., 42, 92, 99, 103, 170.

24. Ibid., 170, 179–82.

25. Josiah Ulysses Young III, "Existential Aptness and Epistemological Correctness: West and the Identity of the "Lord," in *Cornel West: A Critical Reader*, ed. George Yancy (Malden, Mass.: Blackwell Publishers, 2001), 168.

26. Ibid., 35.

27. Ibid., 33; Eduardo Mendieta, "Which Pragmatism? Whose America?" in *Cornel West: A Critical Reader*, 99; Howard McGary Jr., "The Political Philosophy and Humanism of Cornel West," in *Cornel West: A Critical Reader*, 284. Young, "Existential Aptness," 168.

28. Cornel West, *The Cornel West Reader* (New York: Basic Books, 1999), 101.

29. Tricia Rose, *Black Noise: Rap Music and Black Culture in Contemporary America* (Hanover, N.H.: Wesleyan University Press, 1994), 19–34, 59, 101–6, 125–26, 131–32.

30. Joy Degruy Leary, *Post Traumatic Slave Syndrome: America's Legacy of Enduring Injury and Healing* (Portland, Ore.: Uptone Press, 2005).

31. Ibid., 69.

32. Abel Meeropol (Lewis Alan, pen name), "Strange Fruit," in Billie Holiday, *Anthology: Lady Sings the Blues* (Ojai, Calif.: Creative Concepts Publishing, 1976), 111–13. Billie Holiday popularized this song in 1939.

33. Leary, *Post Traumatic*, 129.

34. Ibid., 136–47.

35. Ibid., 142.

36. bell hooks, *Killing Rage: Ending Racism* (New York: Henry Holt, 1995), 16–20.

37. Ibid., 12.

38. Thandeka, *Learning to Be White: Money, Race, and God in America* (New York, Continuum, 1999).

39. hooks, *Killing Rage*, 19.

40. Ibid., 4, 8, 11, 19, 47, 57, 61.

41. Robert E. Hood, *Begrimed and Black: Christian Traditions on Blacks and Blackness* (Minneapolis: Augsburg/Fortress, 1994), xi, xiv, 25, 43.

42. Ibid., 18, 19, 73, 80, 83, 89, 90, 91, 181, 183.

43. Jon Michael Spencer, ed., "Preface," *The Theology of American Popular Music; Black Sacred Music: A Journal of Theomusicology* 3 (Fall 1989): v.

44. Andrew Greeley, *God in Popular Culture* (Chicago: Thomas More Press, 1988), 13–14, 16, 87.

45. Ernst Bloch, *Essays on the Philosophy of Music*, trans. Peter Palmer (Cambridge: Cambridge University Press, 1985), 227, in Spencer, "Preface," vi.

Note that prior to the 1960s, both church and society accepted the "hidden cracks" of racism, sexism, and classism as the status quo. Further, both church and society usually ignored the ramifications of these "cracks" (e.g., denial of certain people's humanity and legal violence against minorities).

46. Jon Michael Spencer, *Theological Music: Introduction to Theomusicology* (New York: Greenwood Press, 1991), xi.

47. Ibid., 162. See James W. Button, *Blacks and Social Change: Impact of the Civil Rights Movement in Southern Communities* (Princeton: Princeton University Press, 1989), 77. Button analyzes and documents changes caused by the effect of the civil rights movement within Southern communities from the 1950s to the mid-1980s. Theomusicology—not limited to but conducive to the study of Christian, African American cultures—must account for "the actual lack of liberation at levels and in areas that elude national attention" and must explain those nuances in music that scholars have difficulty articulating.

48. See Manfred Clynes, "The Communication of Emotion: Theory of Sentics," in *Emotion, Theory, Research, and Experience*, ed. R. Plutchik and H. Kellerman (New York: Academic Press, 1980), 271–300; Manfred Clynes, "The Living Quality of Music," in *Music, Mind, and Brain: The Neuropsychology of Music*, ed. Manfred Clynes (New York: Plenum Press, 1982), 47–82.

49. The term *manifest destiny* in the nineteenth century was used to claim that the United States was destined, even divinely ordained, to enlarge its territory throughout the North American continent, from the Atlantic to the Pacific Ocean.

50. The Roots are the house band for *Late Night with Jimmy Fallon*. See http://www.latenightwithjimmyfallon.com/about/the-roots (viewed April 30, 2010).

51. ?uestlove in *The Wall Street Journal*, http://online.wsj.com/article/SB10001424052970203609204574318291134732278.html (viewed April 27, 2010).

52. The Reverend Dr. Herbert Brewster is a composer, minister, songwriter, poet, and community leader who composed the original "How I Got Over" and other gospel songs recorded by Mahalia Jackson.

53. Afrika Bambaataa uses music to promote peace among gangs.

54. The Roots (featuring Truck North, P.O.R.N., and Dice Raw), "Walk Alone." *How I Got Over*. Def Jam Records, 2010.

55. On the origin of P.O.R.N.'s name, see http://www.okayplayer.com/interviews/latest-interviews/p.o.r.n.-_and_-truck-north:-say-hello-200805075663/ (viewed April 27, 2010).

56. The Roots, "Walk Alone."

57. "The Greatest Hip Hop Groups of All Time," Mtv.com; see http://www.mtv.com/bands/h/hip_hop_week/2007/groups (viewed April 27, 2010).

58. *Shaolin and Wu Tang* is a 1981 film directed by Hong Kong martial artist Gordon Liu.

59. Russell Guess, Personal Interview, April 2010.

60. Robert Christgau, review of *The Tao of Wu*, by RZA, *Rolling Stone* (October 2009).

4. G.O.D. (Gaining One's Definition)

1. Erwin Raphael McManus is an author, speaker, activist, filmmaker, and innovator, who specializes in the field of developing and unleashing personal and organizational creativity, uniqueness, innovation, and diversity (www.erwinmc manus.com).

2. James H. Cone, "Black Theology in American Religion," *Theology Today* 43, no. 1 (April 1986): 6–21.

3. Linda E. Thomas, ed., *Living Stones in the Household of God: The Legacy and Future of Black Theology* (Minneapolis: Fortress Press, 2004), x–xiv.

4. Jeremiah Wright, "Doing Black Theology in the Black Church," in *Living Stones in the Household of God*, 13–15, 23.

5. Karen E. Mosby-Avery, "Black Theology and the Black Church," in *Living Stones in the Household of God*, 33–36.

6. Alice Walker, *In Search of Our Mother's Gardens: Womanist Prose* (New York: Harcourt Brace Jovanovich, 1983), xi.

7. See http://illusionsmanoj.com.

8. "Ella Fitzgerald, the Voice of Jazz, Dies at 79," *New York Times*, http://www.nytimes.com/1996/06/16/nyregion/ella-fitzgerald-the-voice-of-jazz-dies-at-79.html?pagewanted=4 (viewed May 1, 2010).

9. Clara Ward, composer, "How I Got Over," 1951. It was performed by Mahalia Jackson in 1961 and won the Grammy for Best Gospel Song in 1967.

10. Martin Luther King Jr.'s "I Have a Dream" speech, delivered in Washington, D.C. on August 28, 1973, is one of the civil rights activist's most popular and resonant deliveries of his career.

11. Scott Yanow, "Ella Fitzgerald—Biography," http://allmusic.com/cg/amg.dll?P=amg&sql=11:71r67ui0h0j3~T1 (viewed March 16, 2007).

12. David Pilgrim, "The Mammy Caricature," Ferris State University. October 2000; see http://www.ferris.edu/jimcrow/mammies.

13. Jo Ann Gibson Robinson, *The Montgomery Bus Boycott and the Women Who Started It: The Memoir of Jo Ann Gibson Robinson* (Knoxville: University of Tennessee Press, 1987), 107.

14. See Ella Fitzgerald's official website: http://www.ellafitzgerald.com/about/biography.html.

15. See "Vicki Smith's Tribute to Ella Fitzgerald" online at http://www.vickie smith.com/ella.htm.

16. Nicolson, Stuart, *Ella Fitzgerald: A Biography of the First Lady of Jazz* (New York: Da Capo Press, 1995), 179.

17. "Vicki Smith's Tribute to Ella Fitzgerald."

18. An old "one hundred" is a metaphor for traditional, classic hymns, often sung to long meter. Long meter is a poetic meter with four-line stanzas in iambic tetrameter with alternate rhyme scheme a-b-a-b.

19. This tension is not unique to black worship; consider the use of trained choirs to edify passive worshipers by the beauty of Christmas services (the popularity of sing-along *Messiah*s demonstrates the lack of worship in the aforementioned flaccid observances).

20. W. E. B. DuBois, *The Souls of Black Folk* (New York: Boomer Books, 2008), 159–74.

21. Ida Mukenge, *The Black Church in Urban America: A Case Study in Political Economy* (Lanham, Md.: University Press of America, 1983), 1, 6.

22. Michael Battle, *Black Church in America: African American Christian Spirituality* (Malden, Mass.: Wiley-Blackwell), 2006.

23. William D. Watley, "Introducing the African American Churches," in *Readings in African American Church Music and Worship*, comp. and ed. James Abbington (Chicago: GIA Publications, 2001), 27–38.

24. John Hick, "The Problem of Evil" in Alan Richardson and Alan Bowden, eds., *The Westminster Dictionary of Christian Theology* (Philadelphia: Westminster Press, 1983); David Hume, *Dialogues Concerning Natural Religion*, ed. H. D. Aiken (New York: Harper, 1948), 66.

25. Henry Louis Gates Jr., *Figures in Black: Words, Signs, and the "Racial Self"* (New York: Oxford University Press, 1987), 14–25. For example, thinkers who use reason to support racist theories include David Hume, Immanuel Kant, Georg Hegel, and Thomas Jefferson.

26. T. W. Tilley, "The Problem of Evil" in Joseph A. Komonchak, Mary Collins, and Dermont Lane, eds. *The New Dictionary of Christian Theology* (Philadelphia: Westminster Press, 1983); Kenneth Surin, *Theology and the Problem of Evil* (New York: Basil Blackwell, 1986), 2, 8; Ronald M. Green, "Theodicy" in Mircea Eliade, *The Encyclopedia of Religion* (New York: Macmillan, 1987); John Hick, *Evil and the God of Love*, rev. ed. (San Francisco: Harper & Row, 1977), viii.

27. See John Rawls, *Justice as Fairness: A Restatement* (Cambridge, MA: Belknap Press, 2001).

28. Michael Walzer, *Spheres of Justice: A Defense of Pluralism and Equality* (New York: Basic Books, 1983).

29. Robert Nozick, *Anarchy, State, Utopia* (New York: Basic Books, 1977).

30. Barack Obama, Commencement Address, Southern New Hampshire University, Manchester, N.H. (May 19, 2007).

31. Barack Obama, Commencement Address, Knox College, Galesburg, Ill. (June 4, 2005).

32. Jamal Joseph, *Tupac Shakur Legacy* (New York: Atria Book, 2006).

33. The Love Movement is an effort promoted through www.diddyblog.com and designed by Sean Combs to promote the social gospel of Jesus by challenging young web visitors to get out and do something with their faith in God. The subtitle for the blog is "dream, believe, do, then repeat."

5. Put Down the Pimp Stick to Pick Up the Pulpit

1. Quotation from Bishop Don Juan, known as the spiritual guide for many Hip Hop recording artists.

2. Bishop Don Juan's Best of the Best Contest is found on his website: http://www.thebishop.us/default.html

3. See http://www.apollotheater.org/artists/leviticus.htm (viewed August 1, 2010).

4. Kevin White, phone interview, July 31, 2010. The Reverend Kevin White is the youth pastor at Greater Mount Zion Baptist Church in Austin, Texas.

5. Don E. Saliers, *Music and Theology*, Horizons in Theology (Nashville: Abingdon Press, 2007), 5.

6. Ibid., 7–14.

7. Melva Costen, *African American Christian Worship*, 2nd ed. (Nashville: Abingdon Press, 2007), 105–19.

8. J. Wendell Mapson, *The Ministry of Music in the Black Church* (Valley Forge, Penn.: Judson Press, 1984), 19–21.

9. White interview.

10. Ibid.

11. Tommy Kyllonen, *Unorthodox: Church, Hip Hop, Culture* (Grand Rapids, Mich.: Zondervan, 2007), 109–23.

12. Leona Nicholas Welch, *Tupac, Rahab and Them: A Call to Compassion and Commitment Toward Those Often Unheard, Untouched, and Unsung; Ultimately, Unloved* (Columbus, Ga.: Brentwood Christian Press, 2005), 10–16, 19, 20, 27.

13. White interview.

14. This and the following epigraphs in this section are taken from a personal interview with Jerome Washington in August 2005.

15. MosEL, "Vent." *Just Thinkin Out Loud.* MosElmusic, 2010.

16. Peter Drucker, *Post-capitalist Society* (New York: HarperBusiness, 1993).

6. Jesus Walks

1. Lyrics from "Jesus Walks" from the album *College Dropout* (Roc-A-Fella Records, 2004).

2. As quoted in an interview with Thomas Golianopoulos, *The Source* (April 2004): 101.

3. Diallo Smith, personal interview, June 23, 2010. Diallo Smith is a pastor, theologian, and graduate of Perkins Theological Seminary and Wilberforce University.

4. See their website at: http://youthspeaks.org/word/ (viewed May 1, 2009).

5. Ibid.

6. John H. McWhorter, "Up from Hip Hop," *Commentary* 115, no. 3 (March 2003): 62–65.

7. Evelyn L. Parker, *The Sacred Lives of Adolescent Girls: Hard Stories of Race, Class, and Gender* (Cleveland: Pilgrim Press, 2006), 161–79.

8. Daniel White Hodge, *The Soul of Hip Hop: Rims, Timbs and a Cultural Theology* (Downers Grove, Ill.: IVP Books, 2010), 159–75.

9. Carl Kenney, "REV-elution: 'Start Snitchin'" (August 14, 2007), http://rev-elution.blogspot.com/2007/08/start-snitchin.html (viewed August 17, 2010).

10. David White and Matthew Mistal, "Choices," in *Way to Live: Christian Practices for Teens*, ed. Dorothy C. Bass and Don C. Richter (Nashville: Upper Room Books, 2002), 171–86.

11. Hodge, *Soul of Hip Hop*, 180–226.

12. Brett Esaki, "Desperately Seeking Silence: Youth Culture's Unspoken Need," *Cross Currents* 57, no. 3 (Fall 2007): 387–89.

13. Lisa Silberman Brenner, "Blackface as Religious Expression," *Cross Currents* 53, no. 3 (Fall 2003): 460–61.

14. Carol Lakey Hess and Marie Hess, "Creativity," in *Way to Live*, 95–110.

15. Emily Saliers, Don Saliers, Mark Monk Winstaley, and Liz Marshburn, "Music," in *Way to Live*, 261–73.

16. William J. Brown and Benson P. Fraser, "Hip Hop Kingdom Come," *Christianity Today* (January 8, 2001): 48–52, 54.

17. Douglas LeBlanc, "Rap's Demon-Slayer: T-Bone Brings Hip Hop Swagger to Spiritual Warfare," *Christianity Today* (April 23, 2001): 11.

18. Jeff Stickler, "Hip Hop Church Rocks the Message," *News and Observer* (April 8, 2010); http://www.newsobserver.com/2010/04/08/426519/Hip-Hop-church-rocks-the-message.html (viewed August 15, 2010).

19. Kevin White, phone interview, July 31, 2010.

20. Pamela P. Martin, LaTrese E. Adkins, Tuere A. Bowles, Simone T. Robinson, and Sheretta T. Butler-Barnes, "'Does Heaven Have a Ghetto': The Gospel and the Gangsta, in the Religious Socialization of African American Adolescents," chapter in manuscript in press, *Revolutionary Rhetoric: Consciousness and Contemporary Hip Hop*.

21. Garth K. Baker-Fletcher, "African American Christian Rap: Facing 'Truth' and Resisting It," in *Noise and Spirit: The Religious and Spiritual Sensibilities of Rap*, ed. Anthony B. Pinn (New York: New York University Press, 2003).

22. Ibid.

23. Martin, Adkins, Bowles, Robinson, and Butler-Barnes, "Does Heaven Have a Ghetto."

24. Pamela Martin, *African American Faith Communities Project Newsletter* 1, no. 1 (July 5–July 31, 2004): 2.

25. Ibid., 2–4.

26. Cornel West's Twitter webpage: http://twitter.com/CornelWest (viewed August 2010).

27. Alanna Nash, "Siegfried and Roy: The Night of the Tiger Attack," *Reader's Digest* (April 2004); http://www.rd.com/family/siegfried-and-roy-tiger-attack (viewed April 2004).

Epilogue

1. Ben Detrick, "Why Wyclef?" *The New York Observer* (August 10, 2010), http://www.observer.com/2010/daily-transom/why-wyclef (viewed August 10, 2010).

2. Tim Padgett, "Wyclef Jean to Run for President in Haiti," *Time* (August 4, 2010), http://www.time.com/time/world/article/0,8599,2008588-1,00.html (viewed August 10, 2010).

3. It was already decided that Wyclef Jean could not run for president.

4. Christina Hoag, "'Rap Teacher' Uses Hip-hop to School L.A. Kids in Algebra," *USA Today* (June 18, 2010): http://www.usatoday.com/news/education/2010-06-18-rapping-teacher_N.htm (viewed January 26, 2011); Eric Hellweg,

Hip-Hop Helps Teach Everything from English to Algebra, http://www.edutopia.org/hip-hop-teaching-classroom

5. Tim Townsend, "Movie Producer Turns to Local Talent for New Hip-hop Movie," *St. Louis Post-Dispatch* (January 15, 2011), http://www.stltoday.com/lifestyles/faith-and-values/tim-townsend/article_22b5e808-fe0a-52ba-b855-a6573ff1c8ed.html (viewed January 28, 2011).

6. Cheryl Kirk-Duggan composed this poem to complete the volume.

9 781426 703010